AVALANCHE

lessons of love

KRIS OCHOA-KEANE
& STEPHEN J. ODDO

Published by Kris Ochoa-Keane and Stephen J. Oddo, San Diego, CA

© 2011 by Kris Ochoa-Keane and Stephen J. Oddo
Printed in the United States of America

ISBN: 978-0-615-52952-3

Edited by Brenda Judy
www.publishersplanet.com

Cover and Interior Design by Carolyn Sheltraw
www.csheltraw.com

Photo of Kris Ochoa-Keane and Stephen J. Oddo taken by Amy Connor Photography
www.amyconnorphotography.com

Authors' Note:
The content of this book is a factual story. The quotes from the written judgment in Chapter 9 are verbatim. However, the dialogue throughout the book, as well as the testimony in Chapter 8, is not verbatim but rather the authors' recollection of what was said. The authors are expressing their personal opinions, perspectives and analyses of all that transpired.

⊖ The paper used in this publication meets the minimum requirements of the American National Standard for Information sciences—Permanence of Paper for Printed Library Materials, ANSI Z39.48-1992.

www.avalanchelessonsoflove.com

This book is dedicated to all those who have struggled through periods of grief. In the most desperate of times, you must look deep inside to find your source of strength. During his times of trial, Archbishop Oscar Romero would recite the following mantra: "I can't; You must; I'm yours; Show me the way." In this loving act of faith and surrender, may you all find peace.

Grandeza

by Annette Ochoa

I was told my whole life about the beautiful glacier that my father saw from his window at the Bugaboos. He told my mother that it was a Spiritual Experience seeing the majestic beauty at different times of the day. It moved him deeply and he saw God in the mountain. This is my interpretation of what he may have seen.

This is for you, Mama.

Love,

Annette

CONTENTS

PROLOGUE

On a warm August afternoon in the summer of 1963, I climbed into the back of our family station wagon and set out on a grand adventure. My younger sister and two younger brothers sat alongside of me as we left our home in Emmitsburg, Maryland, for the strange unknown of Mexico. I was eleven years old and my life would never be the same.

My father had accepted a year-long teaching position in Guadalajara; which, after looking in the atlas, we discovered was right in the middle of Mexico. No one in my family spoke a word of Spanish, so it was with quite a bit of trepidation that we set out on this adventure. When we arrived in Guadalajara, my parents decided that the only way we would learn the language was to attend Mexican schools. We did learn the language, but those first few months were very difficult for me and my siblings. By the time the school year was over and we were ready to return to Maryland, I hated the entire experience so much I vowed never to return to Mexico.

Fate had other plans for me, however. My father accepted another teaching position, so we returned to Guadalajara the following fall. In addition, my father had organized a summer program of studies through the Jesuit University in Guadalajara. He worked with several Catholic universities in the United States to develop a first-rate summer school program, which he founded and continued to direct for the next thirty years. For me, however, the bottom line was that I had to spend all my summers with my family in Guadalajara.

At first, I was angry and upset about having to return to Guadalajara the following fall and then every summer thereafter. In 1966, my father accepted a teaching position at the University of San Diego. I was a teenager settling into a new high school, making new friends and trying to adjust to life in San Diego. Summers in Guadalajara were simply not a top priority for me. But, by the time I graduated from the all-girls Academy of Our Lady of Peace High School in 1970, my attitude towards Mexico had changed dramatically. I actually began to look forward to the summers in Guadalajara. My friends and I had reached the age where we could begin to explore the Guadalajara nightlife, which had no age restrictions. The best part was the Mexican men—I had never seen so many tall, dark and handsome men before, and all of them seemed to have a soft spot for American women.

In the summer of 1970, I was eighteen years old and I felt totally in charge of my life—quite the woman of the world. That was, of course, until I met Alfonso Ochoa that summer. He was twenty-seven years old and the most handsome and debonair man I had ever met—the epitome of a Latin lover. The night of our second date, about an hour after he had dropped me off at my apartment, I was sitting on my bed telling my roommates about what an incredible man Alfonso was when I was interrupted by the sound of guitars and voices singing in Spanish. We figured our neighbors below were playing the radio loud again so, with the typical tact of teenagers, we stomped on the floor. The music continued, however, and even got louder.

"That's not the radio," I said. "The voices sound terrible and they sound like they're coming from outside."

I walked over to the only window in our second-floor apartment, opened it halfway and stuck my head outside. It was Alfonso! My heart nearly beat out of my chest, as I realized he was serenading me. I stared into his eyes as he and his friends played two more songs. I did not even hear how bad they were . . . I just kept staring into his eyes. When they finished, he did not say a word. Alfonso blew me a kiss, then turned and disappeared into the night.

I put my hand over my heart as I turned away from the window towards my roommates. "Oh my God," I said. "I think I'm in love."

When summer ended and I returned to San Diego to begin college, I cried for the entire three-day train ride back to San Diego. I did not know if I would ever see the man of my dreams again. Fortunately, the thought of our being apart was unthinkable for Alfonso as well. Two weeks later, he visited me in San Diego, and for the next two years, we carried on a long-distance relationship between Guadalajara and California. After I completed two years of college, I worked as a flight attendant, in no small part for the free trips to Mexico.

In June 1973, I had a few days off, so we decided to escape to Puerto Vallarta for a weekend getaway. We went to the fanciest restaurant in Puerto Vallarta. Alfonso looked so handsome in his three-piece suit, his long black hair flowing off his collar. His black goatee framed his face perfectly. He talked about all the plans he had for the future, how he would someday be the largest steel mogul in Mexico.

After dinner, we took a moonlit walk on the deserted beach in front of our hotel. We held hands and I felt like the luckiest girl on the planet. We stopped at one point and he turned towards me, brushing the hair off my shoulders. He leaned over and kissed me . . . I melted in his arms. I was in heaven.

Then he reached into his pocket, pulled out a little box, opened it and said in a heavily accented English, "Kris, please marry me."

As I looked into his eyes, then down at the beautiful ring he held in his left hand, I did not hesitate for a second. "Of course I will. I love you so much."

Alfonso and I were married on November 23, 1973, at St. Joseph's Cathedral in San Diego. With all of Alfonso's family and friends flying up from Mexico for the wedding, it seemed like half of Guadalajara was at the ceremony. It was the happiest day of my young life. The candlelight ceremony was beautiful. Alfonso was dashingly handsome and I was madly in love with him. I felt like things had fallen into perfect order for me, and I could not wait to begin my new life as Mrs. Alfonso Ochoa.

I moved to Guadalajara with Alfonso and began what I quickly realized would be a long and difficult task of adapting to life as a young wife in Mexico. I benefited from the fact that several of Alfonso's friends were married around the same time, so we had a group of about eight couples who began married life together. The wives embraced me as their friend and helped me in so many ways during this time of great adjustment. To this day, these women remain some of my closest and dearest friends.

As Alfonso's businesses began to grow, so did our family. After settling down in our new home in Guadalajara, Alfonso and I decided that we wanted to start a family almost immediately. Because of medical problems I had experienced as a child, the doctors had warned me that I might not be able to have children. We found out very quickly that the doctors were wrong. In May 1974, we learned that we would be parents soon. We were thrilled, and our first son, Alfonso Jr., was born on February 1, 1975.

Alfonso was absolutely beside himself with joy. He wanted a son so badly. To a Mexican man, a son is one of the most important things in his life. In the male-dominated society of Mexico, a son is a sign of virility, a sign that the family name and the family bloodline will persevere. When Alfonso Jr. arrived, Alfonso's eyes filled with tears of pride and joy as he held the tiny baby—his son and namesake. All of Alfonso's hopes for the future were transferred onto his son. Even when Alfonso Jr. was still just an infant, many times Alfonso would take the baby with him to the office. I often caught him whispering with intense tenderness and emotion to Alfonso Jr. that all that he had was for him and that he was the reason his father was working so hard. I have never seen such a deep love as I saw in Alfonso for his son . . . and, before long, his sons.

Soon we were blessed with a second son. In late October 1976, Carl Eric was born. From the moment Carl arrived, he was the handsome spitting image of his father. Carl was cunning and dashingly handsome; and, from the beginning, we knew that he had a special gift. Even as a young child, Carl proved to be a shrewd businessman. Armed with his natural good looks and charm, Carl could wheel and deal just about anything. Alfonso sensed this and could not wait for Carl to grow up and join him in the family business. With Alfonso Jr. and Carl, Alfonso felt so lucky to have the sons he knew someday would carry on the family business.

In July 1979, our third baby boy, Christofer, joined his older brothers in the Ochoa clan, and brought us quite a scare. Shortly after he was born, Christofer was diagnosed with a heart disorder called Wolfe-Parkinson White Syndrome, which causes an irregular heartbeat. Several times during the first few months of his life, he nearly died from tachycardia attacks. After one of those incidents, I was holding him in my arms in his hospital room, crying as I rocked him to sleep. A picture of the Virgin Mary on the wall looked down upon us, and I noticed that she seemed to be smiling at us. For several minutes, as I held Christofer close to my heart, I looked deep into Mary's eyes, then heard a soothing voice tell me, "It's not his time. He will be fine. I have great plans for him." Christofer did survive a tremendously difficult first year of life, and has grown into a special young man, with wisdom and understanding well beyond his years.

Over the next few years, two more sons, Jonathan and Nicholas, arrived on the scene to form what Alfonso would call his "Starting Five." Alfonso could not have written a more perfect script—five sons, whom he would teach to hunt, fish, ski, bike, surf and, eventually, work in the business empire he had established. Even when the boys were very young, Alfonso was already thinking about where each son would fit best in the businesses. The boys were Alfonso's dream team. What could possibly have been better than to build a business empire with the knowledge that one day he would be working side by side with his sons? This dream inspired him every day in his work and was a major motivation for much of his success.

As lucky as Alfonso felt about having so many boys, his younger brother, Francisco, must have felt equally as cursed. Many Mexican men, even today, judge their "machismo" by how many sons they bring into this world. I know Francisco must have been frustrated with his track record, especially in comparison to Alfonso's. After his eldest child, Francisco Jr., was born, Francisco and his wife had seven consecutive girls. When they finally had another boy, the child was born with a heart defect and his prospects for surviving beyond his childhood were slim.

I know Francisco envied Alfonso for having so many sons. Although they were brothers and business partners, they were also very competitive and, over the years, I could sense that Francisco worried that Alfonso and his team of sons would ultimately limit his influence in the family steel business. Alfonso never could have envisioned such a scenario because family was too important to him. Still, the birth of each new son probably fueled Francisco's fears.

Meanwhile, having five boys, six if you include Alfonso, in one family made family activities decidedly masculine. When there was a decision to be made about whether to go to the ballet or to the soccer game, the ballet did not stand a chance. Still, I tried to ensure that my boys received as well-rounded an upbringing as possible. With no other women around besides me, sometimes that task proved difficult, which is why I thought it was all the more important that the boys have a little sister. They needed to see how the other sex behaved and lived in order to have their own successful relationships with women in the future. In April 1990, our prayers were answered when God blessed us with a beautiful, healthy daughter, Annette.

I know that Annette was, and continues to be, a very special gift to me and my family from Mary, the Blessed Mother. I prayed to her constantly, and I knew in my heart that my prayers would be answered. I even wrote a letter of petition to the Virgin Mary with my request for a healthy daughter, which a friend took with her on her pilgrimage to Medjujorie, Yugoslavia, the town where Mary is believed to have appeared to five local children on a regular basis beginning in 1981. The letters of petition are placed on an altar and offered to her on a daily basis.

When Annette was born, I truly felt the Virgin's presence with me. When I was wheeled into the delivery room, I even saw a picture of the Virgin of Medjujorie on the wall. The picture was placed on the wall so that, from where I was lying, it was as if she was smiling down on me the entire time. Still, when the baby was being born, I initially thought it was another boy. As the baby's head was coming out, Alfonso said, "This little guy has the face of a boy."

But within seconds, the doctor screamed, "It's a girl, it's a girl!"

There was not a dry eye in the room, as everyone knew how much we wanted to have a daughter. All I could do was cry and thank God and the Virgin Mary for the wonderful family I had been given.

CHAPTER 1

the fall

Tuesday, March 12, 1991, was a day of uncommon beauty and majesty in the mountains of British Columbia, Canada. After the early clouds had burned off, the sun shone brightly, glistening off the peaks and the countless acres of snow and ski runs. After a couple of days of constant snow, the weather had cleared leaving behind the purest and deepest powder a skier could want.

For the nine Mexican men, including my husband, Alfonso Ochoa, who each year planned this heli-skiing vacation in the Bugaboos, the day could not have been more perfect. An overnight snow had left the powder steep and deep—skiing unlike any they had experienced before. The nine friends had traveled 3,000 miles from Guadalajara, Mexico, the day before to reach this skier's paradise and they were anxious to hit the slopes. At the breakfast table, few words were spoken. Pancakes and sausage were swallowed nearly whole to hasten the morning rituals, as this was to be a truly memorable day.

At about 3:30 in the afternoon, after nearly a full day of fabulous skiing, the group reached the base of an exhilarating slope aptly called "Holy Shit." The run down the steep and challenging mountain had left the men gasping for air, but thrilled at their latest conquest. When the last of the group reached the bottom of Holy Shit, the Mexican men, still panting, looked at each other and collectively nodded as if to say, "That's it; let's head back."

Alfonso, however, did not want this perfect day to end. He always wanted more of the good things in life and would never settle for less.

"C'mon guys, one last run. It doesn't get any better than this," he told his comrades in Spanish.

The other eight could not match his energy and began taking their skis off.

This did not deter Alfonso. His adrenaline still pumping, he joined eleven other skiers in the group, most of them from Europe, for one final run down these heavenly slopes.

The skiers that remained boarded a helicopter that would lift them to the top of a run called Bay Street, the final part of which is a powder skier's dream—3,000 feet of undulating terrain with an average inclination of 35 degrees. It was steep and loaded with deep, fresh powder.

Alfonso, looking out the window of the helicopter, waved at his friends, who were boarding another helicopter that would take them back to the lodge. He enjoyed the helicopter rides almost as much as the skiing because he could look out at the grandeur of nature and soak in the beauty that surrounded him. He particularly loved the way the sun reflected off the snow, which he described as millions of sparkling diamonds illuminating the mountainside. In these special moments, his thoughts would always turn to his sons and how he longed to share these times with them when they were old enough. This was the high no substance could come close to matching. This was life!

Alfonso's helicopter landed at the peak of Bay Street's upper bowl, an intermediate run tucked naturally into the side of the glacier. In single file, each skier followed the guide down and through the bowl. Alfonso, as was his custom, followed immediately behind the guide because he felt he learned more from the guides when he could follow directly in their path and see their technique. The other skiers followed behind him. When the group reached the end of Upper Bay Street, the guide instructed the skiers to follow her through an area filled with large chunks of ice and snow that had fallen from a cornice overhang above. This was the only path leading to the beginning of the Lower Bay Street run. One by one, the skiers followed the guide's trail through the maze of ice chunks and reached the top edge of Lower Bay Street.

When the first members of the group reached the top of the Lower Bay Street run, the guide stopped the group and shouted instructions, "Follow me down the right edge of the slope, but don't go out into the middle of the mountain." The guide did not want the group to ski in the center of the run, a 40-degree vertical slope covering more than 2,500 feet, because the large amount of new snow and the extreme vertical drop could make that area dangerous.

Alfonso, who understood little English, picked up a word or two from the guide's instructions, but since he was first in line, he figured he would just follow her. As they began their descent, a German skier, along with a British woman and two Americans, who had been bringing up the rear, were just reaching the spot Alfonso and the others were vacating.

As Alfonso and the others began gliding down the mountain, the German man, in a thick accent, yelled, "What did she say?" Hearing no response and seeing the rest of the group following the guide, the four stragglers paused for a moment, took a deep breath and headed down the hill. Not having heard the instructions, the German skier led the other three out onto the main part of the mountain. There was a sudden, deathly calm and then, without warning, a slab of snow beneath the German man began to move.

"Stop, there's a slide!" one of the Americans above him shouted. But, it was too late.

The snowpack fractured, creating a deep rift across the mountain and causing a massive slab of snow and ice to dislodge and begin spiraling downward. Within seconds, the slide had engulfed the German skier and began gaining momentum for its violent trek down the mountain. The wayward skiers had triggered an avalanche.

When the slide began, Alfonso had reached a point about 100 yards down the mountain, where the guide had stopped to wait for the others. Alfonso first felt a powerful vibration surround him followed by a sensation that the snow beneath him was giving way, much like the roll of an earthquake. He then heard the guide, who was just below him, yell into her radio, "Avalanche!" But, within a few seconds, he and the other skiers were swallowed up in the wall of snow and ice crashing down the mountain. The surge of trees, rocks and Volkswagen-size blocks of ice, moving at more than 100 miles per hour, trampled down the mountain in seconds—depositing its cargo at the base of the run and leaving behind a deathly silence that stilled the mountain.

Alfonso died within seconds of the initial impact from the traumatic blows to his head and body. The autopsy revealed that the initial impact, and the resulting plunge down the mountain, shattered virtually every bone in his body. The wall of snow and ice carried him more than 2,500 feet to the bottom of Bay Street where his body came to rest, under five feet of snow and ice, in a small creek just adjacent to the run. All of the other skiers who were on Lower Bay Street when the avalanche occurred also died, except for the guide, who miraculously survived, and those who trailed the German skier.

When he had arrived at the lodge just a day before, Alfonso had marveled at the beauty and serenity of the Bugaboos. He had confided to a friend that of all the places he had been on Earth, this spot was the most beautiful he had ever seen, and that, if he could choose, this would be the place where he would want to leave this world to be with God.

On that radiant March afternoon, much sooner than he had hoped or expected, Alfonso got his wish.

CHAPTER 2

the avalanche

Three thousand miles south of the Bugaboos, in the Mexican city of Guadalajara, I have just returned from a PTA meeting and am getting ready to go to bed. After checking in on each of my six children and making sure each is asleep, I slip into my pajamas, hoping to enjoy some quiet time in bed with a good book. The sound of the doorbell jolts me out of my deep concentration. I glance at the clock on my nightstand. Who could possibly be here at 10:30 p.m.? Since my husband is out of town on a skiing vacation, and the only late-night visitors we ever have are related to his business, this interruption in my peaceful evening makes even less sense. My palms begin to sweat when I hear my brother-in-law Francisco's voice on the other end of the intercom. He would not be here at this time of the night unless something is wrong.

"I need . . . I need to talk . . . to talk to you . . . right now, Kris," Francisco says in a hesitant voice that cracks with each word.

"Are you okay, Francisco?" I ask. "It sounds like you've been crying. What's going on?"

"Just come down . . . come down here . . . please," he says.

My body grows tense and I begin to tremble as I press the button to let Francisco in through the front gate, then fly down the stairs and out the front door to meet him—a million possibilities are racing through my mind. Out in the yard, I notice that Kico, my husband's cousin who is a priest, has accompanied Francisco. This sets off a panic attack and I scream at them, "What are you doing here? What happened?"

Francisco grabs my shoulders and tries to speak.

"Alfonso . . ." he starts, but cannot finish. I immediately think of the skiing trip and flash to an image of my husband tumbling down a mountain, and then in a hospital bed in a body cast somewhere in Canada. He must be injured badly if Kico is here and Francisco is this upset. I must go to him!

"What happened, Francisco?" I scream. "Francisco! Tell me! For God's sake, tell me!"

Francisco cowers away from me, turning his head towards Kico, but Kico gently pushes him towards me.

"Tell me he's okay!" I plead.

Francisco finally raises his head and I can see in his bloodshot eyes a sadness so deep that I cannot bring myself to breathe. He looks at me and says, "An avalanche . . . Alfonso and eight or nine others . . . dead."

The words reach in and pierce my heart as everything goes black. I fall to the ground as Francisco and Kico watch in shock. Alfonso dying simply is not in the realm of possibility. Injured? Maybe. Dead? No way. I tell myself, "My husband, so strong and healthy, is invincible and will live forever. What are they talking about? Alfonso cannot possibly be dead."

As I lie face down on the rock-paved walkway leading into my home, I begin to scream, "No, no, no . . ." but I can't hear anything coming out. "My God," I think, "I'm screaming and no one can hear me."

I begin to kick and hit the ground wildly with my arms and legs, and Kico leans down beside me on one knee and whispers in my ear, "I'm so sorry, Kris, but Alfonso is with God now. You must be strong."

When I hear these words, I cannot control myself—I jump to my feet and run for the house, through the open front door and into the downstairs bathroom where I fall to my knees and begin vomiting in the toilet. It feels like all my life, all my energy is spewing out of me into the toilet.

Without knowing how I got there, I find myself in my living room with Francisco, his wife, Gabriela, and Kico. They begin explaining the details of the accident as told to them by Alfonso's friends, who were still in Canada. With each word I feel a little more lost, with nothing to hold onto except Gabriela's hand.

"Alfonso had been skiing late in the day after all his friends had returned to the lodge," Francisco says.

"That is so like him—if there are ten minutes of skiing left in the day, he has to ski them. That's just the way he is," I think, as I visualize him attacking the mountain and shouting his joy at conquering the last run of the day. "Why couldn't he have just gone back with the others?"

"Apparently," Francisco continues, "it had been a great ski day—lots of sun and great powder. The whole group had an incredible day."

The vision of Alfonso and his friends becomes clearer in my mind. I see him in his bright red parka, goggles pulled tightly around his head, his blue Bugaboos ski hat with the tassel flopping up and down behind him as he carves his way down the hill. Of course Alfonso is out there on the last run—he wants to enjoy every minute of it. Why couldn't he have just gone back with the others?

"He was skiing on a run called Bay Street with several other skiers when the avalanche hit," Francisco says. "He was carried away in a barrage of ice and snow down the steepest part of the mountain. He didn't stand a chance."

That image, of Alfonso being swept away in a wall of snow, immediately appears in my mind and I begin to lose control again, racing for the bathroom. As I lay on the bathroom floor, my head spinning, holding onto the toilet for support, my mind goes haywire. Why couldn't he have just gone back with the others?

Can this be real? It can't be. It seems surreal, like a horrifying movie up on a big screen. But here I am in the middle of the screen, trying to find my way off. Can this really be happening? There must have been a mistake. Maybe it wasn't Alfonso with the group that was killed. No one thought seems clear, but thousands of them race through my mind simultaneously in a chaotic stream of consciousness until suddenly my mind focuses on the children. My God, the children! How am I going to tell the children their father is dead?

With the help of Kico and Francisco, I wake the oldest boys—Alfonso Jr., who is sixteen; Carl Eric, who is fourteen; and Christofer, who is twelve. My tears and sobbing give away the nature of what I am about to tell them.

"Mama," Carl Eric says, wiping the sleep from his eyes as he puts his arm around me, "what's wrong?"

"Something terrible has happened," I say. "Your father was skiing today . . . in Canada . . . and . . ."

I do my best to stay composed, but the tears race down my cheeks.

". . . and he was caught in an avalanche. Your father . . . he . . . he . . . he was killed."

The words sting as I say out loud for the first time that Alfonso is dead; and the words cut even deeper as they reach my sons. They each take a step back, looks of disbelief overcoming their sleepy faces.

"Your father is with God now," Kico says, but his calming words have the opposite effect on the boys.

Alfonso Jr. begins shouting and hitting the counter. "No, no, no, no . . ." he screams. "You must be lying. My Dad isn't dead. He can't be dead. He's not dead. No, no, no, no . . ."

Kico moves towards him, but Alfonso won't let him near—he turns away and places his head in his hands, and begins shouting through his sobs in barely recognizable words about unfairness and God and skiing and avalanches and God.

Carl Eric and Christofer just look at me as if their world is being snapped in two, then they also begin to cry. I grab them and squeeze each as close to me as I can and refuse to let go. As I hold them and feel their hearts beating so quickly next to mine, I close my eyes and flash forward to the lives that lay ahead for each of my boys without his father. Alfonso is, or was, everything to his boys. Their father, their mentor and their friend. The thought of these boys, so young and fragile, growing up without their father seems unbearable. This cannot be; this just cannot be. I sob as I squeeze them tighter, hoping against hope that this vision of their future will disappear.

At around 1:00 a.m., Francisco mentions that we should break the news to my mother-in-law and sister-in-law, who live next door. So, in a zombie-like state, I walk with Francisco, Gabriela and Kico over to their home. Amazingly, they are both awake. Perhaps they have heard the commotion next door at my place. Pitilla, Alfonso's sister, lets us in and, after glancing at my tear-strewn face, she immediately senses something is wrong. I can't bring myself to say even a word, so while Gabriela tells Pitilla what happened, I walk with Francisco into my mother-in-law's bedroom. She is perched up in bed, as if she is expecting us, with a book opened face down on her lap. Francisco sits at her side with both arms around her and whispers in her ear. She just slumps on his shoulder and begins to quietly weep.

Alfonso is the most beloved of the sons in the family, so the reaction from them is the same—shock, disbelief and tears. Throughout his entire life, Alfonso had been the cement holding the Ochoa family together. Even as a teenager, Alfonso assumed the role as head of the family after his father had taken ill and later died. I can see on the faces of my mother-in-law and sister-in-law the fear and insecurity Alfonso's death is already forcing upon them. Who will take care of them now? Who will take care of all of us now?

When we get back to the house, it becomes clear that word of the accident has spread among our friends and family. Despite the late hour, the house is filling up with people who, like me and my family, are in a state of shock. Some pray, others just hug me and sob in my arms. They all have looks of shock on their faces. Throughout the evening and into the morning, the reaction from everyone is disbelief.

"Impossible," they say. "How many Mexicans die in an avalanche? It's just impossible."

I hope against hope that somehow this shared disbelief and the sheer absurdity of this bad dream will somehow give way to reason and undo what has been done. I wrap myself so tightly in this hope until it feels like the same avalanche that has killed Alfonso is beginning to descend upon me and suck me in with the debris. Without warning, I am being swallowed up in an unbelievable nightmare; yet, with every breath I take, it becomes so much more real.

"But it can't be real," I tell myself again. Alfonso has never so much as broken a bone. Whenever I think of either of us dying, I always envision me dying before him since I have more frailties than Alfonso. But Alfonso, dead? Impossible! "This cannot be happening," I think, as I sit and sob in my living room. I feel the comfort of my friends and family around me, but I have never felt so alone in my life.

It is around 2:00 a.m. when I call my parents in San Diego. When my mother answers the phone, I try my best to tell her what has happened, but all I can do is piece together words and phrases in between the sobs. "Mom . . . Alfonso . . . avalanche in Canada . . . he's dead." When I realize what I have just told her, and feeling my mother's comfort even over the phone, I burst into tears and long for her to hold me just as I had just held my boys.

"Mama, please make this bad dream go away," I say.

"I wish I could, my precious," she says. "I love you very much and will be there as soon as I can."

She consoles me for a few more minutes as best she can, then tells me she and my father will leave on the first flight for Guadalajara in the morning.

<hr />

As night turns into early morning, Gabriela tells me I need to begin thinking about the funeral arrangements. Making plans for the funeral and the retrieval of Alfonso's remains seem beyond my capacity, as the shock of what has transpired makes every movement a struggle, every word a trauma. I feel like I am chained to the floor, weighted down by an ever-growing awareness of the profound changes awaiting me and my children. I sense instinctively that this feeling of overwhelming burden will grow immensely in the days, weeks and months ahead.

We decide that Francisco should go to Canada to retrieve Alfonso's remains. I feel my children need me here with them, and the thought of leaving them behind to deal with some very traumatic and very unpleasant affairs in Canada is unthinkable. Francisco will go, and I will stay behind and plan the funeral with the help of Kico and the family.

Meanwhile, in Canada, Alfonso's good friend, Jaime Gomez, apparently has taken charge of the situation at the Bugaboos. He calls around 5:00 a.m. to offer me his condolences.

"Kris, I am so sorry," he says. "I don't know what to say. One minute, we were waving to him as we got on the helicopter; the next, he's gone. God,

I wish we could turn back the clock and I'd insist he come back with us . . . ah, what am I saying? He never would have come back. He always wanted that last run. Kris, I just wish there was something I could say or do."

I can't respond. I just sit here motionless with the phone pinned against my ear.

"Kris, are you there?" he asks. "Well, none of us has slept here. We still can't believe it. We're just sitting around telling stories about him and pouring the rum in his honor . . . I guess it's helping us get through this up here. Listen, Kris, don't worry about all the details up here. I will take care of everything, and we will come back with Francisco on Friday, okay? Kris, please take care of yourself. You've got to find a way to get through this."

Find a way to get through this? Are you kidding! How in the world am I ever going to get through this?

"Kris, I've got to go," he says. "We'll be back on Friday. Try to keep it together, okay?"

"Okay," I say as I hang up the phone. "Keep it together, keep it together, keep it together," I keep telling myself. I think it will be impossible.

***

I sleep about an hour sometime just before dawn. When I awake, my youngest two boys, Nicholas, who is four, and Jonathan, who is eight, are standing at the side of my bed. After walking downstairs and seeing people everywhere, they had run back up to my room.

"Mama, Mama, what's going on?" they ask.

I hug them both tightly and try to rid my mind of the cobwebs that had collected during my nearly sleepless night. Was I dreaming? Their young, sleep-weary faces stare up at mine.

"Mama, why are all these people here?" Jonathan asks.

"There was an accident, honey," I tell them. "Oh God . . . your daddy was skiing yesterday . . ."

How can I tell them? I hold them close to me and whisper in their ears.

". . . and there was an accident . . . your daddy died . . . he's up in heaven with God now."

Jonathan's face turns ashen and it wrinkles up as he begins to cry. Nicholas takes one look at Jonathan and does the same, not really fully understanding the news.

"It's okay, honey," I whisper. "Everything is going to be okay. Daddy's gone, but mommy's right here. I'll always be here to take care of you."

I wonder how I am going to be able to keep my promises to my little ones.

After a few minutes, I gather myself and go into the bathroom. As I stand before the mirror, I notice the dark bags under my eyes and how puffy my entire face looks. As I stand here staring, the realization hits me that I am now a widow! I clutch at Alfonso's bathrobe, which is hanging on the back of the door, and slump to the floor. It still smells of him. I hold it to my body and refuse to let go, crying into the terry cloth lapel. As I weep, all I can think is, "He is gone. He really is gone."

When I finally muster the courage to make my way downstairs, I find the house and patio filled with people waiting to give me their condolences. It is the Mexican way for friends and family to grieve together nearly every hour until the funeral. While this is an enormous comfort to me, at times during the day, it overwhelms me having a constant barrage of people around all the time. Coffee, tea and refreshments are served day and night by friends of mine. It seems like all the food and refreshments appear out of nowhere. I don't know who is organizing things, but I am grateful nonetheless. I see my friend, Rosa Isabella, in the kitchen and wonder if she is coordinating all the activity as she is barking instructions to the maids. But my mind is elsewhere.

Around noon, the directors of each of my husband's companies arrive to talk with me. Quite unexpectedly, I find myself discussing business with them. They tell me Francisco, who is full partner with my husband in all of the family steel businesses, had given them instructions before he left for Canada to get my signature on some very important documents for the local banks. They explain that I will inherit Alfonso's share of the family business and that I am now Francisco's partner. With Alfonso's death, they say, Francisco wants to show the banks that the businesses will be as strong under Francisco's direction as they had been under Alfonso. They place an inch-high stack of papers in front of me.

"Just sign the papers, Kris," they say.

Emotionally, I am not prepared for any of this. I begin to leaf through some of the documents, but their subject matter is foreign to me. I want to be strong, just as Alfonso would have wanted me to be, but I just can't focus. I do notice, however, the words "debt" and "obligation" on a few of the pages, so I ask what these documents are all about.

"We don't really know, Kris. Francisco just said it was extremely important. Just sign them, Kris, and it will be over with."

One of the gentlemen hands me a pen and points at the places where I should sign. I look around at the faces of the four men, and not one of them will look me in the eyes. "I will have to trust Francisco," I think. "What kind of man would he be if he was not looking out for my best interest and the best interest of my family on the morning after my husband dies? These must be just some routine documents that need to be signed when a partner dies." So, I sign in several places and hand the documents back to them.

As the men get up and prepare to leave, one of them pulls me aside and whispers in my ear, "You've made a wise choice, Kris. No sense in antagonizing Francisco so soon after Alfonso's death."

I have no idea what he is talking about, but I thank him as he hugs me and then walks out the door.

In Canada, Jaime Gomez, overcoming the deep sorrow he feels for his fallen friend, has managed to organize matters so that, by the time Francisco arrives, everything is arranged. Jaime sends his son and another member of the group back to Guadalajara to comfort me, and sends two other members of the group to Vancouver to do the legal work at the Mexican consulate. Another group goes to Calgary to pick up Francisco. Yet, another group stays with Alfonso's body at the funeral home in the small town of Golden. Jaime, under extremely trying circumstances, makes sure every detail is taken care of so the funeral can take place as scheduled on Saturday.

Friday afternoon arrives and I have to prepare to go to the airport to meet Francisco, who is returning with Alfonso's remains. I am dreading the trip to the airport and the traditional all-night vigil with my husband's ashes that will follow. The Mexican custom is for family and friends to remain awake until dawn with the body or remains of the deceased to symbolically accompany the soul on his or her journey to heaven. Normally, the vigil takes place the night someone dies. In Alfonso's case, since his remains have been delayed a few days in Canada, we have planned the vigil for tonight.

As evening approaches, I am distraught. I can't get myself together— I alternate between anger and sorrow, with anger winning out most of the time. I am furious with Alfonso. How dare he go heli-skiing? He knew how dangerous it was. How could he leave me, his wife, without a husband, and his six children without a father? He should not have gone. He should have been more responsible. He should have measured the danger. My rage turns to sadness, however, when I think about the accident itself. What were his last moments on this Earth like? I hope and pray that he did not feel any pain. Did he think of me before he died? What were his last thoughts? I will never know.

I do not know how I will gather the strength to go to the airport. This entire three-day nightmare simply cannot be happening. Up in my bedroom, the rage builds in me as I hurl books and pillows across the room, cursing Alfonso, cursing God and crying. My God, I can't stop crying as I keep coming back to the same question—why? Why . . . instead of going to the airport tonight to pick up my husband after a wonderful vacation, why am I going to the airport to receive his ashes in a sterile container? Someone please turn back the clock, I'm begging you . . .

"I hate you for this, Alfonso," I scream. "But I love you so much. Please don't leave me."

When the time comes to leave, I try to compose myself as I gather the children around me. Rosa Isabella brings them out of their rooms. She has been a godsend. In addition to coordinating the household for the last few days, she has also seen after the children, making sure they are eating and dressed properly. I don't know what I would have done without her. The five boys are wearing their best suits, each with a gold cross from his First Communion hanging around his neck, and I carry our eleven-month-old daughter, Annette. Their faces are somber. They are going to pick up the remains of their dead father. The ride to the airport is a solemn, silent and tearful procession that seems to take forever. However, none of us wants the journey to end, because we know what awaits us.

To my surprise, hundreds of our friends are waiting for us at the airport, all of them dressed in black, standing at the curb in reverent silence. As we pull up to the curb, I look outside the car window and see so many familiar faces: Alfredo Anguiano, the night shift janitor at Alfonso's office, whose family Alfonso had helped out of financial difficulties many times; his wife, Maria, is draped on his shoulder clutching a black handkerchief to her face. Next to them are Alfonso's early business partner, Luis Castro, and his wife, Isabella. My God, we haven't seen them in years. I can't believe how many people are here—there must be nearly 150. I am overwhelmed at how many people have come here to share in our grief.

We make our way through the crowd; I can't bear to look at any of the people surrounding our path. I feel like I might break down right here if I make eye contact, so I keep my eyes focused on the ground in front of me. Still, I can't control the tears flowing down my cheeks as we make our way to the gate. After a couple of minutes, Francisco is the first one to come off the plane. My heart breaks in two as I see him climb down the ramp, carrying a brown wooden box, small enough to fit in a carry-on bag. I realize what he is carrying—it is all that remains of my vibrant and dynamic husband. The man who had been my entire life for nearly twenty years is now nothing more than ashes in a box. I bow my head, place my face in my hand and start to cry. "Breathe," I tell myself. "Just breathe. It just can't be."

When Francisco arrives at the gate, he hands me the box. I can barely grasp it. Almost instinctively, I begin to hug and kiss the box. I know it is not Alfonso but, for the moment, it is all I have to hold on to.

As I hold the box, I just feel like screaming, "This is not fair. I'm too young to be a widow. My children need their father. Please come back. God, please let him come back." Instead, I silently walk back to where the children are waiting, trying to wipe my tears away. The pain in their eyes when they see the box is nearly too much for me to handle.

We all sit together with the box on my lap and cry and hug. Alfonso Jr. is disconsolate; he takes the gold cross from around his neck and fastens it onto the box. "You will always be with me, Dad," he whispers.

The younger boys then follow, one by one, for a moment alone with their father.

I feel a surge of strength when we emerge from the waiting area to see that our friends have cleared a path for us and each of them is holding a lit candle. As a family, we slowly walk with our heads down back through the crowd. I glance up from time to time to see the faces of so many friends, their tears visible in the flickering candlelight. As we walk through, I feel their pain in the sad glances and the tears streaming down their cheeks. They too have loved Alfonso, and have suffered a great loss. I feel weaker with every step and begin to pray just to make it to the curb where the car is waiting. "One step at a time, Kris," I tell myself, as I look back down and focus on keeping my feet moving. "Just get me to the car, God, please! That's all I ask. Just one step at a time."

When we return home, I place Alfonso's remains in the middle of the living room on a large glass coffee table he had made from the trunk of an enormous tree. Adorned with various white flowers and baby's breath, the table looks like a heavenly cloud, with his remains in the middle. I place a portrait of Alfonso just to the left of the box. Before long, the vigil begins. The vigil consists of the saying of the Rosary, readings from the Bible, and testimonials and remembrances of the person who died.

This vigil is the most excruciating night of my life. I remain in the living room until dawn, in a trance-like state for most of the night, losing myself in the rhythmic repetition of the Rosary prayers. I hear bits and pieces of the prayers, ". . . who art in heaven . . . blessed are you among women . . . is now and ever shall be, world without end . . ."

As a Catholic, I have said these same prayers thousands of times before in the belief that somewhere some Almighty Being I called God is hearing them and protecting me. Now, as my mind drifts to Alfonso and the children, the words of the prayers seem hollow. What good are these prayers now? Alfonso is gone forever.

Every so often I open my eyes and look at the people around me, so deep in prayer, their hands joined in a human chain of sorrow. Their love and compassion sustain me through the night. I see the rest of Alfonso's friends who were with him in Canada, and who also returned with Francisco. I get up and walk over to Jaime Gomez and Felipe Vasquez and embrace them.

"You know, Kris," Jaime tells me. "I have never seen Alfonso so happy as he was that day. The skiing was amazing and Alfonso, more than any of us, just seemed to be reveling in it. God, he was so happy."

"I shared a pear with him," Felipe says, "just before that last run. He tried to talk me into joining him, but I was too tired. He had so much energy left; I don't know where it came from.

"I'm so sorry, Kris. I wish there was something we could do, something we could say to make this go away. I feel lucky to be alive, but losing Alfonso the way we did . . ."

We embrace and we both begin to cry. "I'm just so sorry," he says.

I can see the conflicting emotions tearing him apart. I know exactly how he feels.

The funeral is beautiful. The largest church in Guadalajara holds nearly two thousand people, and it is standing room only. The entire church is decorated with white flowers. To me, it looks like heaven. Alfonso Jr. carries the box with his father's ashes down the aisle, followed by me and the other five children. I never thought I would ever see the day when my son would be carrying his father's remains down the aisle of a church. It tears at my heart. Words can't describe the pain I feel with each step down the aisle.

The mass itself is celebrated by three priests, including Kico. *Our Father* is sung beautifully by September, a friend of ours whom we knew through the businesses. The children's choir sounds just like angels.

I am here . . . but I'm not. All I can think about is saying good-bye to Alfonso. It feels like there is no one else in the church or anywhere in the world. Above the altar, I see a beautiful statue of the Blessed Mother, and I can't keep my eyes off her. Suddenly, I see a light streaming out from her extended hands and shining directly in my face. I can feel and even see Alfonso's presence in front of me. He seems to be drawn towards the light, too. With him I sense the presence of angels and the spirits of friends and relatives, including his father. Together, they are all leading him lovingly through this last leg of his journey.

Alfonso stands before me, his face filled with so much love for me that I want to cry. With this great love seems to be a sense of peace, a peace that comes from knowing that his journey is nearly complete. He looks at me and I want to scream, "Don't go! Please!" Yet, I know he must go, the time has come. He smiles and I know he carries our love with him. I realize, for the first time, that he completely understands me, my feelings, my fears, my frustrations, my love. His spirit has transformed him into the perfect husband, the perfect father. He will never leave me. He is part of me and he is part of my children, and will be my friend and husband, and my children's father, forever.

He turns and moves towards the light coming from Mary's hands, but keeps turning back towards me longingly as he gets farther and farther away. He mouths the words, "I will always love you . . ." as the vision of him begins to fade, and he joins his father and the others, and returns to God. I feel all the energy being drained from my body as he slips away. I open my eyes and glance down the aisle at my children to see that the light from the Blessed Mother is also shining on their faces.

"Good-bye," I whisper as I put my face in my hands and begin to cry again.

Outside the church, a line of people are waiting to console me. "It's just too much," I think, as I look out at the crowd of people waiting. One by one, they pass by me, crying, whispering comforting thoughts and then moving on. The words and faces all mix together in an endless stream of condolences. Business associates, friends, relatives, employees, doctors . . . "My God, here comes my obstetrician. I don't suppose I will be seeing him much anymore," I think to myself briefly, and then continue with the next in line. Finally, after what seems like an eternity, the last of the well-wishers pass by.

I go back into the church for a few moments of solitude. I sit in the pew by myself, trying to imagine what life without Alfonso will be like. He has been my partner for so long. I am not even sure I know who I am without him. My likes, dislikes, friends and just about everything about me has been molded by him over the years. The question gnaws at me, "Who am I? Who really am I?" I have no answer. I am terrified—thirty-eight years old with six children, and alone.

After the funeral, I decide that I really need to get away from Guadalajara for a few days. My mom suggests I bring the kids up to San Diego for the Easter holiday, which sounds like a great idea.

Even being in San Diego, I can't get my mind off the accident and all that has transpired. Each night, I have the same nightmare. I see Alfonso and the others at the top of a mountain. A voice in the background, perhaps it's mine, is always screaming, "Don't go out there!" But, the skiers do not listen. They ski right out onto the mountain and get crushed by a wall of snow. Then I see Alfonso crawl out of the wreckage, but his body is mangled and he has no face, just a blank outline where his face is supposed to be. I wake up in a cold sweat with my pulse racing, curl into a fetal position and begin rocking rhythmically back and forth as I cry. Every night, the cycle is the same. Even when I am awake, I can't think of anything but the accident.

One morning at breakfast, while we are sitting in my mom's kitchen, my brother, Steve, asks me a troubling question.

"Kris, doesn't it bother you that Alfonso died the way he did?" he asks. "I mean, I've read some of the articles you have and it sure seems like somebody screwed up, that maybe this was just an accident waiting to happen. I don't know what the law is like in Canada, but I would want to know if this group Alfonso was with did everything they were supposed to do to make sure these things don't happen."

"I'm not sure I'm following you," I say. "You mean like a lawsuit?"

"Yeah, maybe," says Steve, who not surprisingly is in his first year of law school. "I don't know—it just seems like if these people are doing what they're supposed to be doing, accidents like this don't happen. And if they are operating an unsafe program, something like this could happen again, and someone should do something to make sure it doesn't. I don't even know if they were, but it might be worth checking out."

I have never been involved in any type of legal action before, nor do I particularly care too much for lawyers. There is a lot to be said for the Mexican approach of avoiding legal proceedings whenever possible. Mexicans rarely sue each other when conflicts arise because they do not view lawsuits as the proper method for resolving disputes. When Alfonso died, the last thing on my mind was any kind of lawsuit.

After hearing what my brother had to say, and as the reality of what happened is beginning to sink in, my attention is turning to the people in whom Alfonso had placed his trust—Canadian Mountain Holidays (CMH). I know avalanches are a natural phenomenon, like hurricanes, earthquakes or floods. What I am having trouble understanding is why my husband and the eight other victims ever found themselves in such dangerous circumstances. Since skiers do not die every day in avalanches, I feel like I have to know what went wrong. How did nine people, in the hands of a reputable enterprise with qualified ski guides, get swallowed up in an avalanche? Was it simply bad luck or could this disaster have been avoided?

I am taking some time now to read the Canadian newspaper accounts of the accident. In addition, there were articles published in several American magazines, including *Sports Illustrated* and *People*. As I read these articles and learn more about what had happened, I can't ignore the disturbing possibility that the accident that took my husband's life and the lives of eight others did not have to happen. At this point, I have very few hard facts to support my suspicions, but this accident doesn't feel like just a natural disaster.

So, I decide to see what my options are as far as investigating the accident and considering legal action against CMH. My brother, Jim, who has a very level and analytical mind, volunteers to help me and we decide to try to get in touch with a couple law firms in Canada. After some research, Jim locates the two law firms in Vancouver that are considered the best in the field of snow-related accidents. After I return to Mexico with the children, Jim flies to Vancouver to interview both firms. When he returns, Jim calls to fill me in on what he's found.

"Both firms seem pretty well qualified," he says. "I think you probably can't go wrong either way. If I had to choose, I think I would recommend Ross Clark; his firm is called Davis and Company. He actually survived an avalanche a few years ago while he was skiing with CMH, but two of his best friends died in the accident. And Ross has already won a case against CMH."

"They sound pretty good," I say. "So you think I should go with them?"

"Well, the other firm is pretty good too, but I just got a better feeling about these guys," he says. "Ross' associate is Susan Smith and I think you will really like her. She seems like a very warm and caring woman, but also tough as nails. If you decide you want to pursue this, I think she will be a valuable ally in a lot of ways."

"So what's the next step?" I ask.

"Well, they want to meet with you in person sometime relatively soon," he says. "They will either go down to Guadalajara or you can go up there."

I meet Ross and Susan about a month later in Seattle, where I am visiting Joy, an old friend from my days as a flight attendant. As we sit around Joy's living room, I can sense a certain anxiousness in the air as Ross and Susan are eager to get down to business.

"I have to tell you," I say, "that I am not completely sold on the idea of suing CMH."

"Kris, I completely understand," Susan says. "This is a huge decision and really one you shouldn't take lightly. I know in the U.S. people tend to sue for just about anything, but in Canada it's different. We have to know you have a much better than average chance of winning before we will even bring a case like this. Now, from what we know so far, there seems to have been some irregularities, but it's much too early to tell whether you would win or not."

"Susan is exactly right," Ross chimes in. "Even if we investigate and find evidence that CMH was to blame in some way, this will be a very difficult case. The entire legal process, including the trial, will take at least four years, and that's not even including any appeals. I just don't want you think we will just file a lawsuit and they will immediately fork over a lot of money—it rarely works that way in Canada."

"To tell you the truth, I really don't know whether four or five years down the road I will want to be reliving this over and over again on a daily basis," I say. "It's just too hard."

I try to compose myself but the tears begin and I find it hard to slow the tide. Susan walks over and sits next to me, putting her arm around my shoulder.

"Kris, I know you've been through a lot in the last few months," Susan says. "I think you're remarkable for being so courageous. I can't even imagine how hard it's been. We just know that you probably want to know whether this was just an accident, some act of nature, or whether it could have been prevented."

"Well, that's really the reason I'm here," I say through the tears. "The one thing I keep coming back to is needing to know what happened, needing to know the truth—not only for me, but for everyone else who goes on these trips."

"That's what we're here for, Kris," Susan says. "If you decide you want to, we'll try to help you find the truth."

I am as impressed as Jim was with Susan and Ross, both professionally and personally. But, I don't feel ready to make a decision right now, so I tell them I will call them tomorrow and let them know if they should get started.

Joy and I go out shopping to unwind—just like the old days. After shopping for awhile, we stop in a café to have some dinner. As we are sharing a crème brûlée, my favorite dessert, Joy looks me in the eye and asks, "So what are you thinking?"

"I think I'm going to do it," I say. "I got a really good feeling from both of them, and I think this is something I need to do."

"That's exactly what I thought you were going to say," Joy says. "If it was me, I think I would do the same thing. It just all seems too fishy to me."

So, I decide to retain Davis and Company. When I call Ross and Susan, they say they will get busy investigating the accident and will keep me apprised of what they find. I leave Seattle feeling like I made the right decision.

CHAPTER 3
the awakening

I have always been a religious person, a practicing Catholic with very strong beliefs. Now, as Alfonso's death becomes more real to me every day, I suppose my concept of God and religion centers primarily around the teachings and practices of the Catholic Church rather than on connecting or communicating with God on a personal level. The Catholic Church, especially in Mexico, is very regimented with the promise of heaven tied to following the time-honored rules set forth by the Church. So, I take my family to Mass every Sunday, work on obeying the Ten Commandments and other rules of the Church, and have always felt that in doing so, I am working towards my own salvation.

Everything I have been taught during my many years of Catholic schooling tells me that now, in my moment of crisis, God will be here to rescue me. Since I have obeyed the rules of the Church and have been generally a "good" person, I think I have built up a "grace account" that I can tap into in my time of need. I believe that the better a person I am, the higher the balance in my grace account. I also believe that whenever I need to make a withdrawal from this account, I can, and everything will be better.

My time of need has come now very suddenly and is crashing down on me with Alfonso's death. I keep thinking that this grace I have built up in my account is at my disposal to help me through these hard times with little or no effort on my part. I certainly don't expect it to be easy, but I do expect an outpouring of grace to ease my pain and suffering. I am quickly realizing, however, how naïve I have been in expecting "instant spirituality" without having laid the groundwork in advance. I have no idea how to tap into this grace account, although I am beginning to believe that it will require a type of commitment I have not envisioned. At some level, I sense there has to be the possibility of a deeper, more personal relationship with God; and I know I have probably seen glimpses of such a relationship, but I have no idea how to access it now.

I do not know how to dive into the sea of deeper spirituality, nor was I ever taught how this would come to pass. So naturally, I am lost now trying to cope with the tragic circumstances surrounding Alfonso's death. I continue to pray my Hail Marys and Our Fathers, go to Mass nearly every day, and yet I'm falling deeper and deeper into depression and despair. I keep praying that someone or something will save me. I am sitting here, waiting to be rescued, and seem incapable of stepping up to rescue myself.

—————————————

At a very young age, I saw glimpses of the power of prayer and its potential in my life. Soon after I was born on February 14, 1952, in Washington D.C., my parents were told that I had spina bifida, a spinal cord defect that can cause paralysis. When I was three days old, I had spinal surgery and, while the surgery was a success, several of the side effects of the disease continued until I was six years old.

In August 1953, my family moved to the small town of Emmitsburg, Maryland, where my father began teaching at Mt. St. Mary's College. Over the course of the next two years, I would have two more surgeries at hospitals in Washington, D.C. Just as one of the side effects was brought under control, others would arise. My parents had hoped the two surgeries would cure me to the point that I might be able to enjoy a normal childhood. Unfortunately, more trouble was in store.

After the second surgery, I developed a severe tumor in the bone between my knee and ankle, which required immediate surgery. This time, the stakes were much higher. The doctors told my parents that, more often than not, tumors of this sort were malignant and required complete amputation of the leg. In the middle of the surgery, which took place on Good Friday, 1957, the doctor came out and told my mother that all indications so far were that the tumor was malignant. He was just waiting for confirmation from the lab before beginning the amputation. The results, however, came back negative.

After the surgery, I was placed in a lower body cast and we returned to Emmitsburg. Life was anything but normal for me. The Veterans of Foreign Wars donated a wheelchair to help me get around. My mother even started a preschool so other children from the town could come in and play with me since I was so immobile. My only recollections of this time are of hospitals, doctors and pain.

The problem was the bone simply was not healing from the surgery. I still had a hole the size of a marble in the bone in my leg, so I could not put any weight on the bone for fear it would break. I was carted around in a stroller or a wheelchair everywhere I went and even had to begin the first grade in a wheelchair. I still remember the other children staring at me and my not being able to join them on the playground. In addition, the long-term prognosis was not good. The doctors said the longer it took for the bone to heal, the less the likelihood I would recover fully. There was also the possibility that I would never be able to walk again.

Around this time, my health problems had come to the attention of the Sisters of Charity who worked at nearby St. Joseph's College. Along with a group of students, they helped to organize a pilgrimage and prayer vigil at the tomb of Elizabeth Ann Seton. Mother Seton, as she was called, later was canonized and became the first American saint. For nine consecutive evenings, the group of about thirty people—nuns, students, my parents and their friends—gathered at the entrance to St. Joseph's College and proceeded through the campus to the tomb for prayer sessions.

A few weeks later, my father took me to the doctor. After taking X-rays, the doctor came back out into the waiting area. To this day, I remember his words, "I certainly can't believe it," he said, "but it appears the bone has healed."

I think I must have almost jumped out of the wheelchair. I could not believe my ears. He gave me a splint to wear for a short period of time;

but, after that, I was walking around just like everyone else. In fact, just a few months later, I would walk out on stage as the Queen of Hearts in the school pageant. My parents could not believe their eyes as their first daughter, who almost lost her leg and then looked like she would be confined to a wheelchair all her life, walked out onto the stage with her classmates.

My parents believe God used me as an instrument to work this miracle and that my recovery was an indication that I had some special purpose in my life. They also believe, as do I, that I could not have recovered without the intervention of Mother Seton. When she was canonized, my story was one of those submitted to the Vatican as evidence of her miraculous deeds. To this day, my devotion to Mother Seton remains a focal point of my daily prayer life.

With Alfonso gone, I genuinely believe my faith will step in and save me; but, the longer I wait, the more I come to realize that simply possessing this belief and actually making it happen are two very different things. With my day-to-day reality so dark and sorrowful, I do not know where to turn and there is no manual to teach me the way, or so it seems.

Instead of tapping into my faith as I'd hoped, I'm falling into a self-destructive pattern of depression. It's been two months since Alfonso died and I feel completely alone, hounded by an aching loneliness every minute of the day. At night, my despair worsens. After the children are in bed, with the dead hours of the night hanging over me, my heartache intensifies. The emotional suffering causes me intense physical pain. Every night, as I sit alone in my huge king-size bed, my head begins to throb and I feel sick to my stomach. Just a few months ago, my husband would have been sitting right here with me, talking to me, telling me about his day. Now, nothing!

The pain is so intense that it takes over my entire body to the point where all I can do is sit and cry. It always starts with a few tears streaming down my cheeks, then quickly turns into uncontrollable sobs. My mind always focuses on the question . . . Why? Why is this happening? There has to be a reason but, for the life of me, I cannot even begin to imagine what that reason is. The more I think about it, the more I cry. I feel as if half of my very being has been amputated. Half of me died with Alfonso. I silently scream, "Why, why, why . . ." until it trails off into the night. I fall to the side of my bed exhausted, depleted, unable to do anything but curse God and curse Alfonso. I hate them, and I hate myself. Most of all, I hate being alone without the man I have loved for more than half my life and with whom I had planned to spend the rest of my life.

The hatred always turns into despair—so deep that I begin to question the very faith I've been expecting to save me. Where is God through this ordeal? When I need Him most, I don't see, feel or hear Him. If God is love, where is He? I feel like my despair leaves me alone in a vast desert, searching for just a single drop of water; but, I'm finding no oasis in my sightlines. I am waiting for a sign, anything to break me out of this cycle of depression and despair. I need Him to reassure me that He is with me and that everything is going to be all right. Without his reassurance, I just keep coming back to the same question, "Where are you, God? My search for God, my search for my faith, is proving futile. Should I be looking in a different place?"

To compound matters, it seems Francisco is developing a deep mistrust of me and my family. As Alfonso's widow, I have inherited my husband's share of the six businesses he and Francisco had owned together. The Ochoa business empire consists of several businesses involved in the purchase, processing and resale of various types of steel. From very humble beginnings, Alfonso and, to a lesser extent, his brother, Francisco, had built the businesses into an extremely successful enterprise. And now Francisco finds himself in the unfamiliar position of being in charge and having me as a partner. He does not seem to be handling it too well.

The first sign of Francisco's animosity towards me surfaces about two weeks after Alfonso's death, while I am spending the Easter holiday with my family in San Diego. The day after Easter, I receive a fax from Alfonso's secretary, who is now working for me. Francisco is alerting me to the fact that he is terminating many of the benefits Alfonso and I enjoyed while Alfonso was alive, including payment by the businesses of such expenses as car insurance, country club dues, utilities at our home and a variety of other bills, including my secretary's salary. In the memo, Francisco reasons that since I am not an employee, and not producing anything for the businesses in the way Alfonso had, neither I nor my family are entitled to these benefits. To him, it seems perfectly logical and fair, but I am appalled.

When I return to Mexico, I realize Francisco is relishing his role as the head honcho, something he probably has always dreamed about. The avalanche that took Alfonso out of the equation has left Francisco alone at the top of the corporate structure. I suppose he wants everyone to know he is in charge now. I have always sensed from afar that Francisco is obsessed with greed and power. From what I gathered over the years, from hearing various people talk about his business style, Francisco has created a neurotic existence for himself on his road to wealth and power, fearing and suspecting everyone around him and trusting no one, perhaps even Alfonso. He always seems to pay the price for his choices, however. His wife, Gabriela, tells me that he regularly suffers from insomnia, ulcers, general ill health and loneliness. I suppose he must feel the results are worth the adverse consequences.

This initial action by Francisco against my family sets off a red flag as I realize I must now be his primary source of suspicion. I suppose he views me as his only competition, even though the strain and trauma of Alfonso's death have made me incapable of competing at any level. I do not know where Francisco's seeds of suspicion against me come from, other than from his mistrust of people in general. I have been so wrapped in grief since the accident that I have barely given the businesses a second thought. Perhaps he feels that when I snap out of it, I will want to compete with him for control of the businesses or that I may disapprove of the way he is handling things. I can sense in the way he is beginning to treat me and my family that he resents the fact that, as Alfonso's widow, I am entitled to participate in the businesses at all and to reap half of the rewards. Maybe he feels that I have done nothing to deserve any of these riches and, on top of that, I am a woman and not even Mexican.

Most upper-class Mexicans view Americans with mixed emotions and many times, because I am the only American around, I bear the brunt of their criticism. They resent the patronizing, Big Brother approach the United States has taken towards Mexico over the years and its perception that Mexico is a Third World country. At the same time, they begrudgingly admire American ingenuity and realize how important their neighbors to the north are, and will be, to Mexican economic development.

It is inaccurate to say that the Mexican people envy Americans. Mexicans are fiercely proud of their heritage and rightly so, as they live in a land rich in natural resources, beauty, culture, history and art. While they often poke fun at themselves when it comes to their place in the world order, they are very sensitive to the criticisms and ribbings of others, especially Americans.

I discovered this the hard way when I made the mistake of crossing the line. One afternoon, not long after Alfonso and I had been married, I was with the wives of some of his business associates for a baby shower. The conversation turned to a supposed UFO sighting in the mountains near Guadalajara. One of the women recounted the incident and concluded by saying, "And the government even sent out the Air Force to check it out."

It was common knowledge that the Mexican Air Force consisted of, at the most, a few dozen World War II fighter planes at a small base outside of Guadalajara. The women were about to joke about that when I beat them to it.

"Oh, you actually have an Air Force," I joked.

The women's jaws dropped and there was dead silence. I knew instantly I had inserted my American foot into my American mouth. It would have been acceptable for them to have made the joke, but not me. After an awkward silence, I beat a hasty retreat and apologized, saying that I knew Mexican military services were top notch.

"Okay, okay . . . you don't have to go that far," one of the women said while laughing. "We know they're not; but, just because you're American, don't think that your military is the only one around. There are others."

I got the message loud and clear. From that day forward, I was very sensitive to their Mexican pride and patriotism.

I am certain part of the animosity Francisco feels towards me comes from this common resentment of Americans. He views me as the outsider in so many ways and that translates into my being the enemy. I am sure that Francisco feels that if he does not protect what is his, the aggressive

American widow is sure to come after it. In my current state of mind, following Alfonso's death, he could not possibly be further from the truth. Still, Francisco's initial actions and attitude do make me nervous. I do not know what he is planning, but I know that because of the paranoid way he operates, our working relationship is going to be a difficult one.

After conferring with several of my family members, we decide that the best course of action is to try to find out exactly what I have inherited. The only way to get an accurate assessment of my position with respect to the businesses is to hire an accountant to conduct an audit of the businesses. It's important that I choose someone whom I trust and who is respected in the business community to represent me in my official capacity as partner in the businesses. This will allow me to distance myself from Francisco while still keeping tabs on the businesses. I feel these actions are quite appropriate and reasonable, especially given my lack of business experience, and typical of what any major shareholder in a large corporation might do in similar circumstances. I suppose these actions shouldn't be necessary among family, but the bottom line is I really do not trust Francisco.

After interviewing several accounting firms, selecting one and then hiring an attorney, I am ready to meet with Francisco to discuss these matters. On a beautiful Saturday morning in July, I take the first step towards protecting my interests in the family business. Arriving right on time, I find Francisco waiting for me in his office. The entire complex is deserted except for the two of us. As I take my seat, I notice how sparsely decorated his office is in contrast to Alfonso's office, which reflected his vibrant personality with photos, awards and personal mementos everywhere. Francisco's seems like a morgue. A bookcase behind his desk holds several business-related manuals. Other than the two photos of his family on his desk, the office is devoid of personal touches.

As his eyes look up from his desk to meet mine, I sense immediately that he is not in a good frame of mind. He looks strained, with dark circles under his bloodshot eyes, as if he has not slept well for weeks.

"Are you okay?" I ask. "You don't look too good."

"I'm fine," he snaps. "What do you want to talk about?"

In a very professional and detached manner, I begin to advise him of my decision. "Francisco," I say, "as you know, I don't have a lot of experience in business matters and I'm a little overwhelmed by what I've inherited. So I talked with some of my family members and they think I need to get a realistic picture of where the companies are right now so I can begin planning for the future."

He just sits there silently and looks as if I am speaking a foreign language. As I continue, I sense the rage building inside him. He flexes his lips in and out like a fish until they settle into a tight straight line on his face. I begin to get unnerved, as he appears to be fuming inside, but holding back for now.

"I've decided to hire an attorney to represent me in all these things, and I'm going to hire a company to audit the businesses," I say. "It's the only way I can . . ."

"If that is what you want, you will destroy the companies," he interrupts.

Speaking in nonsensical ramblings, he goes on to explain that certain areas of the businesses simply should not be exposed to outsiders. "Kris, you don't know what the hell you are talking about and if you know me at all, which I guess you don't, then you would know that I simply will not allow this to happen," he says. "Our laundry must be done at home and no outsiders—I don't care who the hell you have in mind—are going to come in and look at my records. It's just not going to happen. Understand?"

His eyes get very small and snake-like as he stands up. Although not large in stature—he stands about 5'7" and is slim—Francisco strikes an intimidating pose when he gets angry. He turns towards the window, then quickly back towards me as he slams his fist on the desk.

"If you do this, you will have me as an enemy," he says. "I am not a good person to have as an enemy. Get my drift? We have creditors . . . Alfonso owed money . . . you may end up in jail or who knows. I'm not a good enemy to have. Think about this long and hard before you make up your mind. This could mean war."

Then suddenly, he changes gears and begins ranting about Alfonso. "Do you know what a lazy son of a bitch your husband was," he says. "The only reason we are where we are today is because of me. Alfonso never pulled his own weight around here. I did everything. If it wasn't for me, we would all be bankrupt. Everything we have is thanks to me, and now you come in here with this shit . . . I'm not going to carry you like I carried your husband, especially if you start pulling this kind of shit. You need to shut up and trust me just like Alfonso should have done. Any other way and I swear to God I'll crush you. You've just got to see things my . . ."

This outburst is more than I can handle. I cannot listen to him disparage my husband, especially when I know everything he says is just plain wrong. My head is reeling and my stomach starts to churn loudly. I stand up while he is in mid-sentence and rush out of the room and down the hall, barely making it to the bathroom before I throw up. My mind is racing, "How can he threaten me, his sister-in-law, and then trash his own brother? What kind of person am I dealing with? What the hell is going on here? First Alfonso's death, now Francisco—that son of a bitch. His ungrounded arrogance amazes me . . . doesn't he know everything he has is because of Alfonso?"

I am angry and confused but, most of all, scared. I know Francisco is deluded and I know he has a violent streak in him. I have heard from a number of people that he has hit his wife and children on occasion; and once even hit his sister. What's to stop him from hitting me, too—or worse? Fear consumes me, as I realize Alfonso is not here to protect me. Oh God, what am I going to do? I don't want a war with Francisco. My children and his are very close and I don't want to endanger that relationship.

Emotionally, I can't handle a power struggle that I know in the long run I will probably lose. Women in Mexico have little place in the man's world of big business, especially in the steel industry, and the fact that I am an American will also work against me. Nor am I inclined to suddenly become a career woman and take over the day-to-day operations of the businesses, especially with six children at home.

I decide to do what I'm sure Alfonso had done with Francisco many times before—follow the path of least resistance. I decide to try his theory that he is a better friend than enemy. I do not trust him; but, in light of his threatening outburst, I feel I have no choice. I leave the bathroom after what seems like an eternity and return to his office feeling totally defeated.

As I walk back to my seat, he blurts out, "Well, what's it going to be?"

"Francisco," I say, fighting back the tears. "I can't believe you would talk to me this way or about your brother the way you just did. It's unbelievable. I don't know what you think is going on, but I am just trying to do what's best for my family. That's all. If you can't understand that, then . . ."

I can't go on as the tears flood down my cheeks.

"After all I've been through . . . and for you to say these things . . . I just don't know . . . I guess . . . for now . . . we'll do it your way . . . no attorney . . . no audit . . . we'll do it your way and see how it goes."

He stands up, a huge smile on his contemptuous face, and sneers, "You've made a wise choice." With that, he extends his hand and I think I'm going to be sick again. As we shake, I pray that I have made the right choice, but I know he knows he's beaten me.

———————————

I desperately want to give Francisco the benefit of the doubt. I almost feel guilty in not trusting him, as if I am betraying the family. I keep harkening back to my husband's promise that Francisco would take care of us. My biggest dilemma is trying to figure out how to deal with Francisco on a day-to-day basis. On the surface, he appears to be living up to his promise to take care of my family. My monthly stipends continue and I am at least nominally participating in the running of the businesses. I attend board meetings, look over reports and do my best to make sense of the information I am being allowed to see.

Beneath the surface, however, I feel like Francisco is still plotting. According to him, all of the businesses are losing money, which he blames on everyone but himself. Francisco has a litany of excuses: the economy is bad, the employees are not working hard enough, Alfonso had not prepared for this downturn, etc. The actual truth is that when Alfonso died, our group of companies was considered to be the second largest steel service center in all of Mexico. The dismal outlook for the companies now seems plausible only because Francisco lacks the business savvy my husband had used to build the companies.

One day in August, Francisco's plans become much clearer. He asks me to come to his office to discuss the state of the companies. I know right away something is fishy as he begins to explain how poorly the businesses are doing.

"The only solution," he says, "is a major capital infusion from the partners. I expect you to contribute $500,000 to the companies right away and I will do the same."

"But Francisco," I say, "you know I don't have that kind of money. Everything I have left is for the children's future."

"What are you talking about?" he says. "You just got the life insurance money from the States. That had to be at least two million. You can use that."

Now I can see where he is headed—he just wants to get his hands on the proceeds from Alfonso's life insurance. We have the same insurance agent, so he must have found out from her that I recently received the checks. For his plan to work, he needs me to believe that the situation is growing more dismal each week. I know I am not being told the truth about the status of the companies, but I have no independent source of information. The only information I receive is from Francisco, and my trust in him is waning daily.

"We need that money, Kris," he says. "It's the only way we'll survive."

"I'll think about it," I say, as I get up to leave.

He grabs my wrist as I turn to leave, and whispers in my ear, "We need that money."

My inner turmoil from Alfonso's death and the tension of my dealings with Francisco has begun to manifest itself in my outward appearance. Even when I am healthy, I am only 5'2" and weigh just 100 pounds. Since Alfonso's death, I have lost about five pounds. When I look in the mirror, I look so thin and emaciated, I scare myself. Every line in my face reflects my pain and confusion, and I am beginning to project an aura of desperation to many of the people around me. I simply do not know what to do or where to turn. I want peace, but I cannot find it. I want to stop crying, but the tears keep flowing. I cry all the time, night and day. The only thing that varies is the intensity.

One of my friends, Anna, has started to pick up the distress signals I am sending out. Anna's husband was a good friend of Alfonso's, and died five months before Alfonso. In June 1990, he was diagnosed with a cancerous brain tumor. By October, he was dead. One day towards the end of summer, she came over to my house for lunch. While we are sitting on my patio, she takes a long look at me and tells me what I probably already know, "Kris, you need help. You remind me of a juggler. You are trying desperately, and futilely I might add, to balance all of your different problems in the air around you. You are carrying so much baggage around that wherever you go, you can barely make it through the door. You need to stop this juggling and let go of the baggage."

"Easier said than done," I think to myself. Anna persists, however, and leads me through an exercise she learned that involved creating and labeling an imaginary compartment for each of my problems.

"In your mind, create all of these different areas for each of your problems and make sure each compartment has a door with a lock," she says. "Make one compartment for Alfonso's death, another for your grieving, another for each of the children, another for the businesses you have inherited and another for the future. Keep these compartments locked, and only unlock one at a time, and only when you absolutely have to deal with that issue. Otherwise, forget about them.

"If you try to deal with all of them at once, like you're doing now, you won't last too long. Your problems would overwhelm anyone, but you have to live in the present, which means taking on each problem individually and dealing with it only when you encounter it. You can't waste your energy dwelling on all of your problems all of the time. If you do, you'll be headed for the loony bin before you know it."

"I feel like I'm already there," I say.

"I know you do, honey," Anna says. "I felt the exact same way after my husband died. I could barely get out of bed in the morning. I just wanted to lie there and cry all day and hope that somehow I would wake up and things would be like they had been. But it never happened. I kept waiting and waiting, but it never happened.

"Kris, I want you to come with me on Monday to a class on prayer and meditation over at the Jesuit University in Guadalajara. A friend of mine teaches it. Have you ever tried meditating?"

"Not really," I say.

"Well, you're coming with me then and I'm not taking 'no' for an answer," she says.

As she goes on to describe the class to me, I look in her eyes and wonder how she can be at such peace with herself and her situation after all that she has been through. For the first time in months, I see peace, love and compassion. I want that same peace so badly, but I am too scared. I have become so dependent on and absorbed in my cycle of pain and tears that I can't see beyond them enough to let go. Besides, what could a prayer class possibly teach me about a religion I have been practicing since I was a child?

"I'm sorry, Anna, but I just don't think it would do any good."

"Let me help you, Kris. God is here, within you," she says as she takes my finger in her hand and touches my heart. "You just can't recognize it right now, but in time you will. You just have to see Him, I mean really see Him. Not words in the Bible or prayers in church. You need to get to know God on a personal, intimate level. When you do, your life will never be the same.

"I know it's hard, Kris, but I really think this will help. The class starts at 10:00 a.m. on Monday. I promise you won't regret it, and what have you got to lose?"

"I just don't know, Anna," I say, fighting back the tears. "I guess I will think about it, but I don't think anyone or anything can help me right now."

I cannot decide whether to go with Anna on Monday. Every time I have just about decided not to go, I come back to the peace I saw in Anna's eyes. Something has enabled her to overcome her pain and sorrow. What can it be? Would I find out at this class? Curiosity and, perhaps, desperation get the best of me and I decide to go. So here I find myself on a Monday entering a college classroom, scared to death. The peace I sense in Anna is too alluring.

When I arrive at the classroom, Anna introduces me to her friend, Susan, who will lead the class. Susan is an American nun originally from Kansas, who has been in Mexico teaching for several years. She seems very nice; but, for one of the few times in my life, I do not have much to say. Words are unnecessary, as Susan immediately picks up on my emotional pain from my appearance and demeanor. I'm sure Anna has told her my story, but she doesn't ask me any questions. She just welcomes me into the class.

I take a seat as far in the back of the classroom as possible. All I can think is, "What am I doing here?" as the room begins to fill up with about fifteen or twenty other women; and, shortly after 10:00 a.m., we begin.

"Happiness comes from within us," Susan says. "It does not depend on anyone else. Everything we need to be happy is inside us. It is our decision how we use it."

"She is wrong," I think to myself. She cannot possibly be more wrong. Can't she see there is absolutely no happiness in me right now? Alfonso is dead and the best parts of me have died with him. There can be no happiness. I am incapable of being happy without him. She is so wrong. I feel like leaving.

"God wants us to be happy," she continues.

"Then where is He?" I think. I have been searching desperately for Him night and day with absolutely no luck. How can He want us to be happy when He won't even show me He's with me?

"If you are making your happiness depend on another person, or on an amount of money, or on material things, you will never find it," Susan says. "Happiness is finding your Self, and after you encounter your Self, then you begin to accept yourself for who you are. Through enlightenment, you will begin to understand who you really are."

My mind begins to drift away from God and back to me. Who am I? I don't have a clue who I am. Sure, I know I am Kris Ochoa, mother of six children, wife and now widow of Alfonso, but what am I all about? I have lots of labels to describe myself, but what do they mean? Is my identity so sewn up in the lives of these other people that I have no separate identity? I feel a little lightheaded and nauseated the more I ponder these thoughts. Then Susan glances at me in the back of the classroom and seems to direct her next words to me.

"Only through silence can you touch the center of your center: God," she says. "Through that encounter you will begin to glimpse who you really are."

Silence. Peace. Silence. Is that what I had seen in Anna's eyes? What is silence? I have experienced my share of silence during the last few months—a silence so deep and painful in the early hours of the morning that I thought it would never end. Is this the silence Susan is talking about?

"Silence," Susan explains, "is in essence meditation or centering prayer. It is prayer from the heart, from the spirit, not from the mind. The mind is a freeway interchange of ideas and emotions out of control. The mind goes so fast and loud that it is like having eight radios turned full blast and trying to listen to each one. The mind is not the most important part of our Self. In fact, most of the time, it is an obstacle to discovering our Self.

"How can we ever hear God or find ourselves with all of that noise disturbing us? The key is to silence both the mind and the brain. This class will be an attempt to teach us to do just that. It will require more than just a part-time commitment. Enlightenment requires daily practice. Everything in life is a process. Slowly you will see the importance of this and people around you will notice a difference in you . . . a change, a more peaceful you."

"Interesting," I think. I certainly have noticed the peace in Anna and Susan. What do I have to lose? I have hit rock bottom and Susan's words are sparking a glimmer of hope, albeit a faint one. She has struck a chord. I don't know what chord, but I have a feeling it may be a special one.

My life and the lives of my children slowly begin to return to normal as we resume our daily routines when school starts in the fall. The days are hectic, filled with transporting the children to and from school and to their many other activities. I try to absorb myself in these tasks because they keep me busy and take my mind off my loneliness. In the evenings, however, after the children are asleep, my imagination runs wild. I create countless scenarios of potential crises my children and I will have to face alone without Alfonso. In the solitude of my bedroom, I am helpless to stop the chain of disasters I am convinced lay ahead in my future.

One night, I even imagine little Annette has cancer. The illusion is so powerful that I go through the entire process in my mind, from her diagnosis to her treatment to her uncertain recovery. "My God," I think, "how am I going to be able to see her through this alone?" My heart pounds and sweat builds on my forehead and upper lip. I try desperately to hold back the panic, but it engulfs me as all I can see is my baby girl in a hospital bed with tubes running through her tiny body, and me, helpless, sitting at her bedside holding her hand.

Somehow I snap myself out of it, but the emotional wreckage the illusion leaves keeps me awake all night. I cannot control my thoughts and I cannot help but wonder why God is putting me through this torture on top of losing Alfonso. Where is my help, my support, my strength?

The next morning, I sit in Susan's classroom, weary and distraught. She begins the class with a story.

"The search for God is like the story of the little fish in the ocean," she says. "The little fish has an extremely important question that had puzzled him for a long time. He decides to ask a bigger, wiser fish, so he frantically swims after the bigger fish to catch up with him. Finally, when he catches up with the big fish, the little fish pants, huffs and puffs, and asks the big fish, 'Big fish, please help me. I have a very important question to ask you. I can't figure out the answer. It is driving me crazy. Please tell me, where is the water in this big ocean we live in?'

"The lesson is obvious," Susan continues. "God is everywhere, just like the water is for the little fish, but most of the time we are oblivious to His presence. God is inside us and outside us; we live and breathe Him as does everything in creation. Our problem is one of awareness. In theory, it seems so simple for the little fish: just look around and water is everywhere. So too should it be simple for us: look around and witness God's presence everywhere. But the steps in between are the hard part."

I realize that the illusions and fears hounding me nightly are my creation, obstacles to my ability to acknowledge and feel God's presence in my life, in nature and in everything. I have created them, and it is up to me to dispel them.

I am learning, however, that the type of awareness needed for me to dispel these illusions and fears cannot be achieved overnight, and my inability to accelerate the process frustrates me. I feel like an ant standing on the edge of an enormous blanket. My limited vision is of the two or three threads of yarn woven together immediately in front of me. To me, this small area appears huge because my vision does not extend any farther—

my entire life, all the pain and confusion, is in those two or three threads. I am not even cognizant of any area beyond what is in my immediate vision. I cannot see the grandeur of the entire blanket—the harmony of each thread woven together so naturally to create the larger existence; the perfection of each thread occupying exactly the space it is supposed to while bonding together to give strength to the whole.

My vision is so narrow that I can't see beyond Alfonso's death, and past the huge void it creates in my life. Nor can I see beyond the turmoil with Francisco. To me, these catastrophes seem like part of some huge cosmic mistake, and I'm not sure I want to see things differently. Can it be that everything that happens, happens just the way it is supposed to happen, as part of some greater plan? Can it be that Alfonso's death, rather than being a cosmic mistake, is just another strand in the blanket of my life and of the lives of my children; and that strand is exactly where it is supposed to be—tightly interwoven with all the other strands? Can it be that Francisco's hostility towards me is also just another one of these strands? Can it be that all these strands, however painful, are connected in some semblance of order, not only in my blanket, but also with the blankets of all other people and nature and God? Can it be that everything is exactly as it should be, and the only way it can be? Can it be . . .

These new ideas represent a radical departure from how I have been viewing Alfonso's death and Francisco's hostility, and they create an inner conflict in me. I feel like I have two opposing forces struggling against each other for center stage in my mind and in my spirit. On the one hand, I have the pain and suffering I've wrapped myself in since Alfonso's death. The cycle of self-pity and depression to which I've become accustomed, while destructive, is known to me, comfortable, secure and hard to break. On the other hand, I have this growing awareness of something much greater out there and in me. I don't know exactly what it is, but I know it is worth pursuing. Like the ant, I stand peering over my three little strands of yarn, desperately trying to get a glimpse of the bigger picture. According to Susan, however, getting that greater glimpse is not easy.

"Cultivating the type of awareness we are talking about comes only at the high cost of reaching out and letting go of your fears," she says. "This is the one and only path to awareness."

Susan's words remind me of a scene from a movie I had seen with the children recently called *Indiana Jones and the Last Crusade*. In this scene, Indiana Jones is searching for the Holy Grail and is close to finding it when his father is shot and critically injured by their pursuers. To save his father, he needs to quickly find the Holy Grail, a sip from which promises eternal life. He finds himself at the edge of a huge cavern with the Holy Grail on the other side. There is no way across the bottomless cavern. The ancient manual that has led him to the Holy Grail tells him he must "leap the cavern" to get to the other side, a span of at least 40 feet. While looking across the cavern, Indiana realizes the leap the manual calls for is not a physical leap, but a spiritual one—a leap of faith. He hears his father in the background say, "You must believe, boy. You must believe."

When Indiana Jones musters the courage and the faith to take that first step out into the cavern, a path appears below him—leading him across the cavern to the other side. Had he never taken that first step, the path never would have appeared. At times, my first steps seem equally as daunting. But maybe I, too, will see the path appear before me.

My steps are small and clumsy, but I feel like something is growing within me, and these steps I'm taking appear to be creating a new path in front of me. With Susan's help, I'm learning to meditate. I always considered meditation silent prayer, but I've learned that meditation is much more than that. My first efforts at meditation are fruitless. I sit for hours trying to *will* myself into relaxing and finding myself in the silence. The harder I try, the more thoughts race through my mind to distract me. Thoughts of Alfonso, of what life would be like if he were still here, of the accident, of my children's futures, swirl through my mind and keep me from focusing. Susan tells me this is normal and to keep trying.

"Meditation involves silencing your mind so that you can see past your fears, and past your worries about the past and the future, to reach a point where you are living in the 'eternal present,'" she says. "These thoughts sidetracking you are to be expected after what you've been through. When that happens, don't fight those thoughts—just let them flow in through your mind and then right out again. Don't dwell on them, and try to regain your focus. Always return to the stillness, that place where all the thoughts and pressures of everyday life don't exist. This type of meditation enables you to experience a communion with your true self and with God."

Finally, one day, I am able to just let go. I am sitting on a chair in my bedroom, eyes closed, and I focus on nothing but the silence. I am amazed at the peace and harmony I feel inside me in the silence of my prayer. Occasionally, thoughts pass through my mind, but all my energy is focused not on my mind, but on my spirit and on the love I am feeling in this communion with my true self and with God. It is truly exhilarating!

The time I set aside each day to meditate is now the most important part of my daily routine. Susan guides me through various techniques of meditation and relaxation, most of which I struggle with at first. She tells me these exercises are intended to help me reach a deeper level of consciousness and awareness. Even so, I don't notice much of an overall change in myself. I look forward to the silent time by myself but, away from my praying, I am just as confused as ever.

My friends, however, notice a subtle change in me. They ask me, "With all that is happening in your life, how can you look so peaceful?" I suppose the inner source of love I am discovering within myself is changing me without my even knowing it. The peace I feel during my meditations is beginning to transform my entire being as I rediscover God's presence within me. Slowly, I am beginning to resonate with the same peace I had seen in Anna and in Susan when I first embarked on this journey just a few months ago.

Around this time, I am asked very unexpectedly to be the keynote speaker at the National Steel Association Convention in Puerto Vallarta. The Association is going to present me with a special lifetime achievement award in recognition of Alfonso's contributions to the Mexican steel industry. They want me to come to the convention to accept the award, and then to address the delegates on the topic of "Success in Life."

I debate for several weeks whether to accept the invitation. I do not know whether I can get up before nearly a thousand government officials and businessmen so soon after Alfonso's death. These men are among the most powerful in Mexico, and Alfonso had been one of their leaders. I am intimidated not only by the idea of the speech, but also by the topic. I am sure they expect me to discuss Alfonso's recipe for success in the business world, a topic I don't feel comfortable talking about. To top it off, the date that they want me to speak, November 24, 1991, would be my eighteenth wedding anniversary, and my first without Alfonso. The whole idea seems much too overwhelming.

The more I think about it, though, the more I see the offer in a different way. This could be a golden opportunity, and perhaps my last one, to share in Alfonso's legacy and to revel in the amazing business success he enjoyed. Perhaps in some way, my appearing at the convention could even enhance that legacy. In addition, having a woman—and an American woman at that—give the keynote address at a gathering of Mexican businessmen simply has not been done. Part of me wants to seize this opportunity—to make Alfonso proud and to share with these men how I feel and what I have learned about the true meaning of success. So with more than a little trepidation, I set out for Puerto Vallarta with a definite purpose in mind.

My palms are sweating and I am trembling as I sit on the stage at the convention waiting to be called. I don't remember ever being this nervous about anything. I sit nearly paralyzed in front of hundreds of Mexican businessmen praying for the strength to get through the speech without crying too much. Just as I am being introduced, the spotlight shines on me and I am lifted out of my seat and up towards the podium, but through no effort of my own. It feels as though angels are surrounding me, strengthening me with their love and support, and guiding me forward with a sense of peace and purpose. What do I have to fear? This message is too important.

I begin by thanking them for the award, which I feel is a wonderful tribute to Alfonso, who worked so hard for so long to be successful in business and in life. I emphasize that success in life is the far more important of the two, a feeling I know Alfonso shared. Since his death, I have come to believe it even more and have developed a new perspective on exactly what success means. I look out at the faces in the crowd and wonder if any of these very "successful" businessmen have any idea of what I am talking about. I pause for a moment, unsure of myself. Then I look out into the spotlights, feel the strength of my angels supporting me, and the words begin to flow effortlessly from my mouth.

> For me, someone who is truly successful in life is someone who radiates peace. That means that the person has totally accepted God's will. It sounds easy, but the simplest things in life many times are the most difficult. When God sends us a difficult situation, most of us complain, "Why me . . . I don't deserve this . . . It's not fair." I know this all too well because it is exactly what I did after Alfonso died.

> When we resist the pain of the situation, it causes us to suffer. When we accept that the pain is part of God's plan, we realize that pain can be tolerated while suffering cannot. Suffering can twist our minds and drive us crazy. To accept the pain is to accept the fact that we must live each moment of life intensely—there is no past, it has gone; there is no future, it's not here yet. The moment we quit fighting or resisting different situations in our lives and see them for what they really are, we don't suffer anymore. We begin to live our pain and soon it too passes. Happiness and security are inside ourselves. If we hang our happiness on someone or some *thing*, we will never find it. Success is realizing that with or without a given person, with or without money, status or possessions, with or without a certain company or business, I will be happy. There are no conditions attached to this type of happiness.

> We believe and have been taught that the more we do, the better we are. If we can do three or four things at

the same time, we are "Superpeople." If I can talk on the phone, make dinner and take care of the baby all at the same time, I am, or so I thought, an excellent mom. But what has happened? I did nothing with my 100 percent undivided attention. Everything was done halfheartedly and with only a portion of my attention. This is not living. It's just "getting by," getting through the day. Half of the time we have very little recollection of many of the things we do in any given day. On the other hand, giving everything we do our undivided attention enables us to live intensely.

I would like, if I could take this moment, to give all of you some advice: Live life intensely. Always be present to the moment. If you live your life with your spouse with this idea, you will be happy.

Many men live in the business world where power, ambition, money, prestige and status are immortalized. We have accepted this as human nature. I am here to tell you it's not. Life changes from one moment to the next. Live your lives as couples fully, for you never know what tomorrow will bring. Sometimes we say things to our partners that we wish we hadn't, and many times we don't say the things we wished we had. All I can say is that I would give anything to have only five minutes with Alfonso . . . and that is not possible.

Live fully and open your hearts to the person or people you love. Communicate what's in your heart because, if that person dies suddenly, then you can go on living knowing that you left no stone unturned and nothing unsaid, that you lived intensely and fully. Because to be able to go on in life, you must be able to lovingly close certain chapters of your life and open other new ones.

To me, that is the essence of success: To decide to live,
and not to remain asleep.

By the end of my speech, I am beginning to cry and I can barely finish through my tears. I am so emotional that I just want to get out of the room, to run away and be alone. The things I have said came from so deep in my heart that they literally have drained all my energy. My emptiness is short lived, however, for just as I finish, the room explodes with applause. I look down to see all of the businessmen standing and clapping, some wiping tears from their own eyes as they applaud. I am so moved, I cry even more, while the applause continues for nearly five minutes.

That evening, the new president of the steel association takes office, and—instead of using his planned speech—he tells the gathering that he has been so moved by what I said in the morning that he wants to comment further. He transforms his entire acceptance speech into a discourse on what should be important in our lives. His message, not unlike mine, is that the love we cultivate in our homes and in our relationships is so much more important than anything that we could ever do in a boardroom.

I leave Puerto Vallarta feeling proud and even a bit in awe of the impact I have made on the group of steel executives. The depth of my newfound spiritual awareness and my ability to share that awareness with others moves me greatly. The last eight months have been as difficult a period as I can imagine. And the future . . . well . . . who knows what that will hold. For the first time, however, I feel like I have taken those first few steps out into the unknown, but with an awareness that I am not venturing out alone. Alfonso is with me, as are my own guardian angels. Their presence not only helped me get through the speech, but is also pointing me towards a greater awareness of who I really am. Maybe I have always known at some level they have been with me, but I am just now beginning to accept and appreciate their love. While I cannot see where exactly my path is leading, my growing awareness is making the first few steps much clearer.

CHAPTER 4
the betrayal

A few days after I return from Puerto Vallarta, Ramon Beteta, a friend of Alfonso's, calls me and says he wants to talk about something very important. Ramon had been Alfonso's personal account executive at the bank in Guadalajara and knew our finances inside and out, so I assume that is what he wants to discuss. When he arrives the next day, he startles me with his candor.

"Kris, I know what's going on between you and Francisco and I want to help," he says.

"My God," I think, "nobody is supposed to know about this."

"Look, I know what Francisco is doing to you because I've been there before. When my father died, his family completely took advantage of my mother—she was an American, too. They shut her out of the family business and she didn't get nearly what she had coming, and I can see the same thing is happening to you."

"Oh, Ramon," I say, "I am so relieved. Every time I've tried to get anywhere with Francisco, I just get shut down. I told him I needed somebody from the outside to take care of my affairs and he threatened to have me thrown in jail. I just don't know what to do."

Ramon suggests that I form a team around me to develop a strategy for protecting my interests. He suggests the team consist of Ramon, Pepe

Levy, our good friend Ernesto Gomez Ibarra, and an attorney he knows and trusts, Ignacio Gonzalez Luna. By this time I have seen enough to know that I simply cannot trust Francisco to do what is right. However, I do implicitly trust the men Ramon suggests, which brings me a feeling of transitory relief. Perhaps, with their help, everything is going to be all right after all.

After lunch, Ramon asks to see all of the paperwork from the businesses that I have with me. So I go up to my room and bring down three boxes full of various papers that I had been accumulating from Francisco. Ramon spends two hours going through all of the files before he comes across something that catches his eye. He gets a very serious, troubled look on his face as he reads through the papers in this particular file.

"Kris, is this your signature?" he asks, as he hands me several documents.

"Yeah, it is. Why?"

"The date on these is March 13 . . . that son of a bitch was after you the morning after Alfonso died," he says. "I can't believe this!"

"After me for what?"

"Kris, do you remember signing these documents?"

I take a quick look at them, but they don't look familiar. "No, not really," I say. "Wait a minute. I do have a vague recollection of several of Francisco's assistants visiting me the morning after. Yeah, they said Francisco had given them some documents for me to sign before he left for Canada. They said something about needing to show that the businesses were in good hands with Francisco. I don't really remember too much about it—all that time is kind of a blur to me."

"Kris, I don't know how to tell you this, but these documents you signed put you personally on the line for $7 million of the companies' debts."

"So is that bad? What does that mean?"

"It means Francisco has you over the barrel," he says. "It doesn't mean you owe the money right now. But, when these debts come due, and if the businesses aren't in a position to cover them, the banks could come after your personal assets."

"Oh my God," I say, as I grasp my hands to my face and lean forward. "Are you telling me that he was scheming to get me just hours after Alfonso died?"

"It sure looks like it," he says.

I suddenly remember numerous conversations I had with Alfonso in which he would always tell me that if anything happened to him, I would still have Francisco to take care of me. So, naturally, when Alfonso died, my instinct was to trust Alfonso's promise and assume Francisco would look out for me and my family's best interests. Despite my misgivings about Francisco's nature and his honesty, I didn't think *even he* was capable of this type of treachery.

This contrary reality hits me like a cannon ball. Only twelve hours after my world had been shattered by the news of my husband's death, while I was disoriented and incoherent, and incapable of focusing on anything other than coming to terms with what had happened and the implications for me and my family, Francisco had screwed me. Then, suddenly, everything begins to fall into place and make sense.

Alfonso's death meant that, for the first time in his life, Francisco was number one in the family and in the businesses. I do not doubt that Francisco mourned the loss of his brother in some way, but I also believe he saw an opportunity and he seized it. So, when I least expected it, on the morning after my husband died, Francisco began his efforts to consolidate his power.

As Alfonso's widow, I inherited his share of the six businesses he and Francisco owned together. Although Alfonso had become one of the most successful businessmen in Guadalajara, his business empire had very humble beginnings. After dropping out of school at the age of seventeen, Alfonso worked for one of his uncles in the steel business. By paying close attention to his uncle, Alfonso learned the basics of how to distribute steel and, before long, decided to go out on his own. With a 5,000-peso loan (about $600 U.S. at the time) from his mother, Alfonso started his own steel service business. In the beginning, he delivered steel orders on his bicycle. As his experience and knowledge grew, he began to build a reputation as a hard-working, honest entrepreneur.

By the time we were married in 1973, Alfonso had built a strong foundation for his business. He had made enough to put both his brothers through school, to support his mother and to provide for our growing family. Alfonso valued his family deeply and wanted his steel business to be a family enterprise. When Francisco finished college, Alfonso asked him to join the business as an accountant. Over the years, this relationship developed into a fifty-fifty partnership between the brothers in their ever-expanding steel conglomeration.

By 1979, Alfonso's business encompassed three steel service centers in Guadalajara, and plans were made to expand even further. The main business was the purchase and resale of raw steel. The expansion plans called for the creation of a steel processing plant for the cutting and preparation of construction-type steel and a wire production plant. Both these businesses came to be successful entities in the early 1980s through Alfonso's leadership. Alfonso seemed to have come full circle in the late 1980s when he expanded into the bicycle business. As the mountain bike craze was just beginning, Alfonso and I arranged to be the exclusive distributor in Mexico of Diamond Back bicycles through a company we called Cyclos. Finally, at the time of his death, Alfonso was making the final preparations for the establishment of a $120 million steel mini-mill. He had negotiated all of the details with the government, and President Carlos Salinas de Gortari had agreed to participate in the groundbreaking ceremony.

Alfonso's success in business and in life was due to his persistence and his uncanny ability to make his sometimes impossible-sounding plans come to fruition. He quite simply would not take "no" for an answer and nothing was impossible for him. Although never a good student, Alfonso had business vision. He was an expert negotiator with a keen business sense. He also had the ability to surround himself with executives who shared or at least understood his vision and who were able to help him implement his plans. Alfonso had a magnetic personality, which drew people from all walks of life to him. His love of life was invigorating.

Unfortunately, Francisco possessed none of these attributes. Whereas Alfonso had vision, Francisco was a bottom-line numbers cruncher. He possessed none of the creativity or delegation skills his brother possessed. I believe Francisco envied Alfonso's personality and popularity. As their wealth grew, the reputations of the Ochoa brothers headed in opposite directions. Alfonso's reputation in Guadalajara as a businessman and as a humanitarian brought him to the forefront of the city's business community. During harsh economic times in Mexico, when the peso was constantly being devalued, Alfonso always found the time and the money to assist the less fortunate by donating steel for shelters, contributing generously to charities, and, in general, treating people with respect and dignity.

Francisco, on the other hand, was obsessed only with his own personal wealth. His entire existence seemed to revolve around how to get money, how to keep it and how to keep others from getting as much as he had. Whereas Alfonso viewed money and wealth as a means to live and enjoy the type of life he wanted for himself and his family, Francisco viewed the acquisition of wealth as the ultimate goal, in and of itself. He treated people as objects with little regard for anyone's well-being except his own. Employees of the companies would always comment to me that while it was a pleasure to work for Alfonso, it was a nightmare to deal with Francisco.

One story of a former employee shows in particular the type of businessman and person Francisco had become. Alfonso and Francisco were about to celebrate the twenty-fifth anniversary of their business with a huge celebration, which would attract many national, state and local dignitaries. Amidst the hoopla, Alfonso remembered that one employee had been with him from the beginning and he wanted to honor that man for his years of loyalty. In addition, Mexican law requires businesses to give employees who have been with the same company for twenty-five years a sizable bonus in recognition of their loyalty. When Alfonso approached Francisco with the idea of doing something special for this employee, Francisco told him he had fired that employee a few months earlier. Alfonso was incredulous.

"After twenty-five years, you fired him just like that and without consulting me?" Alfonso said.

"You fool," responded Francisco. "What's wrong with you? Can't you see that I saved the company thousands of dollars?"

After the celebration, Alfonso investigated the matter and discovered that several missing files were planted in the loyal employee's desk, giving Francisco a pretext for firing him to avoid paying him the bonus. Alfonso tracked the man down and, out of his own pocket, gave him a part of the bonus he was to have received.

I had heard numerous other stories from friends and business associates of Alfonso's who claimed to have been victims of Francisco's devious business practices. Some were taken in stock deals, others in loans with exorbitant interest rates and still others in risky investments that somehow never provided returns except for Francisco. I never broached the subject of Francisco's ethics with Alfonso, who seemed to have a blind spot when it came to his brother's shortcomings.

Francisco's obsession with wealth probably had its roots in his family's unusual history and his sibling rivalry with Alfonso. Alfonso and Francisco were born into a wealthy family in an era when most of Mexico's elite lived in a closed and self-contained society, as there was no middle class in Mexico. A few powerful and privileged families owned and ran most of Mexico, while the majority of the population lived in terrible poverty and had virtually no formal education. The voice of the elite class was President Porfirio Diaz, whose policies bolstered the rich and kept the poor uneducated so they would remain subservient. The aristocrats, including Alfonso's and Francisco's grandparents and parents, never mingled with the lower class, preferring to remain on their rural hacienda in the state of Jalisco. One of the byproducts of this isolated and closed society was the limited pool of eligible young men and women available to court and marry. Accordingly, marriages between cousins were not uncommon.

Such was the case with Alfonso's parents, who were second cousins, and separated in age by twenty years. Alfonso's father was twenty years old, when, as family legend has it, he went to see the new baby girl and, upon taking the baby in his arms, said, "One day I'm going to marry this girl." Twenty years later, he did. The marriage was not the first, nor would it be the last, between relatives in Alfonso's family, and I believe this trend has much to do with the history of mental illness and instability in the family; it is in the genes. Alfonso's youngest brother, José, spent many years in and out of mental institutions before committing suicide in the late 1970s.

I will never be able to fully explain what was going on in Francisco's head after Alfonso died. I do believe, however, that Francisco's family history may have played a role in the disturbed mental state he developed, including the venomous attitude he would display when speaking about Alfonso after his death. The seeds of sibling envy and jealously were planted early in Francisco's life and never disappeared, even after Alfonso died.

As a child, Francisco stewed in Alfonso's shadow, resentful of the attention his more popular brother received. The jealousy that developed created a temper in Francisco that often sent him into furies of rage. When they were teenagers, Francisco broke Alfonso's nose in a fist fight that got out of hand. As the brothers grew into adulthood, and as they became business partners, their working relationship developed relatively well; but, the accolades Alfonso regularly received over the years must have fanned Francisco's jealousy.

When Alfonso was alive, Francisco's primary role in the businesses was as the accountant who kept the companies' books. Alfonso and I received several hints over the years that Francisco manipulated the numbers to his advantage. Even though the brothers were supposed to be earning equally from the businesses, Francisco's wealth always seemed to dwarf our own.

On one occasion, Alfonso asked me to deposit some money from a completed business deal while I was in the United States visiting my family. Alfonso gave me equal amounts to deposit in his account and in Francisco's account in the same bank. In theory, each brother took an equal amount of money out of the businesses to deposit in these accounts. Since most of the personal expenses for our family and Francisco's family were paid by the businesses, Alfonso always assumed these accounts had similar amounts. After I deposited the money in each account, the teller inadvertently gave me balance figures for both accounts, and I nearly fell to the floor: Francisco's balance was nearly three hundred times greater than the balance in our account.

Alfonso was enraged and confronted Francisco with this information. I do not know exactly what transpired, but when I asked him about it, he just told me that we had everything we needed and to forget about it, which was Alfonso's standard response whenever we discussed anything related to Francisco and money. I know this tore Alfonso apart inside, as he always felt that family relationships meant more than everything. Francisco was his only living brother and that was what mattered. On the other hand, he had to know Francisco was cheating him. This part of Alfonso's life was so personal and troubling that he never shared with me his true feelings about this aspect of his relationship with Francisco. I know, however, that Alfonso never resolved this conflict before he died and, unfortunately, I am left to deal with what remains. The bottom line is that Francisco has come to view me as a threat to his now unquestioned authority and to his acquisition of even more personal wealth he believes will flow from that authority.

When Alfonso was alive, I never went too far in questioning his relationship with Francisco because his standard response to me was true—we did have everything we needed. We lived the life of the privileged, wealthy class in Mexico. We traveled all over the world, especially to the best ski resorts and we purchased vacation homes at resorts throughout Mexico. We were truly blessed. Because of our good fortune and in the interests of family harmony, I believe Alfonso chose the path of least resistance and let Francisco be Francisco. Now I am walking down the same path my husband did before me, feeling I, too, will pay the price.

Shortly after the accident, I had gone secretly to a dear friend of our family for advice and counsel. Pepe Levy was one of the most well-respected businessmen in Guadalajara. He owned a large chain of pharmaceutical companies and he was respected throughout Mexico for his business success. Pepe lost his wife, a dear friend of mine, to cancer just two months before Alfonso died. Because of our common circumstances, we shared a natural bond. As a friend and an advisor, Pepe promised to help me sort through the maze of information I was now receiving as a partner in the businesses. He would review the business reports Francisco had been giving me and periodically would tour the companies. Pepe was shocked by the business reports, which showed utter chaos and a complete lack of organization in the companies. Pepe could not even speculate about the precise condition of the businesses, but concluded that what in early 1991 had been a thriving business, by winter it resembled a dying enterprise.

Now, with the latest information Ramon has uncovered and his suggestion to take action, I decide the time is past due to stop letting Francisco walk all over me. Just after the New Year, I advise Francisco of the existence of my new team. I deliver the news by phone as I do not want another face-to-face confrontation. This time I am prepared for the worst, or so I think. My brother, who is visiting from the United States, and Ramon are by my side when I make the call. I know Francisco is living in paranoia and fear, and that if he gets mad enough, he might go over the edge. When I tell him, he loses control. Twenty minutes after I hang up on his rantings, he is outside my house with a huge stick banging on the gate trying to get in. The night watchman does not let Francisco through the gate, insisting that he leave immediately. This just makes Francisco angrier as he paces up and down the street in front of my house and periodically yells some profanity before returning to ring the bell. He hits the bell about fifty times in succession and then just leaves his finger on it for what seemed like five minutes.

When this strategy does not work, he storms next door to my mother-in-law's house and tries to sneak through her backyard into my backyard. However, he is thwarted again, as the gate is locked. I had placed a lock on the gate a few weeks before when my mother-in-law, who has Alzheimer's, wandered into my backyard and fell face first into the grass. When I found her, my first thought from seeing the way she was lying was that she was dead. Fortunately, she had just tripped and then fallen asleep. Still, the incident scared me; so, for her own safety, I placed a lock on the gate. Now that lock is preventing her only living son from terrorizing me. As I look out my bedroom window, I can see him, his face red as an apple, yelling and trying to break through the lock. He is still at the gate twenty minutes later, foaming at the mouth, when he apparently gives up for the moment. Before he leaves, however, he places his index finger through the fence, shakes it towards my house and says, "This is just the beginning!" I know now that the war has begun.

The repercussions are immediate and severe, as I am ostracized from the businesses. I am given no information on the state of affairs, and any employee who speaks with me is summarily reprimanded or fired.

Alfonso's former employees look at me with sad eyes as their allegiance is divided. I understand their conflict, so I also understand when they follow Francisco's orders: they have bills to pay and mouths to feed, and cannot afford the consequences of siding with me.

I am also cut off from any financial support from the businesses. Of course, my personal relationship with Francisco has deteriorated to the point of open hostility. The families have stopped seeing each other, and my children are devastated because Francisco does not allow his children to play or associate with my children in any way. Francisco has ten children, all of whom have been very close with my children, and those relationships have ended abruptly. In addition, the families' visits to my mother-in-law's house have even been coordinated so as not to overlap.

Meanwhile, my team and I meet at least twice a week to develop a strategy. First and foremost, we need to get accurate information on the businesses. We feel the only way this will occur is to confront Francisco in person and demand access. So, Ramon calls Francisco to set up a meeting. After berating Ramon for nearly five minutes on the phone, Francisco reluctantly agrees to a meeting.

The meeting takes place on a warm January morning, ten months to the day after Alfonso's accident. While I drive with Ramon to the offices, he tries to calm my nerves by assuring me that this is my opportunity to show Francisco that I am not going to allow him to treat me this way. I know Francisco too well, however, and hold out little hope for success. We meet Ernesto, Ignacio and Pepe in the lobby and then quickly are escorted to the conference room where Francisco is waiting.

We learn immediately that Francisco has formed a team of his own. At his side is a sleazy Argentine lawyer whose gaudy silk suit and condescending smirks evince an underworld aura. Three of his staff also sit in on the meeting, flanking him at the long conference table. Francisco calls the meeting to order and, before anyone can say anything, he begins an hour-and-a-half discourse in which he rambles on about how he carried the businesses through the difficult times despite Alfonso's many failings. I suppose the more someone repeats a lie, the more he believes it himself, and Francisco seems very convincing. I can see by the passion in his eyes that he has created a new reality for himself and that he expects everyone else to buy into his little piece of fiction.

Numerous attempts by Ramon, Pepe and Ignacio to interrupt and initiate a dialogue are met with a right-hand slap in the air in their direction and a curt, "I'm not finished. These are my offices and you will listen to what I have to say."

Finally, after nearly two hours of Francisco's ramblings, Pepe motions for us to leave. We stand up and, one by one, file out of the room.

Francisco explodes. "Get back here. You called this meeting and I'm not done yet. Get back here," he yells as his associates try to restrain him from coming after us.

Following the meeting, my team members get absolutely nowhere with Francisco. We can't get any information on the companies, much less any balance sheets. Ramon and Pepe make repeated calls to Francisco and his people to request a variety of documents. The response is always evasive: "We will get that to you tomorrow," or "Francisco is working on that," or "Francisco is the only one who can authorize that." The end result is that we receive no information —the frustration is mounting on all fronts.

———————•-•-◆-•-•———————

During my discussions with my advisors, we begin to formulate several possible courses of action to end the stalemate. First, I can try to buy out Francisco's part of the businesses. However, there are several obstacles to this option. My advisors feel that Francisco, if he were to sell out, would make such exorbitant demands that it would be impossible to reach any kind of settlement. In addition, even if he were to sell, I would then have to assume the role as the head of a conglomeration of multi-million dollar steel businesses, and I am not sure I want that responsibility.

One morning, I receive a call from the wife of an executive with one of the government-owned steel mills. This particular steel mill is one of our primary suppliers of steel and we are one of its top customers. She asks me to have coffee with her that afternoon. I assume she wants to see how I am doing and to offer me her condolences in person. We meet at one of the local coffeehouses and, after the formalities, she gets right to the point. "Francisco," she says, "is not running the businesses properly."

As she continues, her words confirm my suspicions. She goes on to tell me that her husband and the other executives from the company think Francisco is running the businesses into the ground, and that her husband has asked her to bring a proposal to me.

"You know, Kris," she says, "my husband and his associates were very impressed by what you did last year in organizing and co-chairing the National Steel Convention in Acapulco. With their help, they think you can bring the businesses back to where they were when Alfonso was alive. They will back you up financially if you are interested."

For one of the few times in my life, I am speechless—flattered, but speechless. The steel business, especially in Mexico, is a man's world, so I am stunned by this offer. I sit there in silence for a few moments, trying to gather my thoughts.

"That's an incredible offer," I finally blurt out. "And I'm so grateful for the support and confidence your husband and his associates are showing in me; but, I just can't do it. I have six kids at home and no husband. I'm just not ready to make the kind of sacrifices that would be needed to make things work. My children need me too much. They have already lost one parent and they don't need to lose another one to the business world."

As I drive home, the magnitude of the offer begins to sink in. This offer came from the highest ranking government steel businessmen in the country. Under different circumstances, perhaps my answer would also be different. But the more I think about it, the less I can envision taking on the businesses full time and still having enough time to devote to my six children. After all we have been through, my children must come first at this point. I know I've made the right decision.

My only other options are to sell my interests in the businesses to a third party or to Francisco. We begin to explore the possibility of selling to a third party and we actually find some local businessmen who are very interested. Francisco, however, catches wind of our efforts and quickly alerts us to a provision in the companies' by-laws that requires the consent of both partners before a sale to an outsider can proceed. Francisco makes it clear he will never agree to such a sale.

So, for the time being, we continue on with the status quo. Francisco, however, is stepping up the pressure on all fronts. My secretary's desk is constantly being ransacked and no one in the office will even speak to her. All of our file cabinets have been searched, as is her daily planner. I think he's even tapping our phone conversations. Francisco is obsessed with knowing what our plan is and what strategies we are developing.

I have never been able to understand the type of paranoia Francisco feels. I have never done anything to give him the slightest hint that I want anything of his. All I want is my share of what Alfonso worked so hard to create for his family so that I can care for my family. Why am I such a threat? The only explanation I can come up with is that Francisco's obsession with power and wealth makes the cost of accomplishing this quest irrelevant. In his warped perception, he must see me as the enemy because I will not place my complete loyalty and blind trust in him, I just can't do that, and the result has been a war I know I have no chance of winning. Even so, I am shocked and dismayed to see Francisco so intent on taking everything away from me and my family.

With this understanding comes the gradual realization that somehow I need to get out of this situation with whatever I can get. I need to get as far away as possible from Francisco and his envy, greed, fears and suspicions. Not only do I feel physically threatened by Francisco, but he also brings out the worst qualities in me. I hate him. He conjures up all of the negative emotions I have been trying so hard to get around through prayer and meditation. Francisco and his attitude towards me and my family have become an obstacle to my own quest for personal enlightenment.

So, not without a little trepidation, I tell my team that I want and need to sell Francisco my interest in the businesses. In my heart, I know I will probably not receive a fair amount, but my mind is still hopeful that this top-notch team I have put together will negotiate a decent deal for me. Ramon negotiates regularly with the Federal Deposit Insurance Corporation because of his involvement and partnership in various banks in the United States. Pepe Levy had an extensive financial background before becoming the Minister of Finance for the State of Jalisco. Ernesto Gomez Ibarra, in addition to owning the largest chocolate factory in Mexico, participated in the North American Free Trade Agreement negotiations, representing Mexico's private sector. I have complete confidence that my advisors are capable of getting me the best deal possible. What puzzles and disturbs me, however, is how we will ever be able to strike a fair deal when Francisco holds all the trump cards on his side of the table.

Ramon arranges another meeting with Francisco during which we are to present our first offer. We want a very formal setting to try to avoid a replay of the last meeting, so we pick a neutral spot—the offices of a reputable attorney who had worked with both Alfonso and Francisco. As Ramon rises to present our offer, Francisco stands up on his side of the table and cuts Ramon off.

"Just one minute," he says. "This is my first and only offer. The only deal I will accept is this: She gives me her interest in all five companies and all twenty-five properties that we now own jointly. She also pays me $600,000 in cash. Then, and only then, will I release her from the $7 million in guarantees she has signed."

When he finishes, he calmly sits down. With a smug smile on his face, he says, "Well, do we have a deal?"

A long silence follows. I do not know whether to laugh or cry. I cannot believe he is serious. This is beyond unreasonable, even for him. It is ridiculous, absurd and maddening. We have calculated the worth of the companies at roughly between $6 and $8 million and the properties at another $6 to $8 million. All of the other items—the cars, boat, and airplanes—are worth about another million dollars. From these figures, we have come up with a reasonable offer. How could he possibly be serious about me *giving him* everything I rightly own and then *paying him* more cash on top of that? I truly believe he has gone mad.

Finally, Ramon rises and begins to speak. "I don't think that offer adequately protects the interests of Kris' family," he says. "What we had in mind . . ."

"I don't care what you think," Francisco interrupts. "Didn't you hear me? This is not a negotiation. That is my first and final offer. Take it or leave it. But if you leave it, beware."

"Look here, Francisco," Pepe shouts. "You can't possibly expect Kris to give up everything her husband worked so hard for . . ."

"He did nothing!" Francisco retorts. "I built these businesses and she has no more right to them than any of you. What's your answer?"

With that, each of my advisors gathers their papers and we walk out of the room. There is nothing more to be said. This is not a negotiation; it is a sham and an insult. We will not participate any further, so we leave Francisco and his cronies sitting around the table. Our answer obviously is an absolute "no" to Francisco's absurd proposal. The negotiations come to a halt following this meeting, although one could argue that they never actually started.

A few days after the aborted negotiations, Ross and Susan visit Guadalajara to share their findings about my legal case against CMH. They have spent nearly a year gathering information about the accident. It's a warm, windy April morning when they arrive at my house to confirm my worst suspicions.

"Kris, we think we have found a lot of evidence supporting the fact that CMH was to blame for everyone dying in the avalanche," Susan says. "It looks like these people, Alfonso included, did not have to die."

When the words come out of her mouth, I immediately feel sick to my stomach. I am filled with rage and even a tinge of disappointment. I no longer want to blame anyone for this accident, but now I have no choice. Nine innocent people lost their lives; forty-two children lost a parent; so many lives have been shattered—all because of CMH's negligence. They need to be held accountable. CMH makes millions each year charging large amounts of money to take people on these heli-skiing vacations, and they have a responsibility to provide for these people's safety. I know this lawsuit won't bring Alfonso or any of the others back, but at least it might help prevent this type of accident from happening again. Perhaps other families will be spared the loss of a loved one if this lawsuit brings the negligence to light and leads to changes in the way companies like CMH operate. This type of negligence is simply not acceptable. When it comes right down to it, I feel a moral obligation to make CMH answer for its actions—I think my choice is clear.

"Well, it sounds like the decision is pretty clear," I say. "Let's do it."

"You know, Kris, as much confidence as we have in this case, it's still going to be a long haul," Ross says. "While we did find a lot of evidence of negligence by CMH, there are still going to be a lot of issues to overcome. When Alfonso arrived in Canada, he signed a waiver absolving CMH of all liability for anything that happens, even if it happens due to their negligence."

"Can they do that?" I ask. "I mean, I'm not a lawyer or anything, but that sure doesn't seem right. How can anyone disclaim responsibility for everything they do by just having someone else sign a piece of paper?"

"I know it's hard to believe, but in some cases they can," Ross says. "The key is going to be finding a way around the waiver, and I think we have a few different options. The waiver was in English, and you've told us Alfonso didn't read, speak or really even understand English."

"Not only that, Kris," Susan chimes in, "we don't think they made any effort to explain the waiver to any of their Mexican guests. They translated them in other languages, but not in Spanish."

"You know, there's no way Alfonso would have even understood what a waiver was," I say. "Here in Mexico, waivers don't even exist, at least I've never heard of them. I don't think Alfonso or any of the others would have even known what they were talking about if they tried to explain it."

"That's good," Ross says. "We're going to have to get some of Alfonso's friends to testify to that. We think we have enough to prove criminal negligence, which is a higher standard that would get us around the waiver issue. But even if we don't, Alfonso's friends will certainly help.

"Kris, I think you should try to contact some of the families of the other victims. These kinds of lawsuits can be extremely expensive and, while our firm will pick up part of the tab, you are going to be responsible for some of the expenses. If some of the other families join in, those costs can be shared."

With my blessing, Ross and Susan leave saying that they will immediately begin to prepare for the filing of a lawsuit.

———————

I immediately send letters to the families of the other victims—four British families, two French families, a German family and an American family—certain that when they find out about CMH's negligence, they will be as incensed as I am and will join in the lawsuit to prevent this type of tragedy from happening again.

As the replies trickle in, I am more than a little surprised. I expected more enthusiasm from the other families, but it doesn't appear that any of them are going to join me in the suit. The German family writes that the wife of the man who died in the accident has suffered a nervous breakdown since learning of her husband's death and her doctors have strongly recommended against any more trauma, so they respectfully decline. Although the families of both the French victims want to join in the suit, both of the men who died had been divorced. They had spoken with Ross and learned that Canadian law doesn't allow a woman who is divorced to bring a wrongful death action. Both French families say they support my efforts, but are likewise unable join in the lawsuit.

The British families initially show some interest in the case. After receiving my letter, John Clifton, who is the British equivalent of an attorney in England and whose wife was killed in the avalanche, calls me to discuss the case.

"You know, Kris, the trip we took to Canada was to celebrate our twenty-fifth anniversary," John says. "I decided not to go with Maggie and our cousins up to the Bugaboos because I'm not that great a skier and I thought it might be too much for me. So, I went to Victoria for a couple of days. I was walking down the street when I stepped into a café and grabbed a newspaper. As I opened the paper, I saw the headlines about the avalanche and my heart almost stopped."

"Oh my God," I say. "And that's how you found out?"

"Well, not quite," he says. "The paper didn't have the names of the people who had died, only that nine people had perished. I wasn't sure what to do, so I went back to the hotel and called the local office of the Royal Canadian Mounted Police. The article said they had been involved in the rescue efforts. They confirmed for me that Maggie and one of my cousins were among the victims. I couldn't believe it. I still can't . . ."

As his voice trails off, I can't imagine the shock and terror he must have felt hearing the news like that. Not that the way I found out was a good way, but at least I had family around. He was by himself in a foreign country, with no idea of what to do and where to go. I wish I could give him a hug.

"I know how you feel, John," I say. "That must have been just a horrible way to find out."

"It was," he says. "And still is. I guess I don't need to tell you that. Listen, Kris, I know you are already on board with this suit. Ross is traveling over here next week to meet with us and bring us up to speed on where things stand. I think he's going to have an uphill struggle convincing us to join in, but we are going to try to keep an open mind. I'm just not sure we want to drag this whole thing out for a long time. But, I will let you know how it goes and I'm sure Ross will also."

Since John was the unofficial spokesman for the British group, I didn't hold out much hope that they would join me in the suit. John confirms my instincts when he calls a week later to give me the news.

"We had a long and very productive meeting with Ross while he was here," John says. "We just weighed the risks and the benefits and decided the former were too great to risk getting involved. In your case, Alfonso didn't speak English and Ross thinks that will definitely play in your favor. Unfortunately, we won't be able to claim that—although the Queen's English is a little different from what they speak in Canada, I think that would be a little bit of a stretch. I think a Canadian court would uphold the waivers for those who understood them, so that would leave us in a bad way. And when Ross said we could be responsible for CMH's legal costs if we're unsuccessful . . . well . . . that pretty much sealed the deal."

I suppose at some point Ross and Susan must have mentioned that possibility to me also; but, at this moment, I can't remember hearing anything about my potential liability for CMH's legal costs. And it scares me.

"I suppose that's one of the risks," I say offhandedly, all the while running legal fee numbers through my mind.

"Kris, I wish you the best of luck. Please keep me apprised of your progress, and let me know if I can help in any way," John says.

I hear him, but it doesn't register. I politely say good-bye and immediately call Ross.

"Ross, this is Kris," I say. "I just talked to John Clifton in London and he told me they are not coming in. He also said I could be responsible for CMH's legal costs. Is this true?"

"Yeah, Kris, that's right," Ross says. "A lot of things would have to go wrong for that to happen; but, yes, that is a possibility. I know we covered that with Jim during the initial meeting and I think also with you in Seattle. Is there a problem?"

"Well, what kind of amounts are we talking about?" I ask. "I mean should I be worried about this, Ross?"

"I wouldn't be, Kris," he says. "We have a very strong case and, like I said, a lot of things would have to go against us for that to happen. I suppose their legal costs could amount to up to $500,000 if it goes all the way to trial. But, under the circumstances, I think it's an extremely remote possibility that you would ever have to pay all or any of that. By the way, have you spoken with the American woman yet?"

"No, not yet," I say. "I've left a couple messages but haven't heard back from her."

I'm saddened that the European families didn't come on board, but I'm certain one of the main reasons is that Europeans, like Mexicans, do not share in the American penchant for litigation. This factor, however, should not prevent the American family from joining in on the suit. So, when I finally get in touch with the widow of the lone American victim, I am doubly surprised by her response.

"Kris, I really believe you are doing the right thing, but I don't think I can put myself through such an emotional ordeal," she tells me. "I just don't think I would have the strength to endure."

"I respect your decision," I say, "but I think you've misunderstood my motivation for starting this lawsuit. I'm not counting on my inner strength to carry me through this; I'm counting on my outrage, my conviction that this type of incident can never be allowed to happen again. I don't know how I'm going to get through it, but I just know I have to."

"I'm glad you're doing it. I really am," she says. "But to me, it's just not worth the effort."

As I hang up the phone, I realize that she had hit the nail on the head—I really did believe it was worth the effort. I simply can't let CMH off the hook for their grievous mistakes. If that means going it alone, so be it.

While I'm comfortable with my decision to go it alone, the stress over the lawsuit has compounded my anxieties over my dealings with Francisco. It just seems like a constant battle on every front, and I feel drained physically and emotionally all of the time. I know these pressures will cause me either to have a nervous breakdown or to go stark raving mad. I feel like Francisco is hounding me and, in reality, he is. One evening, on my night watchman's evening off, I hear some strange sounds out in the yard. I wake my oldest son and, after we call one of my neighbors, we walk downstairs with baseball bats. We must have scared the intruders away; but when I go out into our storeroom, I notice that one of my file cabinets has been rifled through with papers strewn everywhere.

On several other occasions, I know I am being followed. One time, as I am leaving Pepe Levy's house after a meeting, I notice a black sedan following me out of Pepe's neighborhood. I continue for a few blocks, make the normal turns for where I am headed, then notice that the sedan is still behind me. I floor the gas and begin trying to lose my pursuer on the streets of Guadalajara. It's no use—after each turn, the car shows up in my rearview mirror again. Finally, I speed home, my heart racing until I reach the safe confines of my house. I quickly lock the gate behind me and run inside.

This is no way to live. I am losing control of my life and I have to do something to take it back. I spend countless nights sitting by myself on my bed going over and over in my mind the sequence of events that had led me to this point. I wind up just frustrating myself because, to me, everything is unconscionable. In my family's hour of deepest need, how can Francisco stand over us with a dagger? Every nasty thing he does seems to push the dagger deeper into an already open and gushing wound. Why? And why is God allowing this to happen? Am I not due for a break? I have already lost my husband, and now I am going to lose my inheritance and my children's future. These questions and dilemmas are constantly on my mind—and my mind, rather than my spirit, is controlling my being.

Luckily, I have some help to bring me around to a different way of viewing things—less from my mind and more from my heart. Susan, Anna and I have been forming a deep relationship, more than just pupil and teacher. We have developed a strong and unconditional friendship. As the events involving Francisco unfold, I tell Anna and Susan about what is going on and how deeply disturbed I am. At first they are incredulous, staring at me and gaping in disbelief. Anna knows, however, what Francisco is capable of from personal experience. Francisco had cheated her and her husband in a stock deal a few years before her husband died. They never forgot the dishonesty and the disrespect with which Francisco treated them. So, when I speak of what Francisco is doing to me, Anna just shakes her head sadly with a clear understanding of the type of greed and conniving that is at work. It is obvious to all of us that money and power are the sole forces in his life.

The three of us meet privately on a regular basis, giving me the opportunity to vent a little bit and talk through my feelings about what is happening. Both Susan and Anna counsel me on how to keep my head, and, more importantly, my heart, above water. We pray together and then spend long sessions meditating. These sessions give me the strength and the peace to get through the next ordeal with Francisco. I find it so difficult to translate the serenity I feel with Anna and Susan into a more peaceful approach towards dealing with Francisco. Just the mention of his name makes my blood boil! I realize, however, that every time I let him do that to me, I relinquish control. To regain control, I have to let go and trust. Unfortunately, the more at peace I become with the situation, the angrier Francisco gets, and his attacks become more aggressive and vicious.

I believe the most important part of my development at this stage involves tapping into that inner God source of strength that tells me these circumstances are not what life is all about and that they will pass. During such a painful and frightening course of events, it takes every bit of energy and concentration to keep my focus on God. What is there to learn here? I gradually understand that Francisco can never take away the inner connection I've been establishing with God, one based on total trust. Regardless of what happens with Francisco, I have to believe not only that things will be all right, but that I will grow spiritually from the experience. With this realization, I know I have come a long way.

I feel a deep sense of joy and inner peace when I realize I have to accept my situation and trust that, no matter what happens, the core of my being, my relationship with God, will lead me through. That is a huge step for me, as I am being tortured mentally and emotionally by Francisco, and probably will lose most of my inheritance. I am not happy about what Francisco is doing, but I have to trust that all of us are going to get through this. That is an incredibly liberating feeling—one that is very difficult to arrive at, and even tougher to maintain. I don't know how things will unfold, but I am doing my best to let go and trust. I am taking those first few steps out over the cavern and slowly I see a path unfolding a little clearer every day.

⸻ ◆ ⸻

Meanwhile, my situation with Francisco is deteriorating from bad to worse. The negotiations for my buyout go nowhere, as Francisco simply will not negotiate. He wants it all with no consideration for fairness. I know that I cannot go on much longer living in this state of limbo with Francisco hovering over me waiting to pounce. In my prayers, I pray for guidance, some sort of sign of which way to go. On the one hand, this is my children's inheritance—the businesses Alfonso worked so hard to build for them. And on the other hand, Francisco has managed to force me into a corner with $7 million of debt hanging over my head. I do not know what to do.

One afternoon, Ramon calls me and says he wants to come over and talk with me. He arrives about an hour later with Ernesto, Ignacio Gonzalez Luna and two other friends of mine, Paco Verea and Paco Isaac. As we all settle in on the couches in my living room, Paco Verea begins to cry. What now? Here is this grown man and good friend brought to tears by some sort of news I am about to hear. I just put my face in my hands as Paco Verea begins.

"Kris, I've been to see Francisco," he says. "You know he, Alfonso and I have known each other since preschool. I thought maybe I could talk some sense into him about all this. I sat down across from Francisco and told him directly that I wanted him to treat these negotiations as though Alfonso, not Kris, were on the other side of the table from him. I said, 'Alfonso was your brother. If you do something dishonest to Kris, it is as though you are doing it to him. And you know the moment you die, you will meet up with your brother and have to explain your actions. What will you say to him? You will have to admit that you took everything away from his wife and kids. I am begging you not to do that.' He just turned away and said, 'I don't need to listen to this from you. I have nothing more to say to you.'"

There is a long pause. All of the men stare down at their hands while the tears stream down Paco's face.

"That cabrón doesn't give a shit about anything anymore," Paco says.

I feel the fear begin to crawl up my legs and throughout the rest of my body like a boa constrictor slowly squeezing the life out of me. I feel paralyzed. My eyes are bulging out of my head as I grip the side of the couch.

"Francisco has rejected all of our pleas," Ramon says, his words belying the regret and sorrow he was trying to keep in. "In my opinion, you have two options at this point. You could embark on a legal battle against Francisco. Kris, it would be at least five years in and out of court and you know how the court system is here—whoever has the most money wins. Francisco has connections in high places and has the companies' money. He won't lose. You have less influential friends, limited funds and six children."

I close my eyes while I absorb each body blow. The avalanche never seems to end.

"Francisco is offering you a deal," Ramon says. "It's not a good deal, but it's the best we've seen from him yet. He will absolve you from any legal responsibility for the bank guarantees if you give him all your stock in the companies and the properties. He says that you can keep your house that is under construction, your cars and your house in Puerto Vallarta. The total value of these items is about $1 million. This will mean you will have to sell your house and seriously downsize your lifestyle, but you will have Francisco out of your life. I think he will run the companies into the ground anyway, and you will be free of any responsibility for the companies when that happens."

I cannot believe what I am hearing. The companies, the patrimony—what I thought would be my children's future—all go to Francisco for practically nothing. Each of the men in my living room looks at me with compassion and pity. They know I am being cheated and they know there isn't anything anyone can do about it.

"You know, Kris, this is the exact situation my mother found herself in after my father died," Ramon says.

"What did she do?" I ask. I know the answer and I probably already know what my answer will have to be.

"She turned everything over to her in-laws," he says. "She decided that it wasn't worth her health. She needed to move on. Fights take too much of a physical and emotional toll on everyone and she was at the end of her rope. She scrimped and saved to put me through school, and then, as an adult, I made some good investments for her and she is now a wealthy woman. Remember, Kris, what goes around, comes around. You need to think about this, so we will leave you alone; but, Francisco wants an answer by tomorrow."

"Oh, God, please help me," I think as I sit glued to the couch for more than an hour after the men leave. I almost would trade places with Alfonso. He died in the avalanche, but I am still buried alive in the debris. Finally, I get up and call Anna and Susan. They come over immediately, and we spend the night in prayer and meditation. I am praying for guidance, for some sort of sign to identify the right decision. While I am meditating, I have a vision of Alfonso. I see him standing in an endless field of yellow flowers. He looks so young and handsome, and seems so very happy. His eyes have a serene quality to them and there is an aura of happiness about him. He looks at me and I can feel his love. He smiles and says, "Don't you know that I will always take care of you? I will always be with you, always . . ."

The vision lasts only seconds and, as soon as it ends, the tears begin to pour down my cheeks. I immediately know what my decision has to be. I need to move forward with my children as my focus. I need to move away from this nightmare, away from this terrible past, and away from Francisco's negativity and fear-based existence. I need to regroup with my children and to trust in Alfonso, in God and in the universal plan for us. I need to let go, to begin living again and to choose love.

The following morning, I notify Ramon of my decision. He and the others feel I have made both the right and the only choice. He says he will inform Francisco and put the legal aspects of the transaction in motion.

As the day of the actual transfer approaches, I rely even more on my daily prayer and meditation sessions, and focus my energy on this idea of trust. I believe I have begun to learn one of the most important lessons many mystics speak of when they describe spiritual growth: the ability to live in the "I don't know." We spend so much time trying to understand and control our lives that we often do not appreciate the lessons uncertainty can teach us. Totally trusting God means living in a constant and eternal, "I don't know." Living in and accepting this state of "I don't know" is really the only way to completely open yourself up to God and the plan you and He constantly create for you. The moment you deny this uncertainty and place so much stake in a particular outcome, you close the doors to the different possibilities that are life- and love-giving. Living in the "I don't know" means that you open yourself up to any and all possibilities; and, in so doing, even the totally improbable becomes a possibility. It means learning to live.

For me, this is an about face in my nature. For years, I have meticulously planned every aspect of my life, from vacations to my daily activities. Uncertainty was for the unorganized. Now, my future and the future of my family look very uncertain. I can either accept that and, with God's love, find my own way through this uncertainty or succumb to it and let it haunt my every movement. By this time the choice is clear. Many changes lay ahead, and maybe that is what life is all about—change. I realize I still have much to learn.

May 19, 1992, finally arrives and it feels like D-day. Part of me has been dreading this day when all that Alfonso worked for will be lost. I am angry, frustrated and disgusted. However, another part of me is relieved—this will close one of the most difficult chapters in my life, and I feel like I have come out of it with a new understanding of myself. I am bitter, but that is natural given the circumstances and, in time, might fade. I am no longer going to let those negative feelings dominate my life the way they have for the past year.

The plan is for me to sign the paperwork in front of Francisco's lawyers, but not in front of Francisco, as I have no desire to ever see him again. As we sit down at the conference table on the fifteenth floor of my attorney's office, I look out the window and notice the beautiful view of the entire city of Guadalajara. The sun is shining brightly and the hustle and bustle of the city goes undisturbed by the events unfolding in this conference room.

As I sit down at the conference table, I begin to tremble, feeling myself fighting the trust I have so painstakingly nurtured. The reality is setting in; it is directly in front of me in the form of these dreaded documents. Everything that Alfonso worked for is about to be turned over to Francisco, who deserves very little of it. How many times had I heard Alfonso say that all his hard work, all his dreams were for his boys? I suppose it's just not meant to be. Francisco is forcing me to write my children out of Alfonso's business legacy forever. The legacy will be Francisco's to do as he pleases, and it makes me sick to my stomach.

While my attorney prepares the documents for my signature, I rise from the table and walk back over to the window. To my surprise, the sky has turned from blue to gray as storm clouds descend eerily on Guadalajara. When I return to the table, the papers awaiting my signature are laid out before me. I reach into my purse and take out Alfonso's favorite Mont Blanc pen. My hand is trembling, and I struggle to find the strength to raise the pen to the paper. I am signing away the plans Alfonso and I had made for our children. I want to stand up and run out of the room. I know the cruel reality, however, is that I have no choice but to sign. As the pen reaches the paper, a huge crack of thunder strikes, causing everyone in the room to jump. The thunder startles me so much that I drop the pen to the floor. Perhaps that was Alfonso letting us all know what he thinks about what is happening.

As I hold the pen again and begin to sign the first document in the appointed place, the skies open up outside and all hell breaks loose from the heavens. The most violent thunderstorm I have seen in years pounds the Guadalajara afternoon. The rain pours down, accompanied by loud, frightening claps of thunder and bolts of lightning. "This background music is very appropriate," I think to myself.

Everyone in the room seems moved by the natural phenomena outside. The faces of Francisco's attorneys turn ashen. Somewhere inside of each of them they know that what is happening is just plain wrong.

Suddenly, the power is cut and the lights go out. I sit there in the darkness, with the storm raging outside, weeping silently and begging for strength. Moments later, when the lights are restored, I sign the last of the documents. The moment my pen, Alfonso's pen, lifts from the paper, so does the storm outside. It is over; it's time for a new beginning. Alfonso is sending me a clear message: it's time to smell the clean air, rid of all impurities, and to move on. Why are these lessons always so hard? I am drained, exhausted and depleted, but I trust I have done the right thing. I hope with all my heart that I have; but, I just do not know.

⁕⬥⁕

One month later, Francisco sells all of the businesses to one of the biggest steel consortiums in Mexico. He makes a killing. He receives an estimated $10–$12 million in cash over a three-year period. He also keeps some stock in the companies, all the real estate, including the land on which all the businesses are located, and is able to charge the new owners rent on the buildings and properties. Francisco has won and is getting it all. The question I think about quite often is, "What is he really getting?"

I pray that someday Francisco, during his journey in this life, will be able to reevaluate his priorities and find peace in a life based on love and trust rather than on fear and envy. When I think of Francisco, I am constantly reminded of a passage from the gospel of Matthew: "For what will it profit a man if he gains the whole world and forfeits his life?"

CHAPTER 5

the move

As the mother of six children, each born and raised in Mexico, my experiences give me a deep appreciation for the culture, traditions and societal norms operating in Mexico. I've come to understand that there are certain truths and certain ways of doing things that are firmly embedded in Mexican society. These truths are even more real to me after Alfonso's death, as I find myself fighting an uphill struggle to make my own place in Guadalajara as a widowed mother of six. And each of these realities plays an important role in the decision I have made to leave Mexico.

After having lived in Guadalajara for most of my adult life, and as I reflect on my life in Mexico without Alfonso, I realize how little room there is in nearly every aspect of Mexican society for women, especially single women—even those who, like me, have been widowed. The predominating societal rule in Mexico is that it is a man's world. Cultures in Latin American countries historically, and with very few exceptions, have been dominated by men. The man is the focus of everything, from business settings to social interaction to just about every facet of life in Mexico. Another norm that naturally follows from this male dominance is that, regardless of the circumstance, the men who have the most money and the most connections always prevail. Alfonso knew this reality very well, and he and I spent much time cultivating relationships with people in power, both in business and in social settings. He knew that power and the appearance of power had to be fostered so that when the time came to move on to something else, the groundwork had been laid for getting it done.

If I did not fully appreciate the magnitude of these realities before Alfonso's death, my dealings with Francisco certainly have driven them home. Immediately following Alfonso's death, I had envisioned playing some sort of role in the businesses and had even toyed with the idea of running the bicycle business myself. Francisco, however, being the man with the power and the connections, barred all of my attempts at meaningful participation in any of the businesses. My status as a woman, and an American woman at that, limits my credibility and my opportunities. I have realized quickly that Mexico is a man's world, and I simply do not have the resources nor the desire to compete with Francisco's money and power. I am not allowed to be a player in a game that I really don't know I want to play anyway.

I've also come to understand that middle-age, single people have no proper place in the social circles in which Alfonso and I lived. Single people, whether widowed, divorced or never married, comprise a tiny minority of people whom Mexican society just seems to ignore. Everything in our social circle was planned around the couple. I had noticed this long before Alfonso died, because I had several friends who, for various reasons, did not have husbands or wives. There seemed to be a stigma attached to these people, more often through no fault of their own, and they simply were not accepted as members of our social circle.

I notice that slowly but surely I am falling into this same category. As a single person, I am no longer invited to many of the social events involving Alfonso's and my circle of friends. On those rare instances where I am included, I feel completely out of place without Alfonso. Real or imagined, I feel I am treated and perceived differently by people in social settings. I also sense my situation has become a constant topic of conversation. The members of Guadalajara's elite society are a small, tightly knit group of people who make it their business to know what is going on with everybody else. So, my fiasco with Francisco has become the number one topic of discussion at most social gatherings.

A couple weeks ago, I took Nicholas to a birthday party for one of his classmates at school. While the boys played, I sat with the other mothers in the backyard and we talked about the important news of the day—mostly gossip. Naturally, the topic of conversation turned to Francisco, and I immediately began to feel uncomfortable.

"Kris, how can you let him get away with all this," said Angelica. "I just don't understand it—it just seems so wrong."

"Well, from what I heard, Kris did everything she could possibly do, but Francisco was holding all the cards and just wouldn't give in," chimed in Viviana. "You know how he is, but he'll get what's coming eventually."

"Yeah, you know he will, Kris. It'll just take some time," said Karen. "I don't even see Gabriela anymore—she must have dropped out of sight, too."

This is typical of the conversations I find myself in with friends, as it seems like every place I go I am confronted with people who want to know the latest. Some wish me well, while others are just curious. Some offer condolences, while others offer their help. Still others just whisper as I walk by. From the supermarket to the restaurants to the country club to school events, I feel like my life is being played out in public. That feeling gets old real fast, and I want my privacy back. I appreciate the concern of so many people, but I am getting tired of constantly being on guard.

I woke up this morning, after a particularly long night of little sleep and much anxiety, and began to think about what is keeping me in Mexico. I am beginning to realize that, besides the children, who have spent their entire lives in Mexico, there really is very little keeping me in Guadalajara. I own no property, as the house that Alfonso and I were building and that I received as part of the settlement with Francisco has been sold. The house we were living in when Alfonso died and continue to live in now belongs to Alfonso's mother and is right next door to where she lives. Even though Alfonso and I made about $400,000 worth of improvements to the house, it is still her house. With Alfonso gone, and Francisco no longer an ally, the house has become a point of contention. Finally, after much discussion, my mother-in-law has agreed to let us stay in the house rent free for three years. After the three years, I will have to decide whether to stay and pay rent or move somewhere else. The more I think about it, the more I realize that the time is right for a move, a dramatic move out of the city and the country that has been our home for so long.

My primary concern is the children, as Mexico is their home. They all speak Spanish as their primary language and have built lives for themselves in Guadalajara. The oldest three—Alfonso Jr., who is now eighteen; Carl Eric, sixteen; and Christofer, fourteen—are vehemently opposed to any type of move, especially to the United States; but, my studies and prayers tell me that while I have to do what is best for my family, I also have to do what is right for me. As Susan used to tell me, "If mama hen is okay, then the chicks are fine. If mama hen is unhappy, that will pass on to the chicks and then everything will be a mess."

My life in Guadalajara has become a mess and this mama hen is very unhappy. I know part of my desire to move is selfish. I long to be near my parents and my brothers and sisters, to be nurtured and cared for, to return to the nest, so to speak, and to be with people who love me and who will accept me for who I am. I know a move will be traumatic, but I also know it will open up so many new opportunities, especially educationally, for my children.

I feel I am not alone in making this decision to move to San Diego. Just as my moments of enlightenment in the past have revolved around opening myself up to hear and see clearly, I feel as though I have been guided towards this decision by my intuition. I have come to believe that intuition is a God-given gift that points us in positive directions, if we train ourselves to tune into it and listen. The outside world teaches us to value concrete facts, rather than gut feelings, which makes this tuning in much more difficult.

Through Susan's teachings, I've learned to trust my intuitive feelings as messages from God sent through my soul. When I tune in and listen, as I did this morning, I can feel that the move to San Diego is the right choice for me and my family. This is one of the pieces of my life falling into place and I need to let it fall. Once again, I am putting my foot over the edge and allowing God to guide me and show me the way. I need to move on with my life. I no longer want to spend my days surrounded by the remnants of my battle with Francisco. I need to move on, to create a life for me, not as the widow of Alfonso Ochoa, but as me, Kris Ochoa.

The constant reminders about my past make moving forward increasingly difficult, especially with respect to the lawsuit. Shortly after we determined that I would be the only plaintiff, Susan and Ross filed the suit against CMH in the courts of British Columbia. CMH has made it abundantly clear in the days since then that it views this case as much more than some harmless widow bringing a wrongful death suit. Instead, CMH officials are treating this suit as a threat to their entire way of doing business, sparing no expense to defend themselves. CMH has hired a defense team of five attorneys, led by a man with a reputation for painstaking attention to detail. As a result, I am being bombarded almost on a daily basis with requests for information. In fact, it almost feels like I'm on trial. The defense team wants to know every possible detail about me, Alfonso, our marriage, our children, his businesses and our lives together.

Locating and gathering all this information has become a full-time job for me. Clearly, part of the defense team's strategy must be to overwhelm me with requests for information. Each day, I receive urgent faxes from Ross or Susan relaying the defense team's latest requests for various documents. I do my best but, at times, I want to throw my hands in the air and quit. Some of the requests seem so ludicrous: why do they need to know how much my five-year-old son received in allowances in 1987, or how much I give my maids in pocket change for their bus fare when they go home for the weekend? They want copies of every single bank statement Alfonso and I had since our marriage in 1973. They even want to know how much we spent on the upkeep of our show horse, Piece of Cake, which Alfonso Jr. used to ride in competitions, and this amount has to be broken down into what we spend on hay, feed, trainers and veterinarians. Are you kidding me?

They also want to know everything about Alfonso's businesses—everything from property and business assessments to profit statements and future earnings projections. Since Francisco has nearly all the information concerning the businesses, I'm at a distinct disadvantage coming up with everything they've requested. But I've learned that the CMH attorneys seem to also have alternative sources of information. Today I receive in the mail from Ross a packet with twenty pages of interrogatories—questions I am supposed to answer relating to the case, or supposedly relating to the case. A lot of the questions seem to be only remotely related to the case and extremely intrusive. But, after reading the questions, it is clear to me that the CMH attorneys are getting inside information from a source in Guadalajara and my instincts tell me it's Francisco. After my relationship with Francisco ended, I wondered whether he might try to sabotage my case in some way by helping the defense team. Now it's clear he has.

Certain questions in the interrogatories could only have been asked with the benefit of personal knowledge about my family and my relationship with Alfonso. The insight for these questions did not come from me, since I have yet to be deposed, and I know that neither of Alfonso's sisters nor any of our friends has been contacted. The only possible source is Francisco.

One of the interrogatories asks about a specific argument I had with Alfonso just prior to his death over his desire to take our oldest son, Alfonso Jr., with him heli-skiing. I didn't think it was appropriate to take a fifteen-year-old boy on this type of trip with a group of grown men for what I considered a purely adult activity. The other men who regularly accompanied Alfonso on the annual trip agreed with me, citing their unwritten rule that no wives or children were allowed on those trips. When Alfonso got an idea in his mind, however, he was nearly impossible to dissuade. He loved his boys so much that he wanted to share this exhilarating skiing experience with them. We argued heatedly about this issue for several days before he begrudgingly agreed to wait a few years until the boys were older. Now, nearly two years later, I'm being asked about this argument as if it had been common knowledge. The only explanation I can come up with for its surfacing now is that Alfonso must have mentioned it to Francisco at the time, and Francisco must have conveyed that, and God knows what else, to the CMH attorneys.

When it comes time for my deposition, I expect more of the same. Two CMH attorneys and Ross fly down to San Diego and I fly up from Guadalajara for what is supposed to be three days of questioning. We rent a suite at one of the local hotels and spend the day before my deposition poring over thousands of documents, as Ross briefs me on what I should expect.

"Kris, all you have to do is tell your story," he says. "They may try to trick you into saying things they want to hear, but the truth is you've got nothing to hide."

"Well, you know how I like to talk," I say to Ross. "If they want to hear my story, they are going to get more than they bargained for."

"That's fine, Kris, but don't give them any more than what they ask for. And whatever you do, retain your composure and don't take their bait. If they ask you a question you know came from Francisco, keep the answer simple: yes, no or just a couple words. Don't give them any ammunition."

The following morning, in the same suite, I walk in with Ross to meet for the first time the men who have been tormenting me with information requests for the past year. The lead attorney is an older man with a shriveled, well-worn face and glasses. He shakes my hand and, in a smug voice, says, "So you're the reason we're having to do so much work."

I'm sure he is just trying to be cute but, nonetheless, I am shocked at his insensitivity. I feel like lashing out at him, but I maintain my composure.

"I think your clients had quite a bit to do with it actually," I retort coolly.

Seeing his comments did not produce the response he expected, he just nods sheepishly and takes his seat.

As he proceeds with the questions, I discover how they are planning to use all the information they have requested from me. He asks questions about nearly every document I sent them, and his attention to detail becomes so tedious that Ross spends most of his time playing solitaire on his laptop computer. Every single question he asks of me, no matter what the answer, is rephrased at least two more times with slightly different words to see if I will trip up somehow. The defense team pores over each document I gave them, and asks me to describe and explain each of them down to the minutest of details.

"Mrs. Ochoa, I am going to show you a document, which purports to be a financial statement from one of your husband's businesses," the defense attorney says. "Do you recognize this document?"

"It looks vaguely familiar," I say.

"Well, according to this document, this particular business had substantial losses in 1989," he says. "Do you know if this is true?"

"I suppose it was," I say. "I didn't really get involved in Alfonso's businesses, but this was one of his newer ventures and I think they had some problems getting it off the ground."

"So you would say it's accurate that this business was losing money?" he asks.

"I suppose so, at that time," I answer.

These types of monotonous interchanges carry us through most of the first two-and-a-half days until, finally, he gets to the questions I know have come from Francisco.

"Mrs. Ochoa, did you and your husband agree on the decision that was made to move into the home owned by your mother-in-law the December before your husband's death?" the CMH attorney asks.

I look at Ross, and he just nods coolly.

"No," I say.

"Was it a point of contention between you and your husband?" he continues.

"Yes," I say.

"Did you threaten to leave your husband over this decision?" he asks.

"No! Did he really tell you . . ." but I can't finish before Ross grasps my forearm and immediately asks for a break.

Out in the courtyard, Ross tells me what I already know, "You can't give into these guys. You know they're just fishing for leads and hoping you'll crack. We know they've talked to Francisco; now we just have to get past that and not lend any credence to his crazy theories. Just stay composed."

When we go back in, I stick to the script and shut down my emotions. The questioning only lasts another forty-five minutes and, when it's over, I feel like my entire life has been recorded on the court reporter's stenograph machine. As the attorneys are packing up their gear, the CMH attorney throws out another salvo.

"Well, that was a good start," he says. "I think we have at least two or three days more worth of questions. Do we want to come back here, Mrs. Ochoa, or are you willing to come up to our turf?"

"Are you serious," I say. "You can't possibly have any more of your ridiculous . . ." Ross intervenes again just in the nick of time.

"We'll get back to you on that one," he says.

"Mrs. Ochoa, I know you think some of these questions are ridiculous, but you have made some serious allegations against my clients, and all we are trying to do is get to the bottom of all this," says the CMH attorney.

I nod and bite my tongue as we walk out of the room.

When we reconvene in Vancouver, it's just more of the same— answering the same questions and watching Ross play solitaire. In the end, my deposition takes five full days.

------◆◆◆------

On top of Francisco's apparent involvement, the tactics the defense team is using are becoming a little more than I can handle. I've learned through my sources here in Guadalajara that CMH's attorneys have hired an attorney here who, in turn, has hired a private investigator to monitor my activities. This investigator's task is to dig up dirt about me, Alfonso and my family. The attorney and the private investigator are hounding my friends and Alfonso's former business associates for any tidbits of information. Some of these people have cooperated and answered their questions. Those who haven't cooperated, however, have learned how desperate these people are. They have used deceitful phone calls and outright lies to try to trick my friends into revealing anything they can use against me.

For instance, my friend, Viviana, called me last night to relay this story:

"It was last night, Kris, about 7:30, and I get a call from a gentleman who says he's doing an investigation concerning the lawsuit. He says he wants to ask me some questions. I very politely tell him that I'm not interested in talking to him; he says fine, we hang up and I think that is the end of it. Then, just a few minutes ago, I get a call from a man who sounds like he's trying to disguise his voice, but I can tell right away it's the same guy. This time he says he is calling because you have used me as a reference on a credit application and could I verify the financial information on your application. Well, I just hung up and then called you."

"Wow," I say, "it sure seems like they're getting desperate. Thanks for not talking to them, Viviana. I'm sorry they had to bother you."

I call Ross at home and he says not to worry, that they are merely searching for any shred of evidence to show that the descriptions of my marriage and our lifestyle that were beginning to emerge from my deposition are untrue. They can dig as deep as they want, but they are not going to find anything.

The challenges involved in moving me and my six children from Guadalajara to San Diego initially seem overwhelming. We need to make the move by the beginning of the fall school term, so I've set next July as our target date so we will have some time to get settled before school starts. I know I have several months to prepare, but the details still seem staggering . . . the packing, the good-byes, the search for a new house, new schools, new cars . . . How can I do all this myself? My daily prayers turn again to my mantra from Oscar Romero: "I can't; You must; I'm yours; Show me the way." I pray for guidance. I have no idea how I will put this move together, but I have no doubt that the details will fall into place as long as I stay organized and follow my own path.

One of my initial concerns is finding a good school for the children. While they speak a little English with their American uncles, aunts and grandparents, they do not speak or write well enough to jump right in to an American curriculum. So, priority number one is finding a school with strong English as a Second Language (ESL) program. I decide to take a trip to San Diego to look for a good school. My father, who has been a university professor for thirty years, has made appointments for me with every private school in San Diego. My first appointment is at the La Jolla Country Day School. Since I grew up in San Diego, I think I have a pretty good idea of just about all the private schools in the area. To my recollection, La Jolla Country Day is a snobby, elitist school. I don't want my kids in that kind of environment, so I'm not sure I should even go through the motions.

I decide to put my preconceived notions aside and go see the school. Since it is October, the campus is teeming with activity when I pull into the parking lot. I notice immediately what appears to be a very diverse student body—the students seem to come from a variety of ethnic backgrounds. During the tour I am given of the campus by the admissions director, I am spellbound by the facilities. The school is awesome, and has everything I could ever dream of for my children. Despite being a college preparatory school, the emphasis is placed on each child's unique abilities and individuality. I find that my initial impression of the diversity of the student body is accurate as I'm told that 25 percent of the school's students speak a language other than English in the home. I feel this school will be the ideal place for my children to ease into the American educational system without too much of a culture shock.

The school's art, sports, music and science programs seem to be top quality. About 90 percent of the students graduating from La Jolla Country Day go on to college, many to Ivy League schools. I have always been frustrated by the lack of academic ambition in Mexico and it just seems that putting my children in this type of an environment will be a gift that they are certain to appreciate later in their lives.

While I do attend the other meetings my father has arranged for me, I walk away from La Jolla Country Day knowing that this is the place for my children. Back in Guadalajara, I quickly complete the children's applications for enrollment. In January, I receive notice from the school that they have accepted all six children—I instantly become the school's largest ever supplier of children. For the fall of 1993, I will have children in nursery school and grades twelve, ten, eight, five and one. Upper, middle and lower school—I have them all covered. With the costly private school tuition they charge, I think the school administrators are as happy with me as I am with the school.

Now that the decision about where the children will go to school has been made, I can begin to focus on the logistics of the move, contract international movers and begin arranging to have my furniture and belongings sent to San Diego by July 1, 1993. The question now becomes: Where will I send them? I still don't have a house.

It's April and I decide to begin my house search in earnest. As I board the Aeromexico flight from Guadalajara to San Diego, I keep repeating my mantra, "I can't; You must; I'm yours; Show me the way." I pray the entire flight to San Diego. I have no idea what to do. I trust totally that my path will unfold before me in ways that I am, as of yet, unaware. It is a comfort to feel this trust and to know that I have a celestial team helping me; but, I still have no idea how this is going to work. I probably will have to rent a house close to the school until I can find something that meets our needs.

My parents help me find a real estate agent so we can begin looking at the rental possibilities in La Jolla. The search is totally depressing. Nothing is even close to what I want or need—too small, too big, too expensive, no yard or too close to neighbors. I do see one house that I think would be ideal—five bedrooms, spacious living area, a big yard, beautiful view . . . and total sticker shock! For what they want for rent, I think I could buy a home in Guadalajara.

After a week of futile searching, I am relieved to forget about the house search for a night and enjoy a quiet evening at the La Jolla home of my friends, Isaac and Lorraine Levy. Isaac was our insurance agent and, after Alfonso died, he was instrumental in helping me deal with collecting the proceeds from Alfonso's life insurance, and in helping me redraft my will to remove Francisco from the position of trustee of my children's estate.

As I pull into the driveway of their lovely home, I envy them. Months earlier I had been to their house for the first time and could not help but think how perfect this home would be for my family. The house is so beautiful, with a phenomenal view of San Diego, and it is centrally located on Mount Soledad overlooking La Jolla and San Diego. As I look at the wall surrounding the house, it seems so safe and well protected, and quite a contrast to the uncertainty that seems to be dominating my daily routine. I pray that I might be able to find a home similar to this one. During dinner, Lorraine asks me about my search and I confess that it is not going well.

"Kris, you ought to buy this house," Isaac says completely out of the blue. I am stunned, and cannot speak. I just stare at him, with my mouth open wide.

"What do you think?" he asks. I looked around and tears well in my eyes as I think of the possibility of living in this beautiful home.

"I'd love to Isaac, but I think this is a little out of my ballpark," I say. "I don't see how I could afford it."

"Sure you can," he says matter-of-factly. "I'll talk to the people at my bank and you can take over my loan. We've been wanting to sell this house because we want something larger, and this seems like the perfect opportunity."

Ecstatic, I cannot believe what I am hearing. "It can't be this easy," I keep telling myself. But it is, and by the time I'm ready to go back to Guadalajara, my sister-in-law, Cheryl, has put all the paperwork together and all I have to do is sign. She says escrow will close right around the date I had targeted for the move, so it seems, once again, things are falling into place.

From the San Diego end, the move is going much smoother than I expected. I feel so much love and support from my family and friends; everyone is helping me make the move as easy as possible. I believe my celestial team is working overtime to help me put everything together. The Guadalajara end . . . that's a different story.

After the fiasco with Francisco, I have given up any hope of getting back any of the furniture that had been in Alfonso's several offices. Now that it's time to move, I guess I should at least try to reclaim the furniture from his personal office at the corporate headquarters. We picked out that furniture together during our last trip together to San Diego. The design and decoration of his office was one of the last projects we did together. The two pieces of furniture I would like back are the leather couch and the matching chair we bought at a furniture store in La Jolla, then had shipped to Guadalajara. Both the sofa and the chair are a rich hunter green—beautiful pieces of furniture that are both elegant and comfortable. Alfonso especially loved the chair. When he would have a meeting in his office, he would always sit in that beautiful green chair and seat his clients on the sofa. To this day, I can see him in that chair, with his leg crossed and a warm smile on his face.

The furniture obviously has a lot of sentimental value for me, and I think it is only fair and right that I should take the furniture to our new home in San Diego. I asked the attorney who had helped prepare the buyout to ask Francisco if I could take the furniture. Francisco's reply did not surprise me. Of course I could take the furniture, Francisco told him—just send him a check for $30,000 and the deal would be done. What an outrage—he is trying to sell me my own furniture! I've told a few of my friends about this latest incident, and they are likewise appalled. Several of them have even called Francisco to ask him to reconsider. Francisco is adamant, however, and will not give me the furniture.

Then the impossible happens. It's 11:00 p.m. on a warm June evening, less than a month before we leave for San Diego. I have already started packing, and this is the only time I have to myself to organize things, so I am in my closet, packing up some of the family's winter gear. When the phone rings, I think, "Who could it be at this hour?"

"Kris?" the voice on the other end asks.

"Yeah, this is Kris."

"This is Luis, I work with Francisco," he said.

"What do you want? You know it's past 11:00—why are you calling me this late?" I ask.

"Well, Francisco told me to call you," he said. "Do you want Alfonso's furniture? I've been told to bring it over if you do."

"Is this some kind of joke?" I say.

"No, ma'am, I have it all loaded, but I thought I should call before I came over."

"You know, I really don't think this is funny. Did Francisco put you up to this?"

"I don't know what you mean ma'am," he says. "I was just told to load up the furniture and bring it over. If you don't want it, I guess I can unload it and go home."

He is sounding so polite and sincere that I believe him.

"Okay," I say, "bring it over."

I hang up the phone and immediately call my gardener and ask him to come over and to bring a few friends, just in case this was some sort of gag. At precisely 11:30 p.m. the doorbell rings and Luis walks in with two other workers from the company. They unload every single piece of furniture that was in Alfonso's office, including the chair and the sofa. For the life of me, I can't figure out what prompted this lone act of decency from

Francisco. However, I do know that the furniture will fit beautifully in my house in San Diego, and I can almost see Alfonso sitting in this beautiful green chair in my new living room, smiling at me.

When Luis and his men are finished, he walks over to me, hands me an envelope and says good night. As I watch him pull out of the driveway, I open the envelope—it's a bill from Francisco for $250 for the workers' time.

Much more important than the furniture are my children. They remain incredulous and uncooperative, and cannot believe that I am ruining their lives in this way. The three oldest are leading the opposition, feeling the move is totally unnecessary. They cannot begin to comprehend my motives and can only see that I am taking them away from everything and everyone they love. My heart goes out to them because I know how difficult all this change is for them. First, they lose their father, and now they are being forced to move to a foreign county. I know they cannot see past this pain to the world of opportunities that will open up before them in the United States. Still, I know in my heart that my decision is a good one.

Their opposition, however, is getting more pronounced and more vocal. Finally, I decide I must sit down with the three of them to pretty much lay down the law; so, one evening, I take the three of them out for tacos to discuss their attitude.

"Look guys, I know you don't understand my decision on this," I tell them. "But, you are going to have to trust me on this one. I know it's going to be hard—it's going to be hard for all of us. I didn't want your father to die anymore than you guys, but when he did, it changed everything forever."

I can see the tears start to well up in Christofer's eyes and looks of frustration and rebellion emerge from the older two boys.

"We've lived our entire lives here," Alfonso says. "We have friends, girlfriends, cars—our whole lives are here. And you're forcing us to leave all that behind so you can move back to your home—not our home—your home. It's just not fair."

"You know," I say, "sometimes life doesn't seem fair, but part of growing up is learning how to deal with things you don't really want to do. I know it's not going to be easy, but just think of the all the opportunities waiting for us—new friends, new schools, your grandparents and aunts and uncles. If you give it a chance, you might even like it."

I can tell I'm getting nowhere. They are just sitting, munching on their tacos, tuning me out . . . all except Carl Eric.

"I'm not going," he says. "I don't know what I'm going to do, but I'm not going. I'll run away if I have to, but I'm not going." Then he gets up and walks out of the restaurant.

I start after him, then stop. He's just going to have to come to terms with this on his own. With the other two, I decide the only thing do is to pull rank.

"You are coming with me and that's just the way it's going to be," I tell them. "I am the head of this family and I've decided that this is what's best for the family. All of you are members of this family and I expect your cooperation and support. I'm sorry if you don't agree, but this is the way it's going to be."

We don't talk any more about the move in the weeks that follow until the day before the move, when Carl Eric, as promised, runs away. I panic as I realize that I am leaving the country the next morning and my sixteen-year-old son is nowhere to be found. I can't just leave him behind in Guadalajara, a city of more than six million people, with no money and nowhere to live. I call all of his friends and all of his friends' parents, but nobody has seen him. Finally, at about 3:00 in the morning, he shows up at the house to collect his belongings. I know this is my last and only chance to reach him, so I approach him with so much love in my heart.

"This is all just too much," he tells me. "I don't mean to be making things hard for you, Mom, but I just can't do this. Not now, maybe never. But for sure, it's just too soon now."

I feel so much compassion for him, but I don't know what to say. My heart aches for him as I can feel his pain.

"Carl, your entire family is moving to San Diego tomorrow," I say. "Your mother, your four brothers, your baby sister . . . Do you know how much you will miss them if you are here and they are there? Do you know how much I would miss you?"

Carl puts his arm around me and holds me tight as I start to cry.

"What if we worked something out just for awhile, maybe a year or so and then I will move up with the rest of you," he says.

"But where would you stay, who would take care of you?" I ask.

"I've already talked to my friend Antonio and his parents. They're cool with me staying there through the next school year."

"Are you serious? You've already talked to them about this?"

"That's where I've been all day. I know that now is not the time for me to leave here. I can't explain why, but I just know it. Can't you see that?"

I look in his eyes and I can see exactly that. He's so young, but he has matured so much in the time since his father died. He's not a boy anymore, but a young man. I give in and agree to let him stay in Guadalajara, but only under certain conditions to which he agrees. He can stay in Mexico with Antonio's family for one year and go to school, but he has to maintain a B average. At the end of the school year, he has to rejoin his family in body and in spirit in San Diego.

We hug and cry. My tears are tears of relief: the crisis is over and Carl is okay. Most importantly, I have my son back.

Saying good-bye to my friends is almost as difficult. They all believe that my move will be a temporary one. They all keep saying that they know I will be back; that I am too Mexicanized to survive in the United States. I don't argue with them, but, in my heart, I know they are dead wrong. I know that without Alfonso, I have no reason to stay in Mexico. I know this is the right decision. I know I will see my friends again, but I will never return to live in Mexico again. My children, once they became adults, may choose to return to Guadalajara, and I will definitely support that decision if they so desire. But my purpose for being in Mexico revolved around my husband. Without him, it's time to find my own path.

On the afternoon we arrive in San Diego, I stand alone in the kitchen of my new house. My house: it has such a great ring to it. I have never in my life owned my own house, and this beautiful house belongs to me. This is the beginning of a new life for me and my family, and I find that totally amazing. Alfonso had always purchased all of our homes in the past and then advised me later. But this house is mine from the very beginning. I am so excited! I look around and feel proud of myself and proud of my children. This is our new beginning.

While the children are unpacking their clothes, I stand in the empty kitchen in the middle of the afternoon waiting for the moving vans to arrive. I can hardly contain my happiness. My smile must be wider than it has ever been. As I stand here savoring the moment, the kitchen light suddenly turns on. I look around and see no one, so I just walk over to the switch and turn it off again. "Strange," I think . . . "maybe a short." As soon as I turn it off, it switches itself right back on again. This is one persistent short. I walk to the light switch on the other side of the kitchen to turn off the light. As soon as I turn it off again, the light switches on again. I turn off the light a couple more times only to have it turn on by itself again. What is going on here? Then it dawns on me that maybe this little occurrence has nothing to do with the electrical system of my house. I look around and smile.

"So you approve of the house, Alfonso?" I say. Then suddenly, the light blinks on and off for about three minutes.

"I'm so glad you like it," I say, smiling and laughing. "I guess I did good, huh? Maybe it's because I had such a good teacher."

The light continues to go crazy for about another minute. Then it stops blinking for good.

It feels so good to know Alfonso has given me and this home his blessing.

CHAPTER 6
the new life

Living in San Diego is proving to be full of adjustments for all of us—everything from eating to recreation to home life. The change in lifestyle, especially for my children, is quite dramatic. They have visited the United States, and San Diego in particular, many times, but all of these visits were for a week or two at the most. Now they find themselves uprooted, living in a new neighborhood, a new city, a new country. So, I am glad I decided to give the children a few months to adapt to their new environment before school starts in the fall. The children are spending the summer testing out their new surroundings and, more often than not, finding them lacking in comparison to the lives they left behind in Guadalajara.

My children, for example, having been raised to enjoy hunting with their father, often would set up target practice after school in the backyard of our home in Guadalajara. They would spend hours in our huge canyon of a backyard playing in ways that, for the most part, were quite appropriate for the type of area we lived in. Backyard target practice and many of these other activities, however, are not as acceptable in our new La Jolla neighborhood. In fact, many of the activities my children enjoyed in Mexico are off limits or much more difficult to enjoy in these new surroundings. Not surprisingly, my children are quite bored with life in the United States, and I can't really blame them.

We are spending most of the first few months here as homebodies as we slowly adapt to the American way of life. Running a household is very different for me here than it was in Mexico. In Guadalajara, I had several people helping me with the daily upkeep of the house, and with the cooking and cleaning. I had a full-time helper who made sure the cars had gas, handled all the banking and did many of my errands. In San Diego, I am on my own, which can cause some quite embarrassing situations. For instance, I have never used an ATM before, nor have I ever had to pump my own gas on a regular basis. I'm combining the two today, trying to use my ATM card at a gas station and creating a scene right out of *America's Funniest Home Videos.*

"The lady on pump two," I hear a voice call over the intercom. "Yes, you ma'am. The one in the blue van. You have to pay before you pump the gas. That's it. Slide the card through and insert your PIN number."

"My what?"

"Your PIN number."

"What's a PIN number?"

"Where are you from, lady?"

For the most part, people are very friendly and patient. Still, I am embarrassed repeatedly by my inability to master some of the simple tasks so common in the American way of life.

Grocery shopping is another matter altogether. I can't seem to keep enough food and milk in the house. My kids consume huge amounts of food, much more than I remember they did in Mexico. After just a month or so here, I am getting thank-you notes from the manager of the local Ralph's Supermarket. It seems my weekly grocery bills are setting some sort of record and they want to thank me for my tremendous patronage. In the matter of just a couple of years, I have gone from the frequent shopper list at Neiman-Marcus and Saks Fifth Avenue to the most valuable customer at my local supermarket. What a switch! But after all, that is what the last few years have been all about—change.

Our eating schedule has changed also, as we adapt to the American schedule of breakfast, lunch and dinner. In Mexico, the largest meal of the day, dinner, is served in the early afternoon, while the evening meal is more of a snack. And we quickly have adapted to the American tradition of spending a lot of time in front of the television, especially when *The Simpsons* is on. It is a transition time for all of us and I am grateful for this low-key period, the calm before the fast-approaching storm that will be the beginning of the school year.

———————————

Preparing for the school year is proving to be a formidable task. Since the schools in Mexico required uniforms, we have started from scratch with school clothes. The last few days, I have corralled one child at a time and escorted them to the malls to equip them as well as possible for life at La Jolla Country Day. Cool shoes, stylish backpacks, state-of-the-art school supplies—I figure with all my children are about to go through, I want them to be well armed and as well prepared as possible. They are very nervous about starting school and making new friends. I am even more nervous for them. From my own experiences thirty years ago when I moved to Guadalajara, I know what kind of difficulties lay ahead.

It's the day before school starts, and I'm headed by myself to an orientation session for parents whose children are just beginning at Country Day. At this meeting, the teachers and staff explain what they expect of the parents and the students, what the work load will be like, the types of social activities offered and other details involving their approach to the children's education. As I look around the room, the other parents look like they feel as nervous as I do. These parents probably only have one child, who already speaks English. My children will have so much more to overcome. I feel so badly for them, because I know this is going to be very hard for all of them.

When the moderator ends his talk with the school's motto, "Try and care," I feel the dam that's holding back my emotions begin to give way. I quickly leave the amphitheater and rush to my car, where the dam explodes into a torrent of tears. For the first time, I have serious second thoughts. As I watch the other parents make their way to their cars, I have to wonder whether I have done the right thing taking my children away from Mexico. Will they make new friends? Are they going to be able to handle the difficult transition? Will Alfonso Jr. be accepted into his class of seniors? All of these questions, none of which have readily apparent answers, overwhelm me. I just sit here at the wheel of my minivan and cry. What have I done? My poor children. What was I thinking? What am I about to put them through? The tears will not stop. I feel like the weight of the world is perched on my shoulders . . . and school starts tomorrow.

I drive down to the beach to watch wave after wave roll in and crash on the deserted shore. Slowly, I begin to calm down. I try to adjust my thinking and my emotions, if not to embrace, then at least to tolerate this seemingly overwhelming uncertainty. Just as I am learning from the changes in our lives, so too will my children learn from the difficulties ahead. These transitions and adjustments are part of their paths, their growth process. I know each person has his or her own path, quite distinct from anyone else's. The lessons we learn in this life usually come from our own personal experiences along that path and, more times than not, these experiences are painful.

Why can't we learn the easy way? Why must it be so difficult? I've decided that will be my first question to God when I die. Why can't we take a learning pill or something easy like that? Why does it have to be so hard? Why is it even harder to watch your children suffer? As parents, we love them so much that we want to shield them from any suffering. But as I have come to realize, that would be shielding them from life itself—depriving them of their opportunities to grow as young people and learn from their experiences. Certainly, these next few months are going to be hard for all of us, but my own lesson is going to have to be learning, once again, to trust and to let go—to somehow not only tolerate, but to embrace this uncertainty. All I can do is be there for them with love and support. This is their chance, their opportunity to learn about themselves.

In the months that follow, the adjustments are difficult. More than a few times, my children plead with me to let them return to Mexico. But as the school year progresses, they are acclimating and, although they will never admit it, they seem to be enjoying at least some aspects of their new surroundings. Every so often, a pleasant surprise will pop up and reaffirm my faith. Jonathan runs for fifth grade class president. Though he doesn't win, he receives a standing ovation from his class for stepping forth as the new kid and giving his best. Also, Christofer has become the star of his seventh grade basketball team.

The most pleasant surprise of them all, however, is Alfonso Jr. He has come to symbolize Ochoa family unity to the rest of the school. On his breaks, he drops by the nursery school to play with Annette or he brings snacks to Nicholas, who is in the first grade. He attends all of his little brothers' athletic events, while playing varsity basketball himself. He is always there, watching out for his younger brothers and sister. His efforts do not go unnoticed. The teachers, coaches and administrators always comment to me what a responsible and family-oriented young man he is. I am so proud.

When Alfonso Jr. graduates from high school in June 1994, I know his father will march right beside him to the music of "Pomp and Circumstance." I'm sure Alfonso will beam with pride as his first son graduates from high school and prepares to begin college at the University of San Diego in the fall. This is the first step in the fulfillment of Alfonso's greatest hope for his children—that they receive the best education possible and attend college.

However, within a short period of time, the teachers and administrators at La Jolla Country Day begin to notice that Nicholas and Jonathan have learning differences that are slowing their progress. With the help of the director of the school's learning center, both boys go through extensive testing and the results are at once encouraging and disheartening. Both boys have very high IQs, but both also have great difficulty reading and even greater difficulty printing. They are diagnosed with Attention Deficit Disorder (ADD) and Dyslexia. These conditions, I am told, have only recently been found to be hereditary.

When I hear that, memories of my husband make me think he probably suffered from these same types of learning disabilities and help me to understand Alfonso in a totally different light. I always assumed his inability to read and write well came from his lack of formal education. These shortcomings always embarrassed him and he went to great lengths to cover them up. He learned to compensate brilliantly by having people, like his executives and his secretary, help him through difficult situations. With this revelation, my admiration for Alfonso grows. To overcome this impairment and still achieve what he did makes his accomplishments even more impressive.

Now my children will have to overcome these same difficulties. The big difference is that the learning problems Nicholas and Jonathan have are being identified early enough so they will receive help. They will be given the opportunity to adjust and to learn thanks to the tremendous advances being made in the area of learning difficulties. With special tutoring and a strong support system, I hope they will be able to overcome the learning problems that had so embarrassed their father.

The best way for me to support the children during these transitional years is to be as visible as possible around school. Just knowing their mom is not too far away serves as some sort of comfort to them, so I get involved in as many school activities as I can. However, my question is, "Which ones?" I know my children's strongest points involve sports and athletics, so the Booster Club seems like a natural choice. After attending my first Booster Club meeting, I know I've picked the right organization. The Booster Club is run by Mary Jo Landry, Cathy Rubenson, Pippa Dinger and Vickie Mogilner, ladies who, within a short period of time, become very close friends. We plan homecoming activities, run bake sales and generally do all we can to support the athletic program. More importantly, we have a lot of fun.

The ladies in the Booster Club are exactly what I need to help in my personal adjustment to life as an American Mom. The Booster Club moms are supportive, friendly, and they help me tremendously through some trying high school times with advice and encouragement. For instance, Mary Jo was instrumental in helping to get Alfonso Jr. accepted by the other members of his senior class. Since he was the new kid in a class that had been together for quite a while, he had difficulty at first making new friends. But Mary Jo had her son, Chris, take Alfonso under his wing, introduce him to his group of friends, and include him in all their activities. The change in Alfonso was dramatic—it's amazing what a few good friends will do.

I feel the same way as the Booster Club becomes a big part of my social life as I immerse myself in my children's activities. Their acceptance of me for who I am, with no preconceived judgments, eases my transition greatly. Unlike in Mexico, I do not feel stigmatized by my status as a middle-aged, single mom. With these women, I am just one of the girls. I have not felt this way in a long time and I relish it. I feel like I have come a long way since March 12, 1991.

One of the hardest things to get used to in San Diego is the burden I carry on a daily basis of having to "tell my story." In Mexico, all of my friends knew about the accident and how Alfonso died, and most also knew about what happened with Francisco. In San Diego, moving into a new neighborhood, school and parish mean inviting many new people in my life. Instead of being able to leave behind the painful details of our family history, it seems like everywhere I go, I get into conversations with people who naturally ask about my husband. Despite all the time that's passed, I still find it terribly difficult to go into the details of Alfonso's accident, especially with people whom I do not know very well.

One such conversation, however, winds up having wonderful consequences. In the fall, I decide I should register the family as parishioners at the local Catholic Church we had been attending. I kept putting off the visit to the church, however, because I dreaded having to tell my story and the likelihood of breaking down in tears in front of the pastor. When I finally get around to it, my conversation with the monsignor turns out exactly as I had expected. Once I tell him about Alfonso, and the spiritual awareness I had begun to develop through the classes at the Jesuit University and though my meditations, he tells me there is someone who works at the church he wants me to meet. He leads me down the hall to the office of Linda Lepeirs.

Linda and I immediately hit it off. The priest was right—we are definitely on the same spiritual wavelength. She is a very progressive Catholic, and director of ministries at the church. Linda is such a warm, loving and welcoming person; and, after speaking with her for just a few minutes, I feel like we have an immediate bond. I tell her my story, which she listens to with genuine compassion. She recently lost her sister and her closest friend, so she can relate to the pain of loss I am describing. Linda soon becomes my confidant, my spiritual adviser and one of my best friends. She has helped to fill the void I've felt since leaving Guadalajara, away from Susan and Anna. Linda listens with a comforting ear to my many fears and concerns about the new life I am creating for me and my family. She is always there with words of love and support, even when I feel like things are slipping out of control.

Because Linda and I get along so well, I've become very involved with different projects at the church. A month after joining the parish, I am elected to the parish council, which I see as a tremendous opportunity to help the church to adapt to the realities of living in a more progressive climate. With the decline of vocations to the priesthood, I really feel as though it is up to the lay people to play a powerful role in this transition. As a member of the parish council, I've started a prayer group for mothers with young children, which meets at my house once a week. I also work with the Christian Formation program, an effort to help educate people about the Church's teachings and developments within the Church. I am excited about the prospect of putting some of my newfound spiritual awareness into practice. Life has presented a series of new challenges and I am enthusiastic about tackling them.

———————

One morning, after I drop the children off at school, I decide to take a walk on the beach. After walking for a few minutes, I sit down in the sand in a very deserted area of the shore. With all the hectic activity of my household, it feels good to be by myself, and to enjoy the solitude. It is a hazy morning and the ocean reflects the gray color of the sky. It is chilly and even a bit damp. I am mesmerized watching the waves roll in, one after the other. As I look out at the ocean, I notice a bright reflection coming off the water. I look up and see a tiny crack in the cloud through which a faint ray of sunshine is shining and illuminating the ocean below. It looks like the rays are trying to expand and beat the clouds away, but the crack is not growing much. The effect the ray of sun has on the ocean below is beautiful—sparkling the crest of the waves as they move through this little patch of sunshine.

I feel something stir inside of me. Slowly at first, but then with more confidence and awareness, I realize this little patch of sunshine is like the happiness growing within me. I can feel the sun struggle to push back the clouds, sometimes with limited success, but, nevertheless, constantly trying, and shining through in some way. I chuckle to myself, "I'm actually happy. I can't believe it. I'm happy." I giggle, hug myself and think, "Life is good," as the rays of sun push the clouds out a little farther.

CHAPTER 7

the new love

Since losing Alfonso, I've had a real hard time envisioning myself ever remarrying or even becoming involved in a relationship with another man. The obstacles seem too daunting. I married Alfonso when I was twenty years old and spent my entire adult life with him raising our family. Now, I am over forty, a widow with six children. Spending the rest of my life without a partner does not appeal to me, but the alternative doesn't sound very realistic given the circumstances. I still feel that Alfonso was the one true love of my life, so I guess I've assumed that the romance and love of an intimate relationship for me died along with him. I just cannot envision myself with another man. The idea seems so foreign to me.

Still, as I continue to settle into my new life in San Diego, some of my friends have suggested very discreetly that it might not be a bad idea for me to begin dating again. Dating? . . . I haven't dated for more than twenty years, since I was in college. The idea of male companionship and adult friendship in theory sounds a little more attractive to me. Getting out of the house without the children once in a while with someone I can relate to on an adult level sounds appealing. But, my first few experiments in dating prove disastrous. So now, in early December 1994, I have pretty much given up on the whole idea.

At La Jolla Country Day there is a lot of excitement these days because our football team has qualified for the city championship game.

The kids are excited, and the game promises to be a fun evening of football and school spirit. I call my friends, Mary Jo and John Landry, to suggest that we sit together during the game.

"Sure, Kris, that sounds great," Mary Jo says. "You know I was going to call you anyway. We've got a friend in from San Francisco and we thought you might like to join us for dinner before the game. He's a really good friend of ours . . ."

My ears hear nothing after the "He." He . . . that means a man. Are they trying to set me up? When Mary Jo said a friend, I just assumed she meant a woman. A man . . . that's an entirely different story. After my recent bad experiences, I definitely am a little gun-shy, so I try to look for a way out of the situation.

"That sounds like a lot of fun, Mary Jo, but with the kids and all, that might be kinda tough," I say. "A couple of them invited friends too, so we've got quite a crew going. Can I take a rain check?"

"Sure, no problem," she says. "You can meet him at the game anyway. He's coming with us. We'll see you on Friday around 7:00."

Mary Jo's tone made it seem more and more like it was a setup, so I am a little nervous as we head to the game. On the one hand, I don't want to be pressured into going out with someone, especially someone I don't even know. Still, I trust the Landrys and really believe they would not put me in an uncomfortable situation. When we arrive at the stadium, we find our seats, and the children scurry off to the snack bar to load up on nachos and cokes and popcorn and anything else they can get their hands on. It's a very chilly night, at least by San Diego standards, so we are all bundled up in our winter parkas.

The game is about to start, and Mary Jo and John haven't arrived yet. As I glance towards the entrance of the stadium, I see them walk along the guardrail towards the area where we are sitting. With them is the nicest looking man I have ever seen. Could he be their "friend?" He has kind of a preppy look, which seems to suit him perfectly, at least from a distance. The Landrys and their friend climb up to where we are sitting and join what is now a group of about ten of us from the Booster Club. John introduces me to his friend, Dick Keane. That introduction will be the extent of our conversation tonight. Mary Jo quickly sits down beside me and the men take their places in the row behind us. The game is exciting, but our team loses. I spend most of my time keeping an eye on my children while trying to cheer on the team. When the game is over, we say our good-byes and that is that.

On the drive home, I think to myself that Dick Keane seems like a very nice man and I would not mind seeing him again sometime. Still, he lives in San Francisco and I live here. Oh well.

On Sunday morning, when I call Mary Jo just to chat, I can hear a lot of activity in the background. She explains that John is taking Dick to the airport, so they are in the middle of a last-minute travel frenzy. The background noise seems to subside so I assume John and Dick have left. Mary Jo, in a sort of hushed voice, says, "Kris, Dick left a letter for you."

"He did?" I say, not knowing how to respond. "What does it say?"

"I don't know," Mary Jo says, "I think you should open it, so I'll stick it in the mail. But you know, it might be . . . well . . . We invited Dick to come down and spend New Year's with us. I'll bet he's asking you to join us."

"Wow," I think almost out loud, "that would be very nice!"

"Well, I will let you know when I read it," I tell Mary Jo before hanging ing up and heading off to church with the children.

I am so excited about the letter that I can barely wait for it to arrive. When it comes on Tuesday, I tear open the envelope, expecting to read an invitation for New Year's Eve. Instead, the note reads, "Kris, I was told to tell you this: You are very loved. Everything is going to be okay."

What the heck does that mean? I reread the note five or six times before I call Mary Jo. "What happened to the date on New Year's Eve," I ask her.

Mary Jo doesn't understand the note either. She chuckles and says that Dick is involved in all kinds of weird stuff like parapsychology and things like that. She suggests I call him to find out what is going on, so she gives me his number and I call.

When he answers the phone, he sounds so nice, just as he did the night of the football game. The conversation just seems to flow and he eagerly tells me the story behind the note.

"After the football game, on the drive home, Mary Jo and John told me about what happened to your husband," he says. "They told me all about the accident, the children, the move, how they met you—all that kind of stuff. For some reason, your story really moved me—I even had to fight back the tears on the drive home. I can't really explain it . . . I still can't, but I went to bed thinking about all that you went through after your husband died and what a struggle it must have been."

"You don't know the half of it," I think of saying, but I let him continue.

"Well, I woke up very suddenly around 5:00 a.m. that morning and I heard a voice telling me to tell you that you are very loved and that everything is going to be okay. It was a very strange experience for me because I heard this voice with such clarity, but I had no idea what it meant and I still don't. I also didn't know quite what to do about it. I mean, I had barely met you and this seemed like such a personal message. So, I decided to let fate run its course—if you called the Landrys' house before I left for the airport on Sunday, then I would take that as a sign that I should tell you about the message.

"Since you hadn't called on Saturday, I thought I was off the hook. But then, just as we were heading out the door for the airport, you called. So, while you were on the phone with Mary Jo, I scurried around trying to find a pen and paper so I could write you a note about the message. I'm sorry for not delivering it in person, but I thought you should know. Does any of this make any sense?"

While Dick was relating his story, I was just sitting there next to the phone with a hand over my mouth, speechless. When he asks me if his story makes any sense, I can barely organize my thoughts, but suddenly things start to click in my mind.

"You know, your message makes perfect sense—in fact, it is the perfect message for me right now and it was so wonderful to hear it from you," I say. "Things have been so crazy lately. I don't know if Mary Jo and John told you that I am suing the ski resort where Alfonso, that's my husband, died. The attorneys I hired in Canada discovered evidence that the guides had been incredibly negligent in taking Alfonso and the others down that run. When I started out with the suit, I assumed the families of the others would join in, but they never did, so I have to go it alone.

"Well, needless to say, I had no idea of what I was getting myself into. The last three years have been absolutely grueling with all this pro-cedural BS going on. It's gotten so bad lately that I just want the trial to be over. It was supposed to start on January 9; but, right before Thanksgiving, my attorneys told me it won't start now until May. This means having to live with all of this even longer . . . I just don't know if I can do it."

"That's incredible, Kris," he says. "Sounds like you have a lot on your platter."

"Yeah, I do my best to juggle everything, but sometimes it just gets too overwhelming. And this is one of those times. I haven't even been able to meditate, which is usually a real important part of my life. Since I heard about the trial delay, I haven't been able to pray, or even think clearly. All I can do is think about the long year ahead and the implications of the trial, and I always wind up crying . . . like I'm doing now. I'm sorry, Dick, I don't mean to be laying all of this on you, but your message kinda opened the floodgates here."

"You know, Kris, it's completely natural for you to be feeling this way," Dick says, as I try to compose myself. "The fear of the unknown can be really hard to get through. You just have to do your best to see through the surface to what's really important."

"Yeah, I know," I say. "That's why your message makes such perfect sense to me. In fact, I bet since I've been unable to pray and have totally blocked things out, the message was diverted to you. Maybe my angels knew you would receive and deliver it to me."

"You know who I think the messenger was?" Dick asks. "I think it was Alfonso."

"Alfonso? Why?"

"I don't know for sure. Obviously, I never met him, but I just have a feeling it was him."

"I don't know," I say. "It's just such a wonderful message . . . I don't know what else to say. You know, I have so much enjoyed talking with you, Dick. This has really made my day. I wish I could talk to you all afternoon, but I'm running late to pick up the kids. Can we talk again, soon? Real soon?"

"Sure, how about I call you tonight?"

"That sounds great. Thank you so much for this wonderful gift. I am so grateful."

As I drive to pick up the kids, I become convinced that Alfonso was, indeed, the messenger. With tears in my eyes, I realize that Alfonso will always be there for me—that somehow he is orchestrating things in a way I cannot understand. I realize once again that I simply have to let go—let go and trust. The message is clear: Everything is going to be okay. Why is it so hard for me to believe this? Time and time again, I have allowed fear to overtake my heart, paralyze me and make me blind to the love that is everywhere. By telling me I am very loved, and that everything is going to be okay, Alfonso is telling me to let go. He will take care of things. I am in total awe of this wonderful message and of the messenger himself. Dick has seemingly come out of nowhere to help me right my course, and he, too, seems to be deeply moved by the experience.

This first conversation or revelation, as it turns out to be, creates an immediate bond between Dick and me. We both feel something very special is happening between us. We talk again that night, and we continue to speak on the phone almost daily. Dick winds up spending the New Year's holiday with his three children in Lake Tahoe, so our meeting is delayed a bit. The following weekend, however, he comes to San Diego and we plan our first date.

I am very nervous in the days leading up to that first date with Dick. It doesn't seem like a first date because I feel I know him so well from our numerous phone conversations. We have talked about everything—his family, my family, our spiritual and religious beliefs, our lives, even back to when we were children—everything has just flowed so naturally with him. Even so, we still had only met face to face once and that had been nearly a month earlier. We decide to meet at an Italian restaurant in La Jolla on Friday evening. When I arrive, I don't see him in the lobby, so I walk back outside to wait. As I glance at the menu posted outside, I hear someone call, "Kris?" I turn around and there he is.

"You know, when you walked by the first time, I thought it was you, but I thought you had black hair," he says.

"I must have been bundled up at the football game that night. It's me though," I say.

"I know—and I am so glad to finally see you, live and in person, instead of over the phone," he says as he puts his arms around me to hug me.

We have an absolutely lovely dinner. He is even better in person! We talk about everything, as if we've known each other for years. After dinner, we take a walk down by the beach, and he reaches out and takes my hand in his. We stop and look out at the waves crashing down on the beach. The nearly full moon glimmers off the turbulent ocean and illuminates his face as he turns towards me. It is a chilly winter night, but I feel so warm in his presence. I look deep into his blue eyes, so deep I think I reach down into his soul where I see a reflection—a reflection of me. My knees almost buckle as he takes me in his arms. When he leans over and kisses me, I feel our bodies and spirits meld into one. I know immediately that sometime, somewhere we have been together before and that our coming together now is no coincidence.

When I pull back, I say, "You know, this just feels so right."

"I know," he says. "I think we've been here before."

We wind up spending the entire weekend together. On Saturday night, we go out to dinner again and then to the movies. I can feel the sparks fly between us every moment we are together. On Sunday evening, Dick and I go to dinner with the Landrys. The weekend has been amazing. I have felt like a schoolgirl with a crush the entire time; every time I look into his eyes, I feel like swooning. At dinner, the Landrys say we look like two kids with a bad case of puppy love. We hold hands, giggle and just stare into each other's eyes. The Landrys can tell something very special is in the air. Since they played the part of Cupid and like both of us so much, they are also very excited.

After dinner, Dick turns away from me, looks at the Landrys and, in a dazed tone, says, "I'm so smitten right now. I don't know what has come over me, but I am totally smitten with this woman."

I blush and giggle like a fifteen-year-old girl and say, "Me too. Can you believe it?"

We all toast to our good fortune. What a weekend!

Dick and I soon discover how difficult long-distance relationships can be, even for the most committed of couples. From the beginning, we know what we are getting into will not be easy, and that it will take a tremendous effort on both our parts to make it work. Initially, the hardest part is the logistics. I find myself spending so much time at the airport either going to or coming from San Francisco or picking him up or dropping him off. We try to spend just about every weekend together so, naturally, we rack up quite a few frequent flyer miles. When we are not together physically, we talk on the phone several times each day. We wake up to the sound of the other's voice, and the last thing we do before going to sleep is to say good night to each other. Before long, I realize that I love Dick very much and that I want to spend my life with him.

This is quite a transformation from my belief just a few months ago that I would be the Widow Ochoa for the rest of my life. But, getting to know Dick is like watching a rose bloom: as each petal unfolds, I am in awe of the beauty I discover in him. He is sensitive, caring and tender, and he views the world very differently than most people I know. He respects nature as an integral part of God's creation, to be treated as a beautiful and wondrous gift. He has raised three children who have grown up to be wonderful adults, and he constantly supports me in my daily trials with my children, always telling me what a good mother I am and how lucky the children are to have me.

Sometimes I have to pinch myself to make sure this is really happening to me. I can't believe my good fortune to have found someone with whom I am so in tune. After four years of being the lonely widow, the single parent, now I have a partner again. It's a wonderful feeling. I confide in him, laugh with him, cry with him and he always is there to support me.

Within a short period of time, we truly become soul mates. The feeling of oneness I had when we first kissed on the beach is nurtured by the growing love between us. I feel as though I have known Dick my entire life and beyond. We flow together at the same pace and agree on almost everything. As time passes, our relationship becomes more meaningful and reaches depths I have never known with anyone before. I've read about this type of man-woman relationship in many books, but I never dreamed that I would find it.

The key to our harmony, I believe, is that both of us respect every aspect of the other's being enough to allow each other the freedom we need to grow as individuals. In that way, Dick and I complement each other perfectly. We allow each other the freedom to be ourselves and to learn about ourselves without any judgment, without any manipulation. We feed off each other and learn from each other while, at the same time, retaining our own identity. We support each other on our own personal path to God and enlightenment. At the same time, we are a couple who shares a powerful bond. We are interdependent—while we love each other so much it is difficult to be apart, we do not need to be constantly together to find ourselves.

My relationship with Dick is a liberating union, quite unlike any relationship I have ever had, and quite different from my relationship with Alfonso. When Alfonso died, my identity was so wrapped up in being his wife and the mother of his children that I had not a clue as to who I really was. When Alfonso said jump, I would always answer, "How high?" Still, I have come to realize what an important role Alfonso played in my own spiritual development.

Shortly after Alfonso died, I had a very powerful dream, which at the time disturbed me greatly. Over time, the dream has become a revelation to me. In the dream, I am in a vast, perfectly still ocean where all I can see in any direction is water. I am just sort of floating, almost like I'm wearing a life jacket, but my feet are not grounded. A few yards away is the sailboat Alfonso and I had owned for many years. I can see the line anchoring the boat, but I can't see up over the boat onto the deck. I see a pebble fall into the water nearby, quickly causing ripples to go out in all directions from the place where it falls. Suddenly, I see Alfonso on the deck of the boat. He looks almost angelic, dressed in vibrant white with a certain aura about him. He looks me deep in the eyes and says, "I could never have given you the freedom that you need."

I shout back at him, "I don't want freedom; just come back."

As the years pass, I realize Alfonso was absolutely right. Our relationship and marriage would never have afforded me the freedom I needed to reconnect with my own spiritual self. As long as we were married, my identity would have been so tied into his and to the children that I would probably never have discovered who I am.

In my years of solitude, however, and through my growing spiritual awakening, I have come to a stronger awareness of who I am. Only in coming to terms with myself could I possibly have entered into the mature type of relationship I have with Dick. Only when you love yourself, can you then love others. When you do not love yourself, you spend too much time filling your own voids with objects and other people. These relationships usually turn out to be disastrous. In contrast, Dick and I mirror each other's souls. What people see in other people, good or bad, often is a reflection of what they see inside themselves. In this way, my relationship with Dick has been tremendously liberating; because together, we allow each other to see the beauty in the other and to grow in that beauty.

I no longer feel like I am the shadow of my husband, unsure of my true identity. I have the confidence in myself to contribute my 100 percent in a relationship and still not lose sight of who I really am. Dick and I are both totally individual and yet fully a couple. This amazing union and our mysterious miracle never cease to amaze me. If it had not been for the monumentally tragic events in my life, I would not be where and who I am today. I am a different person with a totally different level of awareness than I had when Alfonso died. These events in my life have provided me with the opportunity to learn invaluable lessons. We can either learn from them or choose to live the life of a victim, but it is always our choice. God always wants the best for us. Though the lessons are hard and the road is rough, He knows spiritual fulfillment is ours if we choose to rise to the occasion and do the work. Most importantly, we are never doing it alone, as He is always with us, embracing us in His love.

———————

The euphoria over my new relationship with Dick is tempered somewhat by my anxiety over the lawsuit in Canada. So I find myself at a crossroads, and I am not sure which way to turn. I seriously am considering abandoning the lawsuit, as so many things have happened since I first decided to sue CMH. My entire attitude towards the case has changed. Initially, my sense of outrage about my husband's death convinced me that holding CMH accountable for their actions was my only option.

Based on my situation at the time—at least from the standpoint of my ability to finance a good fight and see it through—making the decision to sue was a relatively easy choice. At that point, the ordeal with Francisco had not yet unfolded and I still enjoyed the financial security of Alfonso's business empire. Now, with the events involving Francisco behind us and the move to San Diego, my financial resources have become limited. The lawsuit has already cost me nearly $250,000 in out-of-pocket expenses and that amount continues to climb rapidly as the trial approaches. Additionally, the revelation that I might be responsible for CMH's legal fees and costs—now in excess of $1 million—is staggering. I feel drained both financially and emotionally.

To compound matters, my investments in Mexico are in jeopardy. My financial adviser, Ramon Beteta, just called me to suggest I take my money out of Mexico because a major devaluation of the peso is imminent. Shortly after Alfonso died, I invested the proceeds of Alfonso's life insurance policies in Mexico with Ramon and I left those investments in Guadalajara after the move to San Diego. He now suggests that because of the coming peso devaluation, I invest the money in the United States, which I do. The result, however, is that my interest income is cut by more than half. I have gone from receiving nearly 25 percent interest to just over 10 percent. So instead of being able to support the family on a monthly basis with the interest, I am digging into the principal each month to make ends meet.

Given these circumstances, I can't help but worry about whether I am wise to continue with this expensive lawsuit and its uncertain outcome. Will I waste all the family assets on this very uncertain pursuit? I pace the floor night after night, lamenting the past and worrying about the future.

In addition to these concerns, Susan informs me that the defense team has requested a delay in the start of the trial. The lead defense attorney told the judge he desperately needs back surgery to repair two damaged vertebrae and will be on his stomach for several months. The judge granted the postponement and set the trial date for September 5, 1995. I am livid, as this delay means another few months of putting my life on hold and waiting, while the legal bills continue to mount.

My attitude towards what I want out of the lawsuit has begun to change also. Through my prayers and meditations, I have come to peace with Alfonso's death. I appreciate the gifts of awareness and enlightenment his death has brought me and the new life I have created for myself around this new soulful outlook. The adversarial nature of the lawsuit, however, keeps dragging me back into a bitter, vengeful mode. I am not proud of my attitude, but I can't help myself: I want not only to make CMH pay, but also to punish their attorneys who are making my life so miserable with their constant hounding.

Still, the straw that almost breaks the camel's back is the reaction I get when I tell Susan and Ross about Dick.

"Oh, Kris, I am so happy for you," Susan says, "but I think I better get Ross because this could have an impact on the case."

"Impact on the case?" I think. "What could she be talking about? I just told her I've met the man of my dreams . . ." but before I can finish the thought, Ross gets on the line.

"Hi, Kris," he says. "Susan tells me you have some good news."

"I sure do," I say. "It feels so good to have a man in my life who I can share all these things with. It feels so good, I just want to scream it to the world."

"Well, I think you are going to have to hold up on that for a while, Kris," he says. "Please don't take this the wrong way, but this could not have come at a worse time from our standpoint. I mean, from the standpoint of the case. Your involvement with another man could have quite an impact on the damages portion of the case if the defense lawyers find out."

"I don't understand, Ross," I say. "What could my personal life have to do with this at all?"

"If the defense lawyers find out you are seriously involved with a man, they will argue to the judge that this relationship could produce financial support for you in the future," he says. "Remember, our whole damages claim revolves around the money you lost as a result of Alfonso's inability to provide for you. If you have something or someone else to replace that, they might try to make a big deal about it to reduce whatever damages you are awarded."

I think Ross can tell by my silence that I am upset about this.

"Look, Kris, this doesn't mean you have to do anything drastic, like stop seeing him or anything like that," he says. "I just think that for now, you may not want to, as you put it, 'shout it to the world.' I don't know how many people know about this, but anyone who is going to be a witness probably shouldn't be told right away."

"That's just the people from Guadalajara, right?" I ask.

"Well, we certainly don't want Francisco finding out about it, so just use your judgment and make sure there's no way the info could leak to him through anyone you tell," Ross says. "Just keep a low profile. I don't think they still have you under surveillance, but you never know. Just be careful. We really are happy for you, Kris, even if it doesn't sound like it. We just are trying to look out for your best interests in this case."

I thank Ross and Susan, but, as I am hanging up the phone, I feel violated and upset about these intrusions into my personal life and about having to disguise my relationship with Dick. I almost feel like I am doing something wrong, when I am just trying to live my life. Still, I realize that Ross and Susan are probably right. Since we know Francisco is helping the defense team in one way or another with information, and with the way news travels among my old circles in Guadalajara, I am sure if I tell any of my friends down there, the news will make its way to Francisco somehow.

I talk to Dick about it also and we both agree that it will be in my best interest to play the game for now. At times, this is precisely what it feels like to me: a game. We find ourselves looking over our shoulders everywhere we go. Whenever I go to the airport to pick him up or to fly up to Oakland, I wonder if anyone is watching. It's a very difficult way to conduct a relationship. With the beginning of the trial approaching rapidly, the realization has hit me that Dick will not be able to be with me in Vancouver. I have finally found a partner to share my life, and now he can't be with me when I need his love and support the most. It seems so unfair.

On a professional level, it bothers me tremendously that CMH is looking for ways to shift the focus off what I believe was their negligence. I have to constantly remind myself and others that the reason all this is going on is that we all so strongly believe CMH was negligent in allowing nine people to die. CMH's forays into my personal life smack of desperation, which boosts my confidence in the progression of the lawsuit.

Even though I have learned to accept many of the uncertainties in my life, these latest developments leave me floundering again. The constant worrying about the past, the present and the future has sidetracked my spiritual growth. With all of these things on my mind, I am having trouble focusing on anything. Why, after all I have already been through, can I not find spiritual peace among all these uncertainties?

I'm coming to learn that even when someone experiences traumatic circumstances and manages to overcome them with renewed faith and a deeper spirituality, that person may or may not be prepared for the next trauma. After Alfonso's death, I had learned to let go of my fears. Now, however, I am facing an entirely new set of problems. I want to let go, but I can't. I am allowing my fears about this trial to dominate me and send me near the brink. The stakes are too high for me to just let go. My children's futures are in jeopardy. If things go awry, there will be no one to blame but me.

Before Dick arrived on the scene, these worries stood like a road-block in my spiritual path, preventing me from praying or meditating. I felt depressed all the time, like the burden of supporting my family was dragging me down. I felt completely alone, with no one to turn to for help. Just when I thought I had hit rock bottom, Dick arrived on the scene. I was so consumed with fear about the trial that, initially, I did not recognize or understand Dick's inspirational message. The note Dick sent me after our first meeting said, "Kris, I was told to tell you this: You are very loved. Everything is going to be okay." I am sure that my preoccupation with my financial problems and the trial blinded me to the message, and that I desperately needed some sign to get me back on track.

Unwittingly at first, Dick provided me with the spark I needed to break out of my depression. His message and the relationship we have developed have enabled me to take a step back and see how needless and distracting my preoccupation with the trial has been. How could I doubt for one minute that God is with me on my path and that this lawsuit is just another obstacle to learn from and overcome? How could I have forgotten so quickly to trust and to accept living in the "I don't know?" How easily we fall prey to the distractions of life and lose sight of our foundation, even when we should know better.

Shortly after Dick and I began seeing each other, Alfonso came to me in a dream to help bring these points home. In the dream, Alfonso is skiing with a group of angels on what seems like an endless mountain with all these angels flying along by his side. He is skiing like a professional, taking each turn with Olympic precision, focus and concentration. On one turn he looks up and tries to see what's at the bottom of the hill, and immediately falls and crashes into the snow. The angels pick him up and chastise him, "See what happens when you get too far ahead of yourself. You lose the moment. Stay right here, right now and you'll be fine." Alfonso gets up, dusts himself off and seems to wink at me as he starts down the hill again.

With counsel and guidance from Dick and Linda Lepeirs, I start back down my own hill and march on with the lawsuit. I go forward, but with an enormous attitude change. I turn it over to God. I do not fully understand everything that is happening to me, but I trust both myself and God. I suppose everyone from time to time has to be reminded of how important that trust is, and I feel blessed to have people and angels around to help remind me. Dick is also providing me with the tangible emotional support I have been so lacking. If not for my renewed vigor for life that comes from my meeting Dick, I might be giving up. Dick's love and support help me to put things into perspective and to enjoy life.

Davis and Company also assist me financially. They appear confident about the case and have invested so much in the outcome at this point that it would be folly not to help me continue with the case. They agree to help with legal fees, disbursements and court costs until after the judgment. So, with the trial now just a few months away, I am back on track.

CHAPTER 8
the trial

The trial is scheduled to last six weeks, beginning on September 5, 1995. Coincidentally, September 5 also happens to be the first day of the new school year for the children. How am I going to manage getting the children ready for the school year, arrange for their care and prepare myself for six weeks in Vancouver?

One day in August, Ross calls to say that the trial now probably will last until January and possibly longer. He also tells me that the defense attorney never had the surgery he supposedly needed so badly months earlier when the start of the trial was delayed. "Typical," I think to myself, "just another stalling tactic by the defense team to try to rattle me." I have never understood the reasons for all these stalling tactics, but the defense team certainly have mastered them.

Despite these developments, I try to maintain my composure. From the moment Ross calls, I do my best to let go of my fears. It will not be easy to manage, but since there is no other way, I will handle it somehow.

It's three weeks before the trial, and I'm having lunch with a good friend of mine, Lydia Morales. Lydia has been my father's assistant for several years in the summer program he directs in Guadalajara, and we became close friends during the summers Lydia spent in Guadalajara helping to organize the program. Lydia has just left the University of San Diego following my father's retirement and is currently unemployed.

"You know, Lydia, I just don't know what I'm going to do being gone from the children for so long," I say. "They need a lot of attention, what with school starting and all the other things going on . . . I just don't know."

"Well, I'm not doing anything right now," Lydia says. "Why don't I stay at your place while you're gone?"

"Oh, Lydia, I can't ask you to do that. Six kids, my dear, and they are a handful."

"No, Kris, I really want to. The timing couldn't be better. I'm kinda getting bored not working right now anyway."

"Are you sure about this?" I ask.

"Yeah, I'm sure," she says. "Hey, who knows, it could be fun."

"I don't know what to say. You're an angel. You don't know what a load off my back it is to know my kids will be in such good hands. Thank you so much, Lydia. Thank you, thank you, thank you."

As I sit here with Lydia, I realize that, once again, by letting go, things have fallen into place. I hug Lydia and thank her a few more times, knowing in my heart that she, too, is sent by God. There are no coincidences; everything that happens, happens for a reason. I am so grateful to Lydia for helping me at such a time of great need.

Ross and Susan find an apartment in Vancouver to reduce my hotel expenses. We decide to rent two apartments—one for me and one for all the witnesses who will be flying in during the trial and will need a place to stay. I am responsible for all of the expenses for all of these witnesses. Knowing that a majority of the witnesses are friends from Guadalajara, I arrange to pay for their lodging if they pay for their airfare and food expenses. Each witness has agreed. Ross, Susan and I map out a timetable over the phone to coordinate the arrival and departure of each of the fourteen witnesses, quite an organizational accomplishment.

Before leaving for Vancouver, I also have to organize my own household. I meet with the teachers at the children's school and explain the situation to them. They are very supportive and offer to do anything they can to help me and my children. I am worried about leaving the children, but between Lydia and their teachers, I know they will be in good hands.

My attention turns to stocking the kitchen with two months of supplies. I invade Costco and walk away with two minivans full of groceries. In the face of very few certainties, here's one: my children definitely will not go hungry while I am away.

As the trial draws nearer, I try my best to muster the courage to move forward. I know this trial is going to be one of the most painful and emotional ordeals in my life. I will have to relive not only the accident that took the life of my husband, but also the aftermath that's led to the estrangement of our extended family and to the demise of Alfonso's business empire. I am dreading the rehashing of all the painful memories, of a life that now seems so distant to me. It takes a monumental effort to keep focused and to overcome the fears that constantly plague me. What if I freeze on the stand? What if my testimony is not compelling enough for the judge? What if . . .? What if . . .?

As painful as the trial might be, I know it is an integral part of the path that is unfolding as my life moves forward. This presents a unique opportunity for me to confront once more the fears I've had to face after Alfonso died, fears I have worked so hard to overcome during my spiritual awakening. While I know reliving the accident will be difficult, I pray that truth will prevail at the trial and will release me once and for all from the specter of the accident. I pray not only for the courage to persevere, but also for the awareness to learn even more about myself from this experience.

The most troubling aspect of the trial is the thought of being separated from my children for what initially was supposed to be ten weeks. Luckily, I know Lydia will be wonderful with the children. I have no doubt that she will be able to organize all their transportation to and from school, help them with their homework, and provide them with the love and support they will need while I am not there.

I am scheduled to leave for Vancouver on Sunday, September 3. Susan and Ross want to spend Monday, which is Labor Day, preparing for my testimony, which will begin later in the week. Saying good-bye to my family is traumatic. Knowing the difficulties that await me, I almost feel as if I'm a lamb being sent off to be sacrificed for the higher good. I am trying so hard to be brave because I know the trial will test both my courage and my spiritual development.

When I land in Vancouver, Susan picks me up at the airport, and I am so glad to see her that I embrace her and hold on to her for a few moments. I instantly sense she understands my anxieties and my fears. I look into her eyes and am so grateful that my brother, Jim, had the foresight more than four years ago to hire Ross and Susan. Her understanding, support and comfort make me feel I am not alone. When I look at Susan, I also realize the staggering impact this trial has had on everyone involved in these proceedings. Ross and Susan have spent the better part of the last four years working day and night on my behalf, living and breathing snow reports, depositions and financial statements. Their dedication is awe inspiring, and I truly feel blessed by their efforts. Susan and her husband take me out for dinner, and then to the rented apartment—my home for the next few months.

Despite the beautiful view of the Vancouver shoreline and the sound, it feels strange to be totally alone. I have never in my life lived alone, and now here I am in this strange city, with no car and no family, about to embark on a monumental legal battle against the largest heli-skiing company in the world.

The solitude leads me to think about the accident even more. In the months leading up to the trial, I've found myself frequently having flashbacks to the avalanche. Without warning, when I'd be in a grocery store or at a school event or perhaps just sitting around the house, I would have a vision similar to the recurring nightmares I had immediately after the accident. I visualize tons of snow sweeping down a mountain, carrying away a group of skiers. My pulse races and I freeze, trance like, for a few seconds. Gradually, I come out of it and back to reality, but often not before an embarrassing crying spell. That first night in Canada, those same images constantly race through my mind.

Right up until now, I've held out hope that CMH would offer some sort of fair settlement so the trial would never have to take place. I felt certain that this case would be settled "on the courthouse steps," as attorneys often say. Surely CMH does not want to go through the expense of a long trial with the strong possibility of a judgment against them at the end. But all through the summer, there's been no word from CMH or their defense team.

Finally, while I'm in Ross' office preparing for my testimony, the defense attorney calls Ross, who puts him on speaker phone.

"Hello, Ross," he says. "Tomorrow's the big day I suppose. You ready?"

"Yeah, we're definitely ready," Ross says. "Looking forward to it, in fact."

"Well, I think we have a pretty strong case, but my clients wanted me to present Mrs. Ochoa with an offer, so here goes."

My heart begins racing as he pauses before going into the offer.

"We're willing to settle all her claims for $500,000. That's Canadian dollars, for the record, not American dollars. And each side will be responsible for its own costs. What do you think?"

"Well, it's not exactly what we had in mind to tell you the truth, but Mrs. Ochoa is right here, so I'd be glad to ask her."

I just shake my head in disbelief, amazed at the ludicrous nature of the offer.

"By her reaction, I can tell the answer is no," Ross says. "But I will throw this out there. If your client is willing to pay Mrs. Ochoa $2.75 million in American dollars, then we'd be glad to bypass this whole trial."

"Well, I can tell you that's not going to happen," he says while chuckling. "Guess we'll leave it up to the judge. See you tomorrow."

With that, the die is cast. There's no turning back now—the trial begins tomorrow.

As I take my seat in Courtroom 41 on this first day of the trial, I realize that I am not as nervous as I expected to be. Instead, I feel a certain calm come over me. The months and years of preparation and anticipation are finally evolving into something tangible. The case is finally going to be heard. My calm, however, is short lived.

We rise when the judge enters the court and then, as we take our seats again, I feel a knot begin to turn in my stomach. "Are we ready to proceed," the judge asks, which sends my mind racing in a panic. A spiritual tug-of-war is competing for and draining my internal energy; my mind and soul feel as though they are going to battle. As I close my eyes, a series of conflicting thoughts flow alternately through my mind:

"You should feel proud for being the only relative of the nine victims to bring this case to justice . . .

"If you are at peace with Alfonso's death and you believe our lives are orchestrated in perfect harmony, why are you here seeking retribution . . .

"You need to help make sure this type of accident never happens again . . .

"Why, since everything that happens, happens for a reason . . .

"CMH and these attorneys must pay for what they have put me and my family through . . .

"Love requires forgiveness . . ."

Then, without warning, I hear a whisper.

"Kris, let go. You are loved and everything will be okay."

Startled, I open my eyes and look around. Susan gives me a puzzled look and I realize the voice I heard was internal. Suddenly, I feel Alfonso's presence and the presence of the eight other spirits who left this Earth with him that March afternoon. I feel their energy strengthen me as I realize I am exactly where I am supposed to be, the only place I can possibly be. I do not understand exactly why I am here, but I don't need to know. I need to believe and trust that there is a good reason, and to let go of all the fears.

I look over to the vacant jury box and see the faces of each of the people who died in the avalanche, most of whom I have never seen before. They are the spiritual jury presiding over this case, and their authority comes from a much higher court.

The peace I accept in these first few minutes of the trial proves to be my strength in the grueling first few weeks, which includes my own testimony. One of the reasons I am nervous about testifying is that I fear being overly emotional in front of the judge. I have never been someone who can easily disguise or bottle up my feelings. My testimony will require me to tell the judge intimate details of my life, my marriage, my husband, my children, and our lives together before and after his death. I find it difficult to talk about these matters without crying. I do not want to appear to be a distraught, weak woman, so I worry about crying too much.

My testimony will be a vital element in our case, however, as the judge will base her decision solely on the evidence and testimony presented at trial. She will not conduct any independent investigation. Accordingly,

I will be the judge's primary source of information about my life with Alfonso in Guadalajara. Last night, at dinner with Ross and Susan, they did their best to give me some last minute tips.

"Kris, your responsibility is to make sure the judge receives an accurate and complete description of your lifestyle, your love for Alfonso, your children and everything else you think the judge should know about your life before the accident," Ross told me. "You will have to shape her image of you and your family. If the judge finds you to be an honest, credible witness, our case will be bolstered. If not, we will be in trouble."

"All you have to do, Kris, is be yourself," Susan said. "You'll be a natural, and all you have to do is tell the truth; so, there's nothing to worry about. You'll do fine."

While I appreciated Susan's words of encouragement, it is a lonely feeling being called to the witness stand. Everything I say or do will contribute to the image the judge forms of me and my family. From the clothes I wear, to the words I choose, to the looks on my face when I answer questions—all of these factors will combine to show the judge the effect this accident has had on me and my six children. The tremendous scope of the information I have to cover also makes me nervous about my testimony. There are so many details to remember, so many dates and events to tell the judge about. But as I take my seat in the witness stand, I am comforted and strengthened by the reality that all I have to do is tell the truth. Luckily, I have Ross on my side, and I know he will do a fabulous job of leading me through my testimony, asking all the right questions at all the right times. With him as my guide, I feel confident I will provide the judge with an accurate picture.

My other consolation is that talking is one thing I truly love to do. In the first two hours of my testimony, Ross guides me through a brief background of our lives before the accident. Then Ross asks the question I have been dreading, "Mrs. Ochoa, could you please explain to the court the effect the death of their father has had on your six children?"

Although I knew the question was coming, rehashing the pain that my children endured after the loss of their father is an extremely difficult topic for me to discuss, as it conjures up strong and emotional images of the boys in the hours and days after we learned Alfonso had died. When

I hear the question, I fight hard to choke back tears because I know the descriptions I am about to give will be heart wrenching. Even though I have reviewed my testimony with Ross and Susan many times, I know it will be difficult to convey the depth of the anguish and pain my children suffered after they lost their father.

Fighting back the tears, I begin with my youngest, Annette, the only girl of the six children.

"Annette obviously does not remember her father," I say. "Since she was only eleven months old when he died, she only knows him through photos and what I and her brothers have told her about her dad. It's extremely difficult because nothing any of us could say can ever let her know how special she was in her father's eyes and how much he loved her. I've told her about how he was in the delivery room when she was born and how thrilled he had been to finally have a daughter. And I've told her how since he was so used to having sons, he insisted on wearing his bathing suit when he took baths with her. Little things like that . . . you know, they only had eleven months together.

"She's five now and seems to be doing pretty well. She has nightmares a lot, but she can never seem to explain to me what they are about. She also has anxiety attacks from time to time, especially when I'm away from her for any period of time.

"You know, she was going to be daddy's little girl, his shiny and beautiful little jewel . . . so, yes . . . I would say his death has had a very dramatic effect on her short life."

I have to stop there . . . Just the thought of seeing Alfonso in his trunks in our bath bouncing her on his knee overcomes me. God, I can't go on right now—this is too much. I place my head in my hands and begin to weep.

"This might be a good place to stop," the judge says, looking down at me. "Mrs. Ochoa, would you like a break?"

I just nod appreciatively and fall into Susan's arms when I come down off the witness stand.

"You're doing fine, Kris," she says. "You're doing just fine. I know this is really hard, but you're doing great and you'll get through this with no problem."

"I know," I mutter through my sobs. "It's just so hard."

We walk outside to get some fresh air, and by the time we go back into the courtroom, I have managed to compose myself. So, I resume my testimony talking about how the younger boys, Nicholas, Jonathan and Christofer have tried so bravely to deal with the tremendous sorrow they felt following their father's death.

"Alfonso was such a huge part of his boys' lives," I say. "He was not only their father, but also their hero, the man they most wanted to be like when they grew up. With the younger boys especially, he would take them with him wherever he went—to work, on bike rides, on hunting or fishing trips, just about anywhere. His death has created a huge void in their lives, which I simply can't fill. I'm definitely not the outdoorsy type, so they really miss all that kind of guy stuff they used to do with their father."

When I begin to talk about Carl, I look at the judge and I can see the compassion in her eyes. I feel as though she understands the emotions I am conveying. I was told that she, too, had been a single mother; and I begin to feel that, in some way, this testimony affects her and creates a bond between us. My passionate testimony continues with Carl and Alfonso Jr.

"My oldest boys were definitely hit the hardest by my husband's death. He was their whole life. He was everything to them—their father, their mentor, their best friend, their future business partner, the man who encouraged them to follow their dreams and reach for the impossible, just like he had. All of that died for them on March 12, 1991.

"After the accident, I could barely bring myself to look in their faces . . . the sorrow . . . the uncertainty . . . it just hurt me too much. I really think they began to believe their futures had died with their father. They just could not envision life without him, but now they had to.

"They did their best to be strong for me, I suppose, and for their brothers. But they were so young and so afraid. The pain would catch up with them. Alfonso Jr.'s temper became almost uncontrollable. I think he had so much anger built up inside about losing his father, he just needed some sort of release.

"Carl seemed to turn inward. You know, he looks so much like his father, even his mannerisms are so much like Alfonso's. Sometimes, at the dinner table, I would just stare at him and talk myself into believing he was Alfonso. Carl has such a big heart . . . and they were so close . . .

"The hardest part for me was knowing that . . . knowing that no matter how good a mother I was or how hard I tried, I could never take the place of their father—no one could."

It takes me nearly two days to finish talking about my family and, after such heart-wrenching testimony, everyone in the courtroom seems ready to move on to another area. During these two days, there have been no objections or procedural arguments or any other legal maneuvering, which I'm told by Susan is quite unusual. The courtroom has been silent except for my voice and my tears. Everyone present, including the members of the defense team, seems moved by my genuine pain and anguish.

I am so grateful for the strength I have summoned to tell my story, and for the tremendous support I feel from the presence of my angels, who bolster me with love and energy whenever I seem to need it most on the witness stand. At times during my testimony, I find myself lost in the maze of topics I have been covering, unable to remember the subject of the moment. On the verge of panicking, I close my eyes and call for help from my angels. A feeling of strength and confidence fills me instantly and the proper words begin to flow in response to the questions asked. Much like during my speech to the steel convention in Puerto Vallarta, my angels step in and carry me through various stages of my testimony, guiding me to choose exactly the right words and emotions to convey my feelings. Without their assistance, I could never have testified as effectively about such difficult and emotional topics.

Unfortunately, things are not going as well at home with the children. I know that children who have lost one parent often have nightmares about losing the other, especially when the other parent is away from them. My absence is producing severe reactions in my children, especially the younger ones. Lydia has informed me that Annette is having bedwetting problems and frightening nightmares. She has Lydia call me in Vancouver every night just so she can hear my voice and know that I am okay. It kills me not to be able to pick her up and hold her and tell her that everything is going to be all right. The younger boys are misbehaving in school and refusing to do their homework. I think all of them live constantly with their worst fear—since their daddy had gone away and never came home, what if mommy does the same thing? Poor Lydia . . . she has really got her hands full.

By the time I finish testifying about the children, I feel as if every emotion has been drained from me. I must rebound quickly, however, as I still have a large amount of testimony remaining on other topics. My direct testimony also involves detailed and often tedious descriptions of our lives in Guadalajara, and is anti-climactic compared to the emotionally-charged portraits of my children. I manage to get through it by adopting the same frame of mind I had immediately following Alfonso's death—I take one minute at a time, then one hour at a time, and, before long, the day is over.

When my direct testimony ends, my cross-examination begins. On the morning my cross-examination is to start, I watch as the lead defense attorney opens a six-inch binder and begins reading the first question from the first page. My God, I will be up here for months if he goes through that entire binder! We progress so slowly that it seems like the defense attorneys rarely turn a page. We will never get through this huge volume of questions.

One of the defense team's favorite tactics during cross-examination is to ask me a question and then, after hearing my response, direct me to consider my response to the same question in the written transcript of my pre-trial deposition. My palms sweat as I wonder what exactly I said during the deposition more than a year ago. I can't understand the strategy because, without exception, my answers seem to be consistent with my prior testimony—at least the defense attorneys never tell me otherwise.

In Canada, the law forbids a witness on cross-examination from communicating with her attorneys until the cross-examination is completed. The attorneys refer to it as "being in the freezer." I wind up "in the freezer" for nearly a month. I am not on the stand testifying every day, but my cross-examination is interrupted several times to accommodate the schedules of witnesses coming from Mexico and several of the expert witnesses. Constantly on call, I never know when another witness' testimony will end and I will be called back to the stand. My inability to communicate with Ross and Susan makes the wait all the more difficult, especially since they can't even tell me how I am doing.

Dick is my source of strength throughout this time. Every morning and night, Dick calls me to offer his encouragement and support. I do not know what I would do without him. He is my partner, my cheerleader, my therapist, my shoulder to cry on, helping me keep an even keel. He constantly reminds me to trust and to let go of the fear, guiding me in prayer when I am frightened and giving me the courage to get through the day.

He never tires of listening to me and never gets frustrated with my repeated complaints about the entire process. He also uses long-distance "Reiki," a method of channeling the natural flow of energy to promote spiritual, mental and physical well-being. "Reiki" is intended to restore the natural flow of energy, which is often depleted by illness or traumatic circumstances. Dick talks to me and gets me to relax, while he focuses his energy on giving me strength. Then he lifts his hands, sending his energy to me over the miles that separate us. I can feel the sensation of his energy reaching me, which calms me and strengthens my resolve to persevere.

I also feel the presence of Alfonso next to me, and the loving touch of my late grandmother during these trying days. When I sit in the witness stand, I can almost hear her say to me, "It's okay, honey girl," as she had so many times when I was young and afraid. Their presence helps console me during the difficult portions of the cross-examination when I feel like everyone in the courtroom is against me. I know in my heart that there are powerful reasons behind this task that I have chosen, and I pray for the guidance and enlightenment to see those reasons more clearly.

The first interruption in my cross-examination is the arrival from Mexico of several of Alfonso's business associates and friends to testify. Not only will they testify about their relationship with Alfonso, but their testimony will be vital to one of the most difficult issues in the case: the waiver Alfonso and the others signed when they first arrived in Canada. Apparently, Alfonso and the others filled out and signed registration forms, which included a blanket waiver absolving CMH from liability for anything, including injuries or death resulting from accidents from any cause, even CMH's own negligence. Ross and Susan informed me early on that Canadian courts generally uphold waivers in most cases, except in unusual circumstances. They felt Alfonso's unfamiliarity with the concept of waivers and his inability to read or write in English would constitute such unusual circumstances and would be compelling enough to overcome the presumption that the waiver was valid.

The waiver issue is the backbone of the defense's case. If the waiver is upheld, CMH will be absolved of liability. The defense team's primary contention is that Alfonso had the responsibility to read and understand what he signed. Since Alfonso was a responsible, well-respected businessman, he should have known better than to sign something he did not understand.

There is some merit to this argument, but it's overshadowed by Alfonso's complete unfamiliarity with the concept of waivers, and by the inconsistencies in CMH's waiver policies. For instance, if the waiver was such an important document, why didn't CMH do everything possible to ensure that the guests knew what they were signing? Why wasn't it presented to Mexican guests in their native Spanish language, or at least explained to them by someone fluent in Spanish? We hope these questions will expose the holes in the defense's argument.

Our strongest argument is cultural. In Mexico, waivers simply do not exist and the word "waiver" has no direct translation in the Spanish language. Most Mexicans, including Alfonso and his friends, who accompanied him and also signed the CMH waivers, had no idea what the concept of "waiving one's rights" meant. We also want to show that since the document they signed was written in English (CMH had waiver forms in French and German, but not Spanish), and since Alfonso did not speak, read or write in English, and could not read or write very well in Spanish either, Alfonso—even had he been inclined to read the document—would have been unable to do so. Luis de la Peña, the first of Alfonso's friends to testify, tries to explain this to the judge.

"Your honor, none of us knew what we were signing. We were just told the cards were registration forms that we needed to fill out and sign before we could head to the resort. So, those cards we signed, we didn't even read them. We were all sitting around in the hotel bar and the CMH person gave all of the cards to me because my English was better than the others, and asked me to explain them to the others. So, I handed them around and everybody filled them out, then handed them back to me and I gave them back to the CMH person. I thought . . . I guess we all thought it was just part of the registration process. Actually, Alfonso was so confused, he signed in the wrong place, so the CMH guy made me have him fill out another one and sign again.

"They told us if we didn't sign the forms, we couldn't ski. We came there to ski, so we signed the forms and didn't ask any questions. That was that."

When Jaime Gomez takes the stand, he elaborates on Luis' testimony.

"They didn't explain anything to us," he says. "And I think they knew we couldn't read or understand the writing on the card. I took one look at the small print on the back of the card and said forget about it. I just filled out the card, signed it and gave it to Luis. They certainly made no effort to explain anything about the document except that we had to sign it to ski. The CMH person didn't speak Spanish, so no one could translate it into Spanish for us so I didn't really have a clue. You know, we skied with CMH three times before; and I think on one of those trips, we didn't sign anything. But the ones we did sign were always in English and I don't remember anyone ever translating anything for us."

The end result of all of the testimony is that the Mexican men had little or no indication of the legal importance of the waiver. I think we've made our point.

⸺ ⬦ ⸺

The final interruption in my cross-examination is the testimony of my children. Lydia and all the children fly to Vancouver so the three oldest boys—Alfonso Jr., Carl and Christofer—can testify about the loss of their father. It is so good to see them—I have missed them so much. It has only been a couple weeks, but it seems like months.

While I talked about how the loss of their father has affected the boys in my direct testimony, Ross and Susan thought it would be extremely powerful for the judge to also hear directly from the boys. The boys are nervous about their testimony, but they are putting up a brave front. On the other hand, I'm a nervous wreck. The thought of watching and listening to my children testify about the pain and sorrow they feel over the loss of their father will be excruciating. From the moment Alfonso Jr. begins his testimony, I can barely contain my own emotions. I see the pain written all over his face and hear it in his trembling voice. He barely manages to speak above a whisper, but the words he chooses and the emotion with which he speaks them are powerful and indicative of the strong bond of love he and his father shared.

"My father was the best," he says. "He took us with him everywhere—hunting, fishing, mountain biking, to the beach, skiing. Almost everywhere he went, we went with him, and when he died . . . when he died, all that stopped. I miss him so much.

"I used to get so mad. Sometimes I still do . . . at him, at God, at everybody. It just doesn't seem fair. But nothing's going to bring him back now. It's just not fair . . ."

He stops to wipe the tears welling in the corner of his eyes.

"I'm sorry . . . but he meant so much to me . . . I mean, he was everything in my life . . . I just can't believe they would let this happen. It's not fair . . . It's just not fair."

By contrast, Carl is very composed on the witness stand. He is able to convey to the judge very effectively the dramatic effect the loss of his father has had on his life.

"My father was my mentor, the man I admired and loved so much," he says. "Ever since I was a kid, I really thought that one day we'd be working side by side together in his business. I go to sleep at night sometimes thinking about how great that would have been. Ever since he died, I have been trying to figure out what to do now without him . . . I guess I'm just going to have to keep on looking."

My heart goes out to Christofer, who is the last to testify. He has always been the shyest of the six, so the formal setting of the courtroom is especially intimidating for him. Although it is a nerve-wracking experience for him, especially since the subject matter is so personal and emotional, Christofer does an excellent job.

"I really miss how my dad used to take us all hunting, fishing, skiing and to the beach. We'd go everywhere together and have so much fun," he says.

Christofer struggles at times, biting his lip and wiping at his eyes occasionally, but he paints a beautiful portrait of the wonderful relationship he had with his father. Because of Christofer's health problems as a child, Alfonso always had a very special place for him in his heart, and the loss of that relationship came through clearly in Christofer's testimony.

"My dad was always there to protect me no matter where we were. I knew I didn't have to worry because he would watch out for me and take care of everything for me and my brothers. I really miss that . . . and all the fun we used to have . . . I still can't believe he's gone."

Whether it is strategic or maybe a rare moment of compassion, the defense team declines to cross-examine the boys. Perhaps the direct testimony is traumatic enough. I am so proud of each of them and I know their father is also. I know Alfonso was with them up on that witness stand, guiding them and giving them the strength to tell their stories. Our sons— his legacy—are still the most important thing in the universe to him, and he was there with them when they needed him most.

<hr />

The most difficult part of my cross-examination comes immediately after my sons' testimony. When Christofer finishes, after a brief recess, I return to the stand. As I take my seat in the witness box, the defense team opens the enormous binder, and we pick up where we left off. The first question out of the lead attorney's mouth is, "Mrs. Ochoa, isn't it true that your brother-in-law, Francisco, volunteered to help you by going to Canada from Mexico to recover the remains of your husband?"

Every hair on my body stands on edge, and I begin to feel nauseated. By the tone of his voice, I can tell immediately where he is headed. He is going to try to paint Francisco as a helpful, thoughtful and caring brother-in-law who was only trying to help me with everything he did. As I organize a lengthy rebuttal in my mind, I remember the advice Ross and Susan gave me when we were preparing for my cross-examination—just answer the question. Do not elaborate on anything unless you have no choice.

"Yes," I answer.

"And, Mrs. Ochoa, isn't it also true that it was your brother-in-law who picked you and your entire family up from the airport after your return from San Diego in March of 1991?"

"Yes," I answer again, struggling to hold back my true feelings.

"And again, Mrs. Ochoa, didn't he give you a chocolate cake upon your arrival at home so as to ease your pain and welcome you home?" the attorney continued.

"Yes, he and his family gave us a cake," I say in a barely audible voice as I begin to tremble.

"And, Mrs. Ochoa, didn't Francisco try to counsel you and warn you about the financial position of the companies, warning you that they were almost in the state of bankruptcy at the time of your husband's death?" the attorney posited. "But you, in turn, chose to ignore his counsel and care by turning to your brothers instead, who, in turn, turned you against Francisco?"

By this time, I can't contain myself. The emotion of my sons' testimony in the morning coupled with this ridiculous line of questioning hits me all at once. Hearing the attorney try to paint that conniving scoundrel as the good guy and me as the bad guy is more than I can handle.

"You can't really believe that, can you?" I say in a whisper. "Is that what he told you? Of course it's what he . . ."

But I cannot continue. Bursting into tears, I try to go on, but I am unintelligible in my anger and disbelief. I am completely unaware of my surroundings, lost in this preposterous notion the defense team is offering. Mercifully, the judge calls for a recess. Ross asks my boys to take me outside to get some air. I cry on Alfonso Jr.'s shoulder for fifteen minutes, as the emotional memories of Francisco's betrayal resurface. Even following the recess, we are unable to start up again because I am still too upset and unable to regain my composure.

After what seems like an eternity, the sobs begin to subside and I slowly compose myself. I am indignant and horrified at the very suggestion that I had been the bad guy and that Francisco had been the victim. I am sure that is what Francisco told the defense team. In a way, I suppose, he is a victim—not a victim of anything I did to him, but a victim of his own fears and perceptions. And if he views himself as a victim, it is by his own doing. I suppose in certain respects I have been victimized by the events and circumstances that have altered my life so dramatically. Still, I have tried to move beyond that image of myself and what I have been through, and I vow to myself, right here on the stand, never to allow myself to choose to be a victim again.

By the time we are ready to resume, the defense team has recognized the error of their ways. They completely misjudge my responses to their line of questioning, thinking I would snap and turn venomous. When the opposite happens and they realize their strategy has backfired, they do not know how to proceed. When we are ready to resume, the defense attorneys sit at their table sheepishly, almost ashamed that they had pursued such an absurd line of questioning. After reviewing so much information about Francisco, they must know by now his true character. That is the last I hear of the suggestion that Francisco was the victim.

Despite not having gone through a quarter of their binder, the lead attorney tells the judge he has no more questions for me. I can't believe what I'm hearing . . . it's actually over. My role as an active participant in the trial is now over.

I feel like a huge weight has been lifted from my shoulders, as I realize that although the trial is not over by a long shot, my role from now on will be reduced to that of a spectator. In all, I spend all or parts of nine days on the witness stand. I told my story in as much detail and passion as I could. I tried to paint as complete a picture as possible of our lives in Mexico and since Alfonso's death. I hope the judge found my testimony believable. Now that I'm out of the "freezer," Ross and Susan assure me that I did a great job and that things could not look better for us.

We head back to the apartment, order a pizza and rent a couple of movies for the children; then, I collapse on my bed at 7:00 p.m. Every emotion has been drained from my mind and body, and even the solace of knowing I have done a good job cannot prevent the exhaustion from taking over. I sleep straight through until the alarm clock begins to buzz at 6:00 a.m. It's back to the courthouse already.

———————

The most complicated and most important facet of the case is the negligence issue. If the judge finds that CMH was not negligent, the remainder of the issues is meaningless. Ross and Susan have to prove that a well-estab-

lished standard of care for heli-skiing guides exists, and that the actions of
the CMH guides fell well below that standard. The strategy is to use testimony from snow experts to illustrate what should have been done to ensure
Bay Street was safe before the skiers went out onto the slope, and then elicit
testimony from the CMH guides who were involved in the accident to illustrate how their actions failed to meet these preventative standards.

As the focus in the trial changes from my personal and family life to
the negligence issue, I can feel the energy in the courtroom also change.
As I sit alone in the spectator area listening to the various witnesses, I can
feel the spirits of Alfonso and the other eight victims of the avalanche
around me in the courtroom. It is a difficult feeling to describe, but I know
the spirits of these people are present in this courtroom, eagerly awaiting
the testimony concerning the accident itself. Their presence comforts me
because I know they are here to hear the story of how they were killed by
CMH's mistakes. Their presence also reinforces my belief that I have done
the right thing in making CMH answer for its mistakes. I do not believe
they are here for vengeance, but rather to witness the higher good that
could result from their deaths—the uncovering of past mistakes to prevent
them from being repeated in the future.

The evidence relating to negligence begins with the testimony of our
two snow experts, Dick Penniman and René Boiselle. Since CMH is the
king of the tightly-knit heli-skiing community, Ross and Susan had difficulty finding expert witnesses who were familiar with the heli-skiing
industry *and* willing to testify against CMH. Dick Penniman and René
Boiselle are snow and avalanche experts with very little or no background
in the heli-skiing industry. Ross' task will be to use the testimony of
Penniman and Boiselle about snow safety standards and avalanche prediction, and then have them relate this expertise to the highly specialized
heli-skiing situations in which CMH is involved.

The judge asks Penniman to spend an entire day providing background information on the terminology and scientific procedures involved
in avalanche prediction. Penniman, who teaches college courses on avalanche prediction, takes us all through a basic course in the science of snow
and avalanche. The most compelling testimony involves natural warning
signs that indicate an avalanche is probable in a certain area.

"Common and reliable warning signs of a potential avalanche on a ski run are the indicators of prior avalanche activity, such as the absence of branches on the uphill sides of trees, the presence of specific types of trees that grow in places that avalanche, trees that have been broken off and carried down the mountain by earlier avalanches," says Penniman. "When those signs are there, an informed observer would immediately conclude that the run could be unstable and has the potential to avalanche again."

"And were those types of signs on Bay Street before this group went down?" Ross asks.

"Yes," he says. "According to my review of the guides' deposition testimony and my own inspection of the run, this was exactly the type of indicators that were on Bay Street. This should have been a clear signal that the run was avalanche prone and should be treated with special care. Instead, the guides appear to have ignored these natural warning signs and led the skiers down the hill. My only conclusion is that either they were untrained or completely misread the signs. Either way, the results were disastrous and could have been avoided."

Even after all this time, these words, that the accident could have been and should have been avoided, are very difficult for me to hear.

René Boiselle's testimony is more technical and involves descriptions of the generally trustworthy methods of testing a snowpack for avalanche vulnerability. Boiselle explains to the court the importance of regularly conducting snow profiles of ski runs to learn which runs are safe, and how accepted practice and CMH's own internal manuals require certain tests to determine whether a snowpack is stable. The goal of these tests is to determine the stability of a run by observing how tightly the various levels of snow from different snowfalls have bonded together on top of each other.

"One test that should be performed by advance guides involves digging a large hole in the snow to observe the hardness and stability of the pack through its various levels," he says. "The guides had a profile prepared from the last pitch of Bay Street that disclosed the layers that failed. Guides are trained to perform another rudimentary test called the ski pole test. This test, which is usually done right before a group skis down a run, is executed by thrusting a ski pole deep into the snow. By doing so, a guide can try to assess the type of resistance the pole meets and whether the snowpack has any prominent weak layers. On a run like Bay Street, if the tests reveal any doubt about the stability of the layers, the guide should choose an alternate run. The results of these tests, along with a guide's observations of the physical conditions of a run, should allow a guide to determine with reasonable comfort whether that run is safe for skiing. The tests are even more important when the runs involved are known to be avalanche prone."

"And, Mr. Boiselle, do you know whether these tests or any others were performed by the CMH guides on the afternoon of March 12, 1991?" Ross asks.

"From reviewing the documents, the CMH guides had a profile of the failed slope, which disclosed the failure layer, but I do not know if they referred to it before skiing the run," Boiselle says. "A ski pole test was performed by one of the investigators after the accident and it indicated potential instability at the entrance to the run. The only precaution they appear to have taken was the route followed by the guide leading the first group. It was relatively conservative and did not take the skiers out onto the main slope until they were well down the hill."

The expert testimony lays the groundwork for establishing the sequence of events leading up to the accident. The accident itself will be covered by the two CMH guides who were with the skiers that afternoon. The first guide to testify will be the one who led the group of skiers down Bay Street just minutes before the avalanche. The second will be the leader of Alfonso's group. She was also caught in the avalanche but miraculously survived.

When the guides walk into the courtroom, the moment I have been both anticipating and dreading has arrived. I will meet the last person on this Earth to see Alfonso alive and we will hear her version of what happened. After reading the transcripts of her depositions, I know she has been severely scarred by the accident. Yet, her deposition testimony seemed to indicate that she felt no remorse. I am curious to see how she will act and what she will say when we meet.

From what Ross and Susan have told me, she is quite an intimidating figure: solidly built, a bit gruff, yet well-respected. I was not sure how we would meet, but I knew it would happen eventually. A part of me hopes to have some sort of heartfelt conversation with her to let her know that even though she did not do her job properly, I hold no ill feelings towards her.

I long to feel some sense of remorse from her, to believe she is sorry for what happened. I dream about locking eyes and understanding what she is trying to tell me . . . perhaps that she is sorry, that she has regret and that she performs her job more carefully now.

I am getting settled when the guides walk in and sit directly in front of me. Their backs are so large they barely fit in their seats, and their jackets look strained at the seams. After sitting down, the woman turns around quickly to face me. She thrusts her hand towards me and says, "Kristine? I'm Joss Lang."

I am so startled that no words come out. This woman seated directly in front of me is responsible for Alfonso's death and is the last person to see him alive. Thousands of questions race through my mind, but I am frozen. I manage to raise my hand in her direction, and she grabs it and shakes it vigorously, but I cannot bring myself to look at her. As she continues to grasp my hand, I feel waves of emotions flow between us.

I want desperately to feel her pain and to have her feel mine. I need to feel or hear from her some sort of remorse or sorrow for what happened, but when I raise my eyes to meet hers, I find no such solace. As we lock eyes and connect, woman to woman, for an instant I see in her a lost and confused child, fearful and totally untouched by her spiritual side. Her steely gray eyes, weathered face and defiant smirk convey complete indifference to my plight. She is not only unremorseful, but seems irritated at me for wasting her time with this folly. Her demeanor says, "Alfonso knew what he was doing and paid the price for playing a dangerous game—those are the breaks."

Instinctively, I pull my hand back from hers as tears start to trickle down my cheeks. I grab my purse and race out of the courtroom, confused by the complete lack of emotion I have just experienced and unable to control my sobbing.

I walk, then run down the street outside the courthouse through the rain, blinded by the raindrops and by my own tears. I keep thinking to myself, "I can't believe she's not even sorry; she doesn't even care." I am oblivious to where I am running until I find myself beneath the shelter of a canopy outside a bookstore about three blocks from the courthouse. I try to compose myself, but the impact of what has just happened throws me into crying fits. I notice passersby staring at me, so I take out my sunglasses and turn towards the bookstore's display window. What I see in the next instant shakes me out of my spell.

Holly and Christmas ornaments decorate the exhibit inside the window, but it is a small wooden box in the middle of the display that catches my eye. I feel a warm sensation as I see that the beautifully adorned box is surrounded by hundreds of copies of a small, hardback book entitled *The Christmas Box*. I remember being intrigued by a magazine review of the book I read during my most recent flight to Vancouver only a few days ago.

Now, as I stand in the Vancouver rain, the book calls to me. I walk inside and buy a copy. Since I know I can't go back to the courtroom, I take the book back to my apartment and read it. I am captivated by this story about an elderly woman who had never fully recovered from the heartache of losing her daughter. In the beginning of the book, the woman asks the narrator, "What was the first Christmas present?" The entire message of the book involves the narrator's attempt to answer that simple question. I am about three-quarters of the way through the book when I jump out of my chair to the startling realization that I know the answer. The answer is love; love was the first Christmas gift.

I feel as if my soul has opened deep inside me and love is flowing uncontrollably from it in all directions. Angels fill the room, and are joined by Alfonso, the other eight skiers, my grandmother and an entire cast of heavenly musicians. I see streamers falling from the rafters, as the entire group holds up their champagne glasses for a toast, saying, "She's got it; she's finally got it."

At this moment, I have the clearest thought I have ever had of what life is all about: love. Thoughts about my life, Alfonso's life, the lives of our children and even Joss Lang, crystallize in this flow of energy that almost seems to lift me out of my seat. Love is the now, the then and all the spaces in between; nothing else matters. While circumstances in each person's life are different, they all will lead us to love if we let them. Suddenly, I feel a calm come over me and I feel Alfonso's presence. "Let go," he says. "Let go of the strife. Let go of her."

I immediately kneel next to the chair and pray for everyone involved in the avalanche, and particularly for Joss Lang. In my mind, I encase her in a beautiful white light, while I forgive and bless her, and pray she will open herself to the love that seemed so absent in her during our encounter.

As I finish reading the book and discover how the narrator comes to realize the answer to the question, I reflect on how easily we give in to fear. If we don't choose love, we choose its opposite, fear, which breeds self-pity and embitterment. I clearly see through this wonderful little book that I want to choose love, and that I need to choose love, especially in these most trying of circumstances.

This experience gives me an entirely new outlook on all aspects of the trial, and it gives me a new strength and demeanor during the remainder of my time in court. It is within my power to either grasp needlessly at the happenings in the courtroom or to let them go and just choose love. The choice is always mine. As I go to bed, I also come to realize that all those angels and spirits who helped me celebrate this afternoon were asking me to share my enlightenment. I don't know how I will accomplish this, but I know in my heart that somehow I will. Maybe I will write a book!

———————————————

It's Saturday, so no court today; however, Susan is taking me out to lunch to fill me in on the guides' testimony, which I missed. Susan tells me that both guides admitted they failed to perform any of the required snow assessments on Bay Street. The last profile had been done on February 26 and had shown that there were two layers of weaker snow that could be potentially dangerous. In addition, on the morning of the accident, CMH officials had other indications that Bay Street might be dangerous, as the guides had placed Bay Street on the questionable list at their daily meeting. Nonetheless, at the lunch meeting the guides decided to ski it anyway.

The guides revealed that they had intended to take the skiers down one last run before returning to the lodge for the day, and Alfonso had been the only man in the Mexican group to remain on the slopes for that last run. Prior to skiing down Bay Street, the guide for the first group, who had never skied Bay Street before, radioed the helicopter to ask about the safest route. He recommended taking his group down the run on the skiers' right-hand side of the slope, which our snow experts testified provided better protection from the risks of an avalanche. The first guide followed that route and reached the base of the run safely.

Alfonso's guide, however, allowed the second group to go out onto the main slope of Bay Street. Boiselle had testified that guides can take skiers down exposed runs one at a time, from place of safety to place of safety. This precaution ensures that several skiers are not on a vulnerable slope at the same time. The weight and movement of several skiers might trigger an avalanche. On that fateful afternoon, however, Alfonso's group did not take the conservative route, nor did they go down the slope one at a time. The group proceeded haphazardly down the steepest portion of Bay Street with no instructions from the guide.

Joss Lang testified that after she skied about one hundred yards down the run, she stopped, turned around, and she saw several of them skiing out onto the main part of the run. She decided to wait until they all reached the spot where she had stopped before she gave them a new set of instructions—leaving all the skiers vulnerable in the interim. By that time, it was too late: the skiers in her group never made it to her.

A loud rumble shook the mountain as the snowpack began to separate. Within seconds, the avalanche was pounding down the mountain in full force, swallowing up all ten skiers in a wall of snow, ice and debris. Joss Lang, the only survivor, screamed "avalanche" into her radio a split second before being carried away by the rush. This was probably the last word Alfonso ever heard. The avalanche crashed down upon the guide and the others at more than 100 miles per hour.

When we finish lunch, I decide to walk back to the apartment and enjoy the beautiful fall day and reflect on how the trial is proceeding. I sense that as the negligence evidence against CMH has mounted, the spirits of Alfonso and the others are very pleased. The arrogance of CMH's belief that they had done nothing wrong and bore no responsibility for protecting their guests because of the waivers seems to be withering under the weight of the evidence.

I sit down on a bench along the lakefront, close my eyes and see the outlines of the spirits in the jury box and even hear their conversation. They speak to each other and to me about why they are in the courtroom. The spirits know the accident could have been avoided, but the purpose of their presence is not vindictive. They want to protect the skiers who will come after them, and they want to make certain heli-skiing enterprises are held responsible for their actions. More than anything, the spirits want others to have the opportunity, in an atmosphere that is reasonably safe, to share in the euphoria and soulfulness they experienced while heli-skiing.

Feeling their presence and hearing their thoughts fills me with a sense of wonder and makes me proud of what I am accomplishing. I pray that the end result of this case will be to fulfill the spirits' beautiful wishes by changing the heli-skiing industry and changing the attitudes of the people involved in this case.

Following Joss Lang's testimony, the trial switches gears, as CMH's attorneys begin to present their expert evidence. Their evidence and arguments are very painful for me to hear, and seem to go on endlessly. Many times I cannot bear to listen to their version of the events, and I am offended by their absolute refusal to take any responsibility for what had happened. Particularly galling are the comments of one of the vice presidents of CMH.

"We know going in that there are certain risks associated with heli-skiing and the people who pay thousands of dollars for our services know the risks, too," he says. "We do all we can to prevent these things from happening—and we did everything to prevent this accident from happening—but sometimes they do anyway. But, I have to emphasize that our procedures are sound and in compliance with what the province requires. I am sorry for what happened, but it certainly was not our fault."

After hearing testimony like that, I need to take a walk to calm myself and try to recapture the feelings that so transformed me that rainy Vancouver morning last week. It is a constant struggle to shove fear out of my consciousness and to choose love instead, especially when I hear testimony that runs so counter to what I believe to be the truth. But the inner peace I enjoy, when I am able to, is well worth the effort.

On March 8, 1996, nearly five years to the day of the accident and six months after the trial began, it finally ends. Both sides have presented their cases and have argued their points of law. Now it is up to the judge, and she has to make her judgment based solely on the evidence. She advises the attorneys from both sides that due to the enormous amount of evidence she will have to review, she will probably not render a decision until the end of August, at which time she will issue a judgment and a written opinion.

As we walk out of the courtroom that final day, Ross and Susan invite me to dinner to celebrate. Although I feel relieved that the trial is finally over, I am not in a celebrating mood, so I politely decline. Even though there is a drizzle in the air, I decide to walk back to the apartment, needing some time alone to gather my thoughts and reflect on everything that has happened.

I walk the streets of Vancouver for quite a while. It is rush hour, so the streets are bustling with people headed home after a long day. I wander aimlessly in the afternoon drizzle until I come upon a beautiful old Catholic Church. The gothic style, with huge gargoyles and stone monuments carved into the outer walls, reminds me of the huge cathedrals in Europe, though this one is quite small in comparison.

I walk in, pushing inward the two huge wooden doors, each deeply and delicately carved with scenes from the New Testament. The church is dark except for the daylight that filters through the stained glass windows around the dome. I kneel in the back pew and thank God for the strength to endure the trial and I pray for more strength and guidance in the months that lay ahead.

Out of the corner of my eye, I see the flicker of candlelight in one of the sanctuaries along the side of the church. I walk over to the candles and kneel on the padded knee rest at the base of the collection of fifty or so candles. I strike a match and light nine candles, one for each of the men and women who died on Bay Street. Tears roll down my cheeks as I relive in my mind those last terrifying seconds of their lives. "Please, Lord, let this effort not be in vain."

As I pray, I notice a person get up from one of the front pews and begin walking towards me along the side aisle. I strain to see him through the dim light; he appears to be dressed in monk's attire with a dark hood pulled over his head. "My God," I think, "it's Alfonso!" I close my eyes and see his face so clearly, looking just as he had the day I dropped him off at the airport.

When I open my eyes, he is standing right in front of me. He removes his hood and places his hand on my shoulder. The candlelight flickers off the gold cross he wears around his neck and illuminates his face. "Peace be with you," he says, then turns and disappears into the darkness.

CHAPTER 9
the judgment

It's already September and my anxiety is escalating. I cannot wait for the day when the trial, the conflict and the waiting will be over. The waiting is so difficult, as so many material things depend on this decision. Will I have to sell the house and pull the children out of private schools? Will an adverse judgment drive me into bankruptcy? So many questions, so few answers. The month is nearly half over and still no word from Canada. Susan must be reading my mind as just as I arrive home from dropping the kids off at school, I am greeted by her phone call.

"Hi, Kris, how are you holding up?" she asks.

"Okay, I guess," I say. "Just really getting tired of the waiting. Any clues on when we're going to hear something?"

"I wish I knew. I was in court last week and another attorney with a case before our judge told me she has been assigned several new cases over the summer. She probably has not had the time she needs to write the opinion. It's just a theory, so don't put too much stock in it, but I think maybe the reason she is taking so long is that she's ruling for us on the waiver. If she had returned quickly with a judgment, she probably would have upheld the waiver and decided to ignore the rest of the legal issues."

"Makes sense to me," I say. "But you guys are the experts. I just wish she would hurry up."

"Well, I think she also may be taking a long time to make sure her judgment is appeal-proof and will withstand a legal challenge on appeal. Anyway, hang in there and we will call as soon as we hear anything."

Susan's theory seems logical, but I am going crazy. I need to know.

Finally, on the afternoon of Thursday, September 27, 1996, I am just returning from picking the children up at school, when I walk into the kitchen and notice the little red light on the answering machine flashing. My pulse immediately quickens. In fact, every time I have walked into the kitchen during the last two months and have seen the light flashing, my heart begins to race. Each time, I think, "Is it Ross with the judgment?" When I press the message retrieval button this time, however, I hear his voice. I had specifically asked Ross to deliver the news quickly, in no more than a sentence or two, so the suspense would not kill me. As the message begins to play and I hear his voice, I sit down on a chair in the kitchen and just listen.

"Kris, this is Ross. The judgment is in. We lost on every count. I have not read it yet. I am in Whistler and will be back in the office tomorrow. I'm so sorry. Please call me."

I do not hear another word after ". . . every count." I hurl myself at the answering machine and jam my finger down on the "repeat" button. Maybe I heard wrong; I must have heard wrong! How could this be? I listen to the same words from Ross again. He had followed my instructions to the tee—direct and to the point. We lost. I lost. My God, what am I going to do?

As I sit in the kitchen, I flash back to the evening I was told of Alfonso's death. The same type of disbelief races through my mind and my heart. The same sort of nausea begins to kick me in my stomach. This has to be some kind of mistake; the judge must have given us someone else's judgment. We cannot possibly have lost because I know in my heart we are supposed to have won. We had to win! Justice is at stake. Will this nightmare ever end?

I dial Ross' number in Whistler. He greets me with a stunned "hello," and then proceeds to fill in the details of the bad news his message foretold.

"I've just read the opinion, cover to cover, and I really can't believe it. The judge ruled for CMH on every count. She didn't find that CMH was negligent at all. Here, let me read this part to you: 'Only in hindsight could the CMH guides have been aware of the danger that awaited those nine skiers on Bay Street on the afternoon of March 12, 1991.' As if that wasn't enough, she went ahead and upheld the waiver Alfonso signed anyway, even though she found no negligence by CMH."

"My God," I say. "Was she sitting in on a different trial?"

"It gets worse, Kris," Ross says. "The judge said she would hear arguments on whether you should be responsible for CMH's legal fees, which I'm sure are in the millions. I won't let that happen, Kris, but this still looks pretty bad."

Ross tells me to call him at the office the next day, apologizes again and then hangs up. As if the rulings are not enough, the judge actually might make me pay CMH for their legal fees. I am numb. I cannot move. I just sit here next to the phone and feel my entire world come crashing down on top of me. I bury my head in my hands and start to cry. All I can see is me standing out on that same mountain where Alfonso was five-and-one-half years before. That same wall of snow that carried him away to his death is now crashing down on me again. There is no sound, just the fury of the snow carrying me away. This avalanche, unlike the one on Bay Street, seems to have no end. It just keeps hurling me downward into the state I have come to dread but know so well—the unknown.

I reach for the phone, my hands trembling, and dial Dick's number.

"Honey," I say, barely audible through my tears. "We lost."

My voice disappears as I gasp for breath. He can hardly hear me, but I cannot speak any louder. All I know is he says he is on his way to the airport to catch a flight down to San Diego, and will be here as soon as he can.

"Don't worry, Kris," he says. "Everything is going to be all right. This time you are not alone. We'll figure this out together. We're partners, remember?"

Dick's words are of great comfort, but the shock is only beginning to set in. I was so sure that justice would be served—that justice would mean a winning judgment for me—that I never really considered losing the case as a realistic possibility. I have been so confident that part of my purpose in life was to hold CMH accountable for what happened and to help ensure that it does not happen again. Instead, CMH has been absolved of negligence, and I am left to wonder what has become of my theory of justice. How could the judge find no negligence? Nine people are dead. There is no justice.

After what seems like hours of despair and crying, Lydia and my mother arrive at my house to offer their love and support. They hold me and reassure me that everything will work itself out.

"I'm so proud of you, Kris," my mom says. "You did what you had to do, what you thought was right; and no matter what the judge says, what you did was really important. You know that, don't you? Even though you didn't win, you let those people know they can't be so careless. You've been through much worse than this, sweetie, much worse. It will just take some time."

Dick arrives later in the evening with the same message. His strong arms hold me close to him as he just lets me cry.

"Where was the justice," I whisper over and over again. "Where, where . . . How could this be?"

For five years, my life has been consumed by this trial and the opportunity to make right what I believed was such a grievous wrong. Instead, I am disappointed again, this time by a judge and a system that could not possibly have had justice as its goal.

The shock of the negative judgment takes quite a long time to wear off. For several days, I feel as though I am moving around in a fog, just going through the motions. Everything and everyone is in slow motion. I have no emotion left—I left it all in that courtroom in Canada and it's been delivered back to me in shambles. I need very badly to get away from it all, so Dick arranges for Lydia to take care of the children so he and I can fly up to his place in the Bay Area for the weekend. Through his nurturing and love, by Sunday, I feel a flicker of life somewhere deep inside me. The tasks that await me, however, are staggering.

We spend much of the weekend and the next few weeks planning for the drastic changes that lay ahead. The negative judgment means I can no longer afford to keep my dream home. I bought the house when my finances were relatively stable and the mortgage payments were affordable. With the peso devaluation and the costs of the lawsuit, the mortgage payments have come to dominate my monthly budget. With the negative judgment, Dick and I sadly agree the house has to be put on the market. We call a real estate agent and, within a week, there are prospective buyers prancing through my home.

We also decide it would be unrealistic to continue to pay private school tuition. Jonathan and Nicholas have just started attending a school for children with learning differences and, while they are making steady progress, the tuition is astronomical. It saddens me to think that after finding what I think is the perfect school for my children's special needs, I will be forced to take them out of such a wonderful environment. Nevertheless, I ask the principal at the school to recommend the best public schools for Nicholas and Jonathan. Dick and I then begin looking for homes in the school districts she recommends.

Annette and Christofer, meanwhile, are still at La Jolla Country Day. Christofer is a junior and I cannot bear the thought of him having to start over at a new high school for his senior year. So, we decide to keep Christofer at Country Day until he graduates. Annette, however, will join Nicholas and Jonathan at the public school in the area we choose to live.

These decisions and our realization that we will have to cut back expenses in just about every area leave me weary and wary as we embark on these new challenges. There is so much change and work ahead that it seems overwhelming. I know from experience that this transition will be very difficult. I am so tired of grieving—grieving over Alfonso, grieving over Francisco, and now grieving over losing the lawsuit. I know that with every loss, grieving is inevitable, but I also know that how I handle the grieving will be an indication of how far I have come as a person and as a spirit. In my heart, I know this is true, and I know my family and I will get through this, just as we have survived and learned from the previous trying experiences. Still, I can't help but think, "Why us? Why again?"

For a couple weeks now, there has been a small package sitting on my dining room table. It is my copy of the judge's opinion, which Susan mailed down to me and which I have been conveniently ignoring. The time has come to open it up and read it, so after dropping the kids off this morning, I do just that. I guess my need to know exactly why and how the judge ruled the way she did has gotten the best of me.

As I quickly leaf through the judgment, I come to the paragraph that summarizes the basis of her decision: "The defence evidence was consistent and overwhelming that only in hindsight would the potential for a deep layer avalanche or any avalanche on Bay Street have been recognized."

As I read these words, I think to myself, "What could the judge possibly have been thinking?" I sat through 90 percent of the trial and heard the same evidence she heard. Granted, I may have been just a little biased, but I know what I heard. The evidence relating to negligence was overwhelming. All along, my only fear about losing centered on the waiver. I thought that if I were to lose, the judge would find CMH negligent, but then uphold the waiver. In her opinion, however, the judge did not even find a shred of evidence that CMH had been negligent. I am stunned.

As I turn back to the beginning of the opinion and begin to read each word, I feel something is terribly wrong with the way the judgment is worded. The entire introduction, which describes the accident and my life with Alfonso in Guadalajara, reads as if the judge is going to rule in my favor. There are glowing accounts of me and my testimony, which the judge says she found "entirely credible." There is also an accurate and insightful summary of the impact Alfonso's death had on me and my family.

The legal analysis section reveals that the judge bought the defense team's smokescreen completely. After dismissing our criminal negligence claim rather quickly, the judge explains how ordinary negligence would depend on whether the "mistake" made was the result of an error in judgment or skill, or both, which fell below a reasonable standard in the avalanche forecasting profession. Or if not, were the industry standards unreasonable? The judge's answers to both these questions are a resounding no.

The judge rules that CMH and their guides had no indication that Bay Street would avalanche on the afternoon of March 12, 1991. In doing so, the judge ignores both our expert testimony and the testimony of CMH officials, who admitted that the action of their guides had not complied with the due diligence requirements in their own official guiding manuals. According to the judge, CMH was required to do no more than it did to prevent "mistakes" like the Bay Street avalanche from happening.

The ruling shocks and distresses me. How can she have ruled that this "mistake" was not preventable? The judge basically ignores common sense and well-established legal standards when she endorses the meager precautionary steps the CMH's guides had taken. The only precaution Alfonso's guide took to assure herself that the run was safe was a pole plant she did while she was actually skiing down Bay Street seconds before the avalanche.

To expect any ski guide, as she is skiing, to simultaneously pay attention to her skiing, consciously plant her pole deep in mid-turn and instantly register this data to analyze the stability of the snowpack, to me, still seems ludicrous. This is why the test is properly done standing still. Since the actions of Alfonso's guide did not come close to complying with well-established preventative standards, I am amazed that the judge feels what the guide did was sufficient.

Another troubling aspect of the opinion for me is the judge's treatment of the expert witnesses. Our experts, she notes, had very little or no experience with CMH's operations in the heli-skiing industry. The obvious question is, "How could they?" If they had such experience, they would have been either working for CMH or in the heli-skiing industry.

The heli-skiing industry in Canada is not unlike the medical field in the United States, where finding doctors willing to testify against other doctors is difficult. Likewise, finding experts within the tightly-knit heli-skiing community willing to testify against the industry that provides their livelihoods is nearly impossible. In our case, since no one within CMH or the heli-skiing industry was willing to testify against CMH, we had to look outside that community for our experts.

I expected the judge to have a better understanding of the implications of these rules. When the judge states in her opinion that "no one but the two plaintiff's experts said, even under close cross-examination, 'I would have suspected this avalanche was lying in wait on March 12, 1991,'" I have to wonder what she expected them to say. Certainly she knew experts on both sides were being paid large sums of money to support opposing positions in the case. I hope the judge hasn't failed to find CMH negligent simply because my attorneys were unable to convince CMH's well-paid experts to abandon their positions that they had been paid to support. Unfortunately, that's the message implicit in the judge's words.

What I am left with, after reading the opinion, is a deep and sincere sense of disappointment in the judge. I am convinced the judge, for whatever reason, took the easy way out. Instead of addressing the particular aspects of this avalanche and these victims, she followed CMH's lead and turned the case into a referendum on the viability of heli-skiing in Canada. She acknowledged as much in the opinion: "It was apparent to the Court that CMH treated the matter as if heli-skiing as a commercially viable sport was at issue. As the matter developed, that defence was appropriate." In doing so, I believe the judge lost sight of what this case was all about— one avalanche caused by a CMH "mistake" that wound up taking the lives of nine people on a Tuesday afternoon in March 1991.

My intention was never to put the entire heli-skiing industry on trial; I certainly hoped my lawsuit would produce some changes in the safety arrangements that operators like CMH used, but I never intended to drive CMH and others out of business or make it impossible for them to continue to make substantial profits. Rather, my intention was to show that, on this particular day, CMH and the people who worked for CMH did not do everything they could have or should have done to prevent this particular avalanche on Bay Street from claiming nine victims. I believe the judge lost sight of this part of the case when she focused instead on the industry as a whole.

Her approach, I believe, was not justice, but rather result-oriented rationalization. Words cannot describe my disappointment—not only in the outcome, but more so in the way the outcome was reached. I expected more.

After I finish reading the judgment, I have to get out of the house. I am too upset at the injustice I am so sure this opinion represents. I drive down to the beach to pray and to try to gather my thoughts on what has happened and the challenges that lay ahead. As I sit on the beach alone, in deep contemplation, watching the sun setting into the water, I realize that there is a major difference in the way I am handling this setback. This time, I have developed the trust to know that God is with me.

If I truly believe the message Dick delivered to me nearly two years ago, then the negative judgment in the lawsuit is irrelevant. My winning the case simply was not meant to be. Whether or not I will be "okay" as the message indicated, however, is not dependent on the outcome of this lawsuit. I also realize that I will drive myself crazy trying to understand all of these events in human terms. In God's plan for me, however, they have to make perfect sense. I pray for the awareness to someday come to understand this more fully. I know how important it is to remain connected to my God—the primary source of my strength, my peace and my love.

As I sit on the beach and pray, my words of strength come back to me, "I can't; You must; I'm yours; Show me the way." In my heart, I know that what has happened is not a mistake. I have been told many times that God never comes into our lives through the front door—probably because we do not let Him. As I sit here by myself thinking about how to open that front door, I feel the brilliant sunlight encircle me and enter me through the top of my head. Then, I feel peace fill my entire body. I am filled with the strength to trust, to let go of my fears and to believe that God's love will see me through. I pray for love for everyone in my life, asking God to bless all of those who have been involved in the lawsuit and asking Him to give all of us the strength to move on. It is time to close this chapter of my life tenderly and with love, and to put it away, reach into the bookshelf and open a new chapter. The accident, the tragedy, the trial—all are over. That in itself is a victory.

I am so proud of the courage I have shown to pursue the lawsuit against CMH. Looking back, I now can see the benefit of those efforts, not only for myself, but also for my children. I have taught them through my actions that you should never give up on something you believe in even if it takes all of the courage and inner strength that you have. I also have showed them and myself that I love the legacy of their father and that I would not stand idly by and allow his wrongful death to go unnoticed. I clearly do not understand the outcome, but I trust . . .

One of the most important lessons I have learned during the events following Alfonso's death has been the tremendous difference between what I expect to happen and what actually does happen. Nowhere is this more true than in the judgment I expected to receive from the Canadian court. I expected human justice, which I thought would take the form of a repudiation of CMH's actions and a monetary compensation for me and my family for the loss of Alfonso. What I learned, however, is that human justice and divine justice have very little in common, and that one tiny glimpse of divine justice will make you completely forget about human justice.

As I grow in spiritual awareness, I have come to hold certain beliefs about divine justice. Unlike human justice, divine justice is not vengeful, nor is it punishment or retribution. Divine justice also is not concerned with fairness or equity. Rather, in divine justice, we find harmony and the fulfillment of our spiritual goals. I believe that each spirit before incarnating makes a pact with herself and with God to accept and learn certain lessons in the life she is about to begin. We choose these lessons to help us grow closer to God during our lifetimes.

When human beings begin to recognize these lessons, they reach a greater awareness of their own spirituality and of their relationship with God. This process of spiritual recognition enables us to look beyond our human natures, and beyond the events and circumstances in our lives, to the harmony and beauty of our spiritual selves. In so doing, our focus shifts from human justice to divine justice, which takes the form of cosmic harmony: everything and everyone working together to produce the lessons that enable us to grow as spirits. One of the lessons I am certain I agreed to learn during my lifetime was to gain a better understanding of this concept of divine justice.

Often we see glimpses of divine justice in our lives, usually in hindsight. I often wonder what would have happened if Alfonso had not died on that mountain in British Columbia. Would I have been able or willing to begin down my spiritual path? Similarly, what if Francisco had not betrayed me as he did in Guadalajara? I may never have left Mexico and probably never would have met Dick, who I truly believe is my soul mate. All these pieces and others fit together perfectly to bring me to the point where I am now, the point where I am supposed to be. So I must believe that while this judgment slammed a door in my face, in reality, it also opens a number of new and wonderful doors for me to walk through.

The most difficult aspect of divine justice is trusting that everything that happens, happens just the way it needs to happen for us to grow as human beings and, more importantly, as spirits. As humans, we naturally tend to want to isolate incidents or events in our lives and judge them by human standards. When these events make no sense to us, we spend all of our time and energy trying to coordinate them or control them better so they will be more understandable to us. If we take a step back, however, and try to catch just a tiny glimpse of the larger picture, sometimes we can let go of that incessant drive to understand. In its place, we will find love. We will find that each event is a minuscule piece of a huge cosmic puzzle and that each piece of that puzzle miraculously fits with beautiful precision, harmony and balance with every other piece.

Trust and faith are the key ingredients for reaching this stage of awareness. One of my goals has been to learn to see and accept God's will for me, and to surrender in trust and faith to God. This is no easy task. We are so afraid to totally surrender to God because we fear what we do not completely understand. I believe I have begun to learn to surrender myself to God and, in doing so, I have been able to say, "You, Lord, have taught me the rules to live by, to live with honesty, integrity and love. The rest is up to you. I trust."

With each new experience, and each new trial and challenge, however, our ability and willingness to make that surrender is challenged. We find ourselves so easily trapped in fear of the pain and suffering we are so certain await us in the unknown. The pain and suffering offers a surrender point where each of us can get down on our knees and utter those simple words of acceptance, "I can't; You must; I'm yours; Show me the way." From this acknowledgment emerges a spirit no longer broken, but one totally willing and able to say that nothing in this world scares me anymore, and that anything is possible. That surrender is the ultimate, "Thy will be done."

CHAPTER 10

new windows of opportunity

Nearly everyone I've told about the judgment shares my disbelief in the outcome. The outpouring of love and support from friends and family is overwhelming. Cards, flowers and phones calls have poured in, each with a message of understanding and comfort. Everyone wants to help in any way they can, and these blessings of love and friendship are helping me to put my financial worries into perspective. In fact, the more I get away from dwelling on the judgment, the more windows of opportunity seem to be opening for me and my family.

Just as I was resigning myself to the reality that my diminished financial situation might force me to remove Christofer from La Jolla Country Day just before his senior year, my friends in the financial aid department have come through with a tremendous surprise. They have earmarked a scholarship for Christofer. The scholarship, offered by one of the local banks, will include full tuition and books, with the only requirement that Christofer will have to do his senior project at the bank.

At Country Day, each student spends the last month of his or her senior year working in the community in some sort of job or volunteer work. Christofer has already started to think that he wants to do something in the business arena since he plans to major in business in college. The scholarship requirement fits right in with his plans since it will provide him with some practical experience as he heads off to college. Without my sudden need for financial aid, however, we never would have found out about the scholarship. When one door closes, it seems another is waiting to open.

My older boys also seem to be benefiting in positive ways from the effects of the judgment. Both are in college, busy with their studies, and both have assumed they would be taken care of in one way or another until they established themselves and, in my opinion, have grown a bit complacent. Perhaps our financial crisis is exactly the type of reality check they need. Since we will have to cut back in all areas of expenses, I decide to sit down with the older boys and explain our financial situation and why these cutbacks will be necessary.

"Look guys," I say, "I know we have been used to a pretty extravagant lifestyle, but, unfortunately, things are going to have to change a bit. Dick and I have been going over our finances since the lawsuit ended and we simply can't continue on at the pace we've been going—we'll be broke within ten years."

I see looks of disbelief and shock on their faces, but I decide to continue on.

"It's time you guys begin to get serious about what you want to do with your lives because I simply am not going to be able to support you forever. The bottom line is that you're both going to have to begin contributing to your own support. That's going to mean getting summer jobs and maybe even working during the school year."

"Well, I guess I can do my part," says Alfonso Jr. "I can move into a less expensive apartment in Guadalajara and sell my car."

I am stunned, as he has always treasured his car—it is almost like an extension of himself. He seems to be realizing, however, that more important things are at stake. He needs money to invest in a business opportunity and realizes that the family wealth has run dry. He has some very good ideas and I can hear a new ring of pride in his voice. I can sense that he no longer is waiting for things to come to him. Instead, he seems to be going out and getting them for himself. I feel a tremendous amount of pride in his decision to adjust his priorities.

A couple months later, I decide to visit Alfonso Jr. in Guadalajara for his twenty-second birthday. We have a small party and invite several of our friends, most of whom I have not seen in a long time. One of our friends, Antonio Blanchet, comes up to me and Alfonso Jr. and begins to tell us about how he had met Alfonso Sr. While Antonio was finishing his final year of college, Alfonso Sr. had recruited Antonio to work for him after he graduated. Antonio is now a partner and major stockholder in a very successful Mexican-German company that makes lubricants for heavy machinery. Because of the unique circumstances Antonio found himself in at the time, he had since come to view Alfonso Sr. as his guardian angel.

"Your father, and your husband, Kris, gave me my start in this business," he says. "I don't know whether you knew that or not. He offered me a job with his company when I was about to finish school. I had no money, no job offers, no work experience in his field and no family in Guadalajara. I was driving myself crazy worrying about my future.

"In my time of utter desperation, Alfonso appeared on the scene to rescue me. He took me under his wing, taught me how the businesses operated, and offered me a full-time, prestigious position in one of his new companies. The work wasn't easy, and I worked harder than anyone to learn the ropes, but I've never forgotten the opportunity he gave me. The guidance he gave me helped make me the successful businessman I am today."

When he finishes recounting his story, he pauses, rubs his chin, then turns to Alfonso Jr. and puts his arms on his shoulders. Looking him directly in the eyes, Antonio says, "Alfonso, I want to give you the same type of opportunity your dad gave me. Do you want a job?"

"Yeah, of course I do," Alfonso Jr. says without hesitating.

"Well, I'll give you an entry-level job, just like your dad did for me, and then you can work your way up. I will teach you all I know about Mexican and international business the same way your dad taught me. Then you can take it from there. How does that sound?"

Speechless, Alfonso Jr. just stares at Antonio for a few seconds, then embraces him.

After Alfonso walks away, Antonio tells me he sees so much of himself in Alfonso Jr.

"He's studying international business, right?" he asks. "That's what I studied. And he seems just as unfocused as I was at his age . . . that's when your husband stepped in. He needs a mentor to give him some guidance and it would be my privilege to do that."

"You are really something else," I say. "If he can't learn about business from his father, then learning from you will be the next best thing. Thank you so much for this, Antonio. You don't know how much this means to me."

"Kris, I feel like I owe this to Alfonso. He was so good to me and I only want the best for his children. When I die, I want to be able to look Alfonso in the eye and say, 'Thank you for what you did for me,' knowing that I was able to pass some of that on to his son."

On my flight back to San Diego, I cannot help but reflect on the message Alfonso sent me, now more than two years ago, through Dick, "You are very loved and everything is going to be okay." I can feel Alfonso Sr.'s presence and I know he is watching over his children. Even though he is no longer a part of our physical world, his sons still mean everything to him. I know he will never leave any of us.

As soon as I get home from the airport, another huge surprise awaits me. Carl is nowhere to be found in the house. I ask where he is and his brothers say, "He went to work." Work? I'm dumbfounded. When I left for Mexico five days earlier, Carl hadn't even applied anywhere. I have been prodding him to get a job since our talk. Finally, shortly before I left for Mexico, my funds diminishing and my patience waning, I took the drastic step of cutting off his allowance because he had not worked since the previous summer.

During the previous summer, Carl had developed an interest in biology and was toying with the idea of going to medical school. He loved the lab research in his biology classes and was doing very well with his grades in those classes. The father of one of Carl's friends operated a cancer research laboratory in San Diego and, sensing Carl's interest, offered him a job at the lab. Carl was ecstatic; not only would the work help him financially, but the experience would enhance his prospects for attending medical school. The job was temporary, however, and Carl has not been working since.

When Carl comes in tonight, I play dumb.

"Hi, honey," I say. "How's it going? I missed you."

"Me too, Mama," he says. "Guess what? While you were gone, I applied for a job and was hired at one of the new Italian restaurants in La Jolla. I'm bussing tables. It's not a lot of cash, but it's something I guess. There's something else, too. I did a lot of thinking while you were gone."

I sit here listening with my mouth open. What's he going to say? With Carl being the free spirit he is, the possibilities are endless. Carl quickly ends my suspense.

"I've decided to move back to Guadalajara so I can go to medical school in the fall. With the classes I've had here in biology and our family connections in Guadalajara, I'm pretty sure I can get accepted as a second-year student."

In Mexico, an undergraduate degree is not needed to begin medical school. Rather, the general education requirements are mixed in with the medicine classes to make up the six-year medical curriculum. Apparently, the grandfather of one of Carl's best friends is one of the founding fathers of the medical school and is still actively involved in the administration.

"I've already spoken with him and made some early plans for the fall semester. Since I knew I was going to need money to follow up on this, I decided to get a job right away and start saving some money. I got them to schedule me nearly every night so it won't interfere with my classes during the day.

"Mom, I want to be a doctor more than anything. I'm willing to do whatever it takes."

This from the same son who just a year ago dyed his hair red, wore an earring and wanted to be a waiter in Cancun. Now he wants to be a doctor! Alfonso is definitely working overtime. His two oldest boys, who seemingly were coming into manhood with no direction whatsoever, are now discovering their own paths. I marvel at what, to me, seems nothing less than a miracle. Now more than ever I can see that I am beginning to understand some of the lessons that are appearing in front of me. My faith in the divine justice at the core of each of our individual and collective lives is growing daily as I continually find myself taking a step back to see the pieces falling into place.

As I think about the positive effects the judgment is having on my sons, I begin to wonder whether perhaps all of us had become too complacent waiting on the judgment from Canada. A huge judgment definitely would have made things relatively easy, at least financially, for me and my children. But perhaps lost in all that money would have been the value of hard work and the fulfillment from doing work that you love. I know my husband, Alfonso, worked as hard as anyone I have ever seen, and he always loved the work he was doing. The loss of this judgment could prove to be a tremendous motivational factor for my children. Now they will know that they have no comfort cushion to fall back on; now they will have to make it on their own, which seems, to me, good for their emotional and spiritual development.

While my older sons seem to be adjusting well to all the new circumstances, the transition hasn't been quite as smooth for fourteen-year-old Jonathan. He comes into my room one night, lies down on my bed and just lets it all out.

"Everyone else has an easy life except us," he says. "We lost the trial and now we have no money. Are they going to put you in jail? Why did my dad die? All of my friends have dads, why don't I? And now this . . . why me, why us? What did we do to deserve this? All of my friends have easy lives, except me. I hate my life."

As I slowly rock him, and hold him tight, I try to explain how sometimes when a door closes, a window opens with a wonderful opportunity.

"This is how God works," I say. "We never know exactly what is going to happen in our lives, but we must trust that God is always with us no matter what happens. Life is never easy, Jonathan, even for the people you think have easy lives. They have problems of their own you don't even know about. What we need to do is learn from these problems so we can grow in God's love."

We stay up past midnight talking; and, when we finish, I'm not sure he really buys into what I tell him, but he seems to have calmed down a little.

The next day, I receive a call from Jonathan's best friend. He invites Jonathan to go with him and his father on a surfing trip to Bali, Indonesia—all expenses paid for two weeks. I can't believe it. What an opportunity, and what a gift! His mother assures me that they want to take Jonathan to Bali. She knows all about the outcome of the trial because Jonathan has told them. Her husband has always been a good friend and a mentor to Jonathan, and she feels this would be a good opportunity for Jonathan to unwind and see that the world isn't all bad. I am amazed at the generosity and the beauty of their offer.

Over the course of the next few days, everything falls into place, and with the blessing of his school, and especially his teacher, Jonathan gets ready to leave for Bali. As he is saying good-bye to me right before he boards the plane, he whispers, "You were right, Mom. This sure is one heck of a big window that opened."

As he walks towards the Jetway, I look up to the heavens and utter a silent and grateful thank you to God and my angels. Jonathan seems to be encased in a bright yellow light as he turns to wave one last time before getting on the plane. I see in his face the excitement and the awe this trip has inspired in him. In some way, this trip has opened his heart to the remarkable nature of God in our lives. For him, it is just a beginning.

Windows of opportunity seem to be opening on so many fronts, and it's impossible for me not to see God's hand in all of this. As I pray my traditional mantra of "Show me the way" every morning, the way seems to begin taking shape before me. Certainly this way is not the way I expected or even desired. Still, I can see so many of the pieces coming together to form new adventures and new experiences for me and my family. The way is hardly ever easy, but the results seem to be well worth the faith and hard work.

I have come to believe that perhaps the most important lessons we learn in this life are the most difficult ones, the ones we resist until they are forced upon us. As the shock of the judgment has worn off, this type of lesson begins to make its way into my consciousness. During the entire legal ordeal, I viewed the lawsuit as a win-lose proposition based on an outcome the judge would determine. The result-oriented society in which we live, where greed, wealth and power are held up as admirable, had conditioned me to believe the only way to win was to get a judgment in my favor. Now, my eyes and heart have been opened to a beautiful, but quite different perspective.

As I am meditating one morning, a startling idea races into my consciousness. I open my eyes, smile, and laugh out loud at the realization. I won! Regardless of what the human justice system and the judge in my case had ruled, my faith in divine justice told me otherwise. I won my legal battle with CMH.

When I decided to hold CMH accountable for its actions, my motives were to bring to light the circumstances of the accident in the hope that this type of disaster could be avoided in the future. I realized during the lawsuit that even the most rigorous precautions cannot prevent every act of nature. I still felt that if CMH had better safety regulations, or at least made stronger efforts to enforce their existing regulations, then other families would be spared the loss of their loved ones.

My lawsuit, despite the outcome, forced CMH to address these issues. Every aspect of their operation was scrutinized during the legal proceedings. I hope this exercise helped CMH to develop better safety standards, and I believe it did. Just the other day, Susan called and, in the course of the conversation, she mentioned that she had heard that CMH had completely altered their regulations to establish much more stringent safety standards. In addition, Susan said that Joss Lang, the guide who led Alfonso and the other skiers down Bay Street, was fired.

I also recently received a letter from an official at CMH. While the purpose of the letter was related to the still unresolved dispute over CMH's legal costs, the letter included a heartfelt paragraph about the impact the accident had on the people at CMH. He said even six years after the accident, not a day goes by that the people at CMH don't think about and remember the tragedy of March 12, 1991. I believe him.

So, while I know there is a judgment filed in a court in Vancouver saying CMH prevailed in its defense of a suit brought by Kris Ochoa, I also know that eighty-page document comes nowhere near telling the entire story. That opinion—and I truly believe it is only that, an opinion—is just one piece of the puzzle. I believe I have accomplished what I set out to do.

I am by no means saying this road has been an easy one to travel. I have had many moments of wondering "what next," especially when it comes to the seemingly never-ending legal case. In fact, I have just been notified that the judge has agreed with CMH and has ordered me to pay a substantial portion of their legal costs. So, not only am I out the money I spent on the trial, but now I have to pick up part of the tab for CMH. I am having a very hard time with this concept—I lost my husband, my kids lost their father, and now I have to pay the people who are responsible for this loss. I pray daily for the enlightenment to get past this troubling reality, as this closing part of the lawsuit still seems wrong to me. "Show me the way."

As I look back on the years since the avalanche, I can see Alfonso's death was a crossroads in my life. His death presented me with the opportunity to ask vital questions that, in my previously complacent life, I was not required nor did I seek to ask. I encountered deep and difficult questions like, "Who am I? What am I to learn from these experiences? Have I chosen love in the difficult times in my life? Have I trusted and let go of the fears?" The experiences in my life since Alfonso's death have allowed me to choose a higher level of awareness of God in my life. While it has not been an easy road, it has been my road, and I have actively participated in its creation.

If I were given the opportunity to return to the comfort and complacency of my old life, I would not go back. I believe my life has unfolded exactly as it was intended to, and I choose to live with an attitude of gratitude for all of the experiences that have allowed me to grow into the spiritual being I have become. I am consciously grateful for everything in my life, and my daily prayers begin and end with thanks to God, and to my angels and spiritual guides, for helping me notice and appreciate the wonder and love in every aspect of my life. However mundane or difficult life becomes, I am now confident that each new experience will carry a seed of enlightenment that will enrich my life.

I try to use this attitude of confidence, trust and letting go to help me deal with the difficult challenges that await us, especially the financial ones. With the house on the market, we have looked with little success for homes in school districts with good programs for children with learning differences. Our search for a new home, however, has proved fruitless as all of the homes we look at are either too small or too expensive. Meanwhile, due to lack of interest, I have been forced to lower the price on my home three times, and still have not received a legitimate offer.

These pressures begin to overwhelm me one afternoon, as I sit at the kitchen table with Dick, looking at the numbers. How can we ever do all the things we need to do and still make ends meet? I throw my hands up and cover my face; it's just too much. I feel a little tap on my shoulder and Dick is looking at me smiling. "What in the world is there to be smiling about," I think.

Very slowly, he says, "I know this is hard. It's really hard, but you are not alone. I'm here with you every step of the way. You are my partner and I love you." He pauses a moment, then says, "Maybe this is a good time for my surprise."

When those words leave his mouth, I instantly and instinctively know what his surprise is, as I flash back to one of the most beautiful experiences of my life. Just after the trial, Dick and I decided we needed some time to reconnect since I had spent so much time in Vancouver. We took a cruise in the Caribbean for some much needed rest and some quiet time together. We flew to San Juan, Puerto Rico, where we boarded a luxury liner for a few days of relaxation.

Our suite was absolutely beautiful, with a private balcony where we could sit and watch the endless ocean roll past us. On our first night on the ship, we had a wonderful gourmet lobster dinner in the dining room. When we returned to the suite, Dick took out four candles, lit them and placed them strategically on the balcony table. He then had me sit on one of the chairs overlooking the Atlantic, which shimmered with the diamond-shape reflections of the full moon overhead. Dick sat next to me and began reading the most beautiful love poem I had ever heard, one he had written especially for me.

The poem finished with the line, "I love you"; then Dick got down on one knee, looked deep into my eyes and said, "Kris, I want to spend my whole life with you. I love you so much. Will you marry me?"

I was speechless. Even though we had talked about marriage, I was not expecting this sudden and beautiful proposal. As I was gathering my thoughts, Dick took out a little box and opened it. Inside was a ring. Dick knew I did not want to wear two rings, so this ring surprised me a little until I noticed it was an "impostor ring." Impostor rings are fake rings with glass instead of diamonds, which look very real, but sell for about $20. I looked at Dick and laughed.

"Well, you know I couldn't propose without a ring," he said as he slipped the ring on my finger. "I spoke with your father and he gave me his blessing. What do you say?"

"Nothing could make me happier," I said, "than to spend the rest of my life with you. Of course I will marry you."

The rest of the cruise paled in comparison to that memorable evening, and I carried the joy of the proposal with me as we departed the Caribbean and headed for home officially engaged. So, when Dick tells me he has a surprise and takes a little black box out of his jacket pocket, I have a pretty good idea of what it is. In the box is the most beautiful ring I have ever seen.

"This isn't an impostor ring, is it?" I jokingly tease.

"Well, if you don't want it," he says as he closes the box and pretends to put it in his pocket.

"Get that over here," I say.

It's the same ring we looked at a few weeks earlier, and decided would be my wedding ring. As he takes out the ring and slips it on my finger, so many emotions flow through me. I think back to the first moment I laid eyes on Dick on that cold, blustery night at the football game. There was something so special about him even from the start, and as the love between us grew stronger, I knew we would spend the rest of our lives together.

I feel so fortunate to have been given a second chance at love, especially after the trauma and misery of losing my first love so suddenly. I even feel a twinge of guilt that I am being untrue to Alfonso, until I remember how Alfonso's message had helped arrange the union between Dick and me. Now, as I look into Dick's eyes, I feel like the luckiest woman in the world to be engaged to such a loving, caring and compassionate man.

"How about a Christmas wedding," he says. "My brother and sister will be here and, with your kids and mine, we can have a beautiful family wedding right here at your house. I was thinking it would be so beautiful to be married out on the deck with the ocean in the background. I love you, Kris, and want to spend the rest of my life with you. Money comes and goes. All of this stuff will eventually sort itself out, but I don't want to miss this opportunity of hooking up with my soul mate. We'll figure all of this other stuff out . . . Marry me, Kris."

The ring, the idea of the wedding, the moment and Dick standing there before me, all hit me at once. I scream, cry and laugh all at once, while saying, "Yes, of course, yes!" as I embrace my husband to be.

⟡

It's 3:30 p.m. on December 28, 1996, and I am standing with Dick under an arch of poinsettias on the verandah of my soon-to-be-sold home. The ocean in the distance reflects the scattered sunlight that, every few seconds, peaks out from behind the clouds. My focus, however, is on the man whose hands I am grasping. I cannot believe how lucky I am to be marrying the kindest, gentlest, most loving man I have ever known. The sun breaks through the clouds and, for a magical moment, illuminates us in its light. All I can see at this special moment is the deep blue of Dick's beautiful eyes and all of the love pouring out from them towards me. Then I hear my father recite the words of one of my favorite scripture passages:

> To every *thing there* is a season, and a time to
> every purpose under the heaven:
>
> A time to be born, and a time to die; a time
> to plant, and a time to pluck up *that which* is
> planted;
>
> A time to kill, and a time to heal; a time to break
> down, and a time to build up;

A time to weep, and a time to laugh; a time to
mourn, and a time to dance;

A time to cast away stones, and a time to gather
stones together; a time to embrace, and a time to
refrain from embracing;

A time to get, and a time to lose; a time to keep,
and a time to cast away;

A time to rend, and a time to sew; a time to keep
silence, and a time to speak;

A time to love, and a time to hate; a time of war,
and a time of peace.

~Ecclesiastes 3:1–8 (King James Version)

For everything there is a season and a time for every purpose under
heaven.

CHAPTER 11
the heartbreak

Dick and I have finally found a home of our own, one that both of us have selected as the place to begin our married life together. We buy a beautiful home in a new development just north of San Diego. While it is not La Jolla, it is a wonderful area with good schools and plenty of things to do. There is even a nine-hole golf course running through the development (and our backyard), which Dick and the boys christen before we even finish unpacking. More than anything, the home has come to symbolize the new life Dick and I will share together for the rest of our days.

Our married life is wonderful, exactly the type of loving partnership between equal soul mates I have dreamed of for so long. It's so wonderful, I don't even mind (too much) sending a cashier's check to CMH's attorneys. Despite the judicial ruling that I was liable for a substantial portion of CMH's defense costs, the people at Zurich Canada (CMH's insurance carrier) had a conscience and a cooperative attitude towards dealing with me in my diminished financial state and agreed to accept a significantly lesser amount. For that I am appreciative. Now we are all free to put the accident and the lawsuit behind us and to move forward in peace and love.

Other than the usual growing pains my children inflict on us, I can't think of a time in my life when I've been happier. Having Dick around has meant the world to my kids, and he has had such a profound influence on Jonathan, Nicholas and Annette. With Dick's guidance, Jonathan has thrown himself into golf. Dick's strong work ethic has definitely rubbed off on Jonathan as he practices constantly with Dick, both on the short Par 3 course that runs through our complex and on professional courses around San Diego. Dick even takes Jonathan on a long weekend up to Monterrey to play the Pebble Beach courses—quite a coup for a teenager! Jonathan makes the varsity golf team as a sophomore and letters for three years. Dick attends every match and provides the calm and support that Jonathan needs to flourish. Dick is his coach, mentor, friend and father.

One afternoon last spring, I walked into the kitchen to find Dick and Jonathan sitting silently around the kitchen table.

"What's going on?" I asked.

After a few moments, Dick finally chimed in, "The letter came in the mail today."

"The letter" was the decision from California State University San Marcos, Jonathan's college of choice, about whether he would receive a golf scholarship.

"Oh for goodness sake, Jonathan, open it already," I said. "The suspense is killing us."

With that, Jonathan pried open the corner of the envelope with his fingers and slowly slid the letter out. Slowly—too slowly for my liking—he unfolded the letter and started to read it. Then, without warning, he shouted, "You're looking at the next Cougar baby! Four years, full ride . . . Woohoo!"

Jonathan and Dick stood up from the table and we met in the middle of the kitchen for a group hug. As I squeezed Jonathan's head to my shoulder, my eyes met Dick's and I saw a tear streaming down his face and a smile as wide as a Torrey Pines fairway.

"You did it, Jonny," he whispered in his ear, "you really did it."

As for Nicholas, Dick has become the father that he has dreamt about having. Nicholas was only four when Alfonso died, and although he claims to remember his father, I doubt he has any real memories of Alfonso. Having Dick in his life has given him a sense of security and well-being— like after so much upheaval in his short life, his world is finally stable and headed in the right direction. Nicholas plays golf with Dick and they go for long nature walks. Dick has opened his eyes to the beauty of nature and the need to appreciate and be kind to the environment, teaching him that you really can hug trees and still be a real man. Dick guides him and teaches him to become a loving, caring young man who appreciates the world around him. This also translates into great strides in school—Nicholas' grades have drastically improved since Dick has been around.

Finally, my baby girl, Annette. Not a night goes by when I don't walk into our bedroom and see Annette sitting on Dick's lap while he reads the Harry Potter books to her. A chapter a night is all it takes to keep Annette enraptured. The Harry Potter series has become their getaway time together. I think Annette views herself as Hermoine and Dick as Harry, as Dick leads her through Harry's many adventures each night. She comes to treasure their evenings together and even starts to call herself Harriet Potter.

Dick also coaches Annette's softball and soccer teams. As long as Dick is on the field or in the dugout, Annette feels that she and her team will surely win. Dick loves coaching and is so good with the kids that the love of the game gets instilled in Annette. She learns how to be part of a team and to take losing with grace, dignity and sportsmanship just as she does winning. He teaches her such valuable lessons, lessons that he has lived his life by.

I step back from time to time and feel so lucky to be married to this wonderful man—a man who has taken the bull by the horns with respect to helping raise my children, and has become such a positive influence in their lives. I know they need a dad, but I never imagined they would have such a great one. We are so blessed and I thank God every day for sending Dick into our lives.

It's a lazy Saturday morning and I'm having trouble mustering the energy to get out of bed, preferring to just lay here and think about how much fun Dick and I had last night with our best friends, the Landrys. I think to myself how lucky we are to have such a great life.

I finally stumble into the bathroom, barely looking at myself in the mirror before grabbing my toothbrush and smiling at Dick, who is in the shower. I am brushing away and surveying my sleep-filled face when Dick gets out of the shower, wraps himself in a big fluffy towel and slowly sits on the edge of the bathtub, holding his head between his hands. I glance over my shoulder at him and wonder if he's not feeling well.

"Are you okay?" I ask, as I continue brushing my teeth.

He raises his head from his hands, looks at me with a confused and frightened look on his face and slowly says, "Nibbsy, nubbsy, mibbsy, hibbsy . . ."

I stop brushing my teeth and, while laughing, say to him, "What the heck are you saying?"

He looks at me with those gorgeous deep blue eyes, but all I see is the terror on his face to know he is not joking. This is serious.

"What's wrong, honey?" I say as I rush over to hug him, but he looks perplexed and can't seem to formulate words. I grab the phone and can't think of anything else to do but call Mary Jo.

"Mary Jo, it's Kris. Dick just got out of the shower and seems really disoriented. He tried to say something, but it came out as gibberish. He was fine last night. What do you think this could possibly be?" I ask, sensing that she can hear the fear in my voice.

With no hesitation, Mary Jo says as calmly as she can, "Call your doctor right away, Kris. This sounds like it could be serious. I don't want to alarm you, but you need to call Dr. Wolfe ASAP."

With my fingers trembling, I dial Dr. Wolfe, Dick's primary physician. After getting bounced around for a minute, I am finally connected to Dr. Wolfe and immediately tell him what has happened.

"Kris, don't get dressed, don't do anything except get Dick into the car and get him to the emergency room now," he says. "I don't even want you to waste the time it would take to call an ambulance. Just get in the car and go. I will call the trauma unit and have people waiting for you and I will get there right away. You must not waste time. Every second is vital. Do you understand me?"

"Yes, of course," I say while my mind screams, "No, I don't!" I hang up the phone and stare at it for a brief moment. "What is going on here," I think, as my mind starts to wander through the possibilities. "Focus," I tell myself. "For God's sake, get your head together."

I snap into action with a sick feeling in my stomach and quickly get Dick into a pair of shorts and a T-shirt, and get him down to the car. One look at Dick's face and I know I have to pull it together and be strong for him. He's trembling and looks terrified.

"Don't worry, honey, we'll get you to the hospital to figure this out," I say, trying my best to smile and keep him calm, while hiding my own panic. "I love you, honey. I love you so much. This will be okay."

I feel a wave of nausea overtake me, so I just drive. Thousands of terrifying thoughts race through my mind during the ten-minute drive to the hospital as I replay the conversation with Dr. Wolfe. Dick doesn't speak a word. I try not to let fear get the best of me, while I squeeze Dick's hand tight in mine, and wonder what is going on in the head and body of the man I love so much.

I pull into the carport in front of the emergency room, and as soon as I turn the ignition off, the trauma team is getting Dick out of the car and into a wheelchair. They whisk him away and usher me into the administration office to deal with getting him admitted.

"Do you know where they are taking my husband?" I ask.

"I don't ma'am, but as soon as we get this taken care of, we will get you an update," the attendant says.

"Okay, Cigna . . . his card . . . yes, here it is . . . Richard Edward Keane . . . yes, full name . . . I am his wife . . . yes, of course . . ."

The questions seem to go on forever and I answer them on autopilot until finally she says, "Okay, that's it. Let me take you back to see your husband."

When I walk in the room, he is sitting up on the bed, dressed in a hospital gown, staring down at his hands. I see the confusion in his eyes, but also the trust as I rush over to him, kiss his forehead, hug him and hold his hand. I fight back the tears as I have never seen Dick look so vulnerable. It breaks my heart.

They run a battery of tests on Dick, which takes the entire morning. My brother, Steve, whom I called after we arrived at the hospital, joins me mid-morning and we wait for some word on what is going on, sitting on pins and needles for any news.

After they run what seems to be every test imaginable, Dr. Wolfe comes into Dick's room and pulls me aside.

"Dick has had a stroke," he says, getting right to the point. "He needs to stay with us for a few days so we can run some more tests, but he will survive. We won't know how much damage it has done until a few days pass and we can run some more tests."

"Survive?" I cry. "What do you mean survive? He could die?"

"Strokes can be very serious and we don't know the extent of the one that Dick's had yet, but, yes, I'm confident he will survive this," he responds somberly.

I am stunned and speechless at the idea that this could be life threatening. He was fine just last night, laughing and smiling without a care in the world. Now this!

"I'm going to have a neurologist come by in a few minutes and talk to you about his recovery, but we won't know the extent of the damage the stroke caused for a while," he continues. "Dr. Nelson is the best there is, so Dick will be in excellent hands. He can give you much more information after he examines Dick."

A few minutes later, the neurologist, Dr. Nelson, comes to see us and, after examining Dick, motions for me to follow him out of the room.

"Dick has suffered a stroke to the part of the brain that controls speech and memory," Dr. Nelson says. "It hasn't been very long since it happened so we don't know exactly what damage was done, but once you get him home, you can expect that he will have problems speaking, remembering things, putting complete thoughts together, following a conversation . . . those sorts of things. For him, it will be like listening to a foreign language. He may know what he wants to say but he won't be able to put it together right. It may be very frustrating for him . . . and for you."

I feel dizzy and sick just hearing Dr. Nelson's words. My mind starts to wander as he starts talking about the various treatments and therapies. How can this be? Dick is the ultimate communicator and now this is going to be taken away from him?

"This just isn't fair," I scream silently. "It just is not fair."

"Kris, are you with me?" Dr. Nelson asks. "Look, the brain is an incredible organ and it has the capability to do amazing things. But it's going to be difficult because he's going to have to relearn a lot of the things that you and I take for granted. There's no reason he can't recover from this and lead a normal and productive life. It just may take some time, but I am confident he will get there."

This is exactly what I need to hear. If there's a way to work through this, then we will just toughen up and do it. Dick is a fighter. I have no doubt that we'll get back for Dick the life that this stroke has temporarily taken from him. As I look at him resting in the hospital bed, all I can think is "Bring it on!" I love him so much, and there's no challenge he and I can't overcome together.

⸻ ⬩◈⬩ ⸻

It's been a week since Dick's stroke and my poor husband is clearly not himself. Dr. Nelson called this morning to tell me that after reviewing all the tests, he sees no reason why Dick can't have a complete recovery and, with occupational rehabilitation and speech therapy, he could be back to work in six months. Dr. Nelson explained that one area of his brain had been damaged by the stroke but that the brain is wired so incredibly that new connections are made. What was lost by the stroke can actually be relearned. Still, I look at Dick lying in bed and have my doubts. In the days since he's been home from the hospital, it's like the soul has been sucked out of him. He has no self-confidence; he can't formulate words or sentences; he has no energy and barely wants to get out of bed.

Seeing Dick like this kills me but I tell myself that I must be the strong one. I take Dr. Nelson's prognosis at face value and make myself believe that Dick will improve as time passes. I share the news about Dick's prognosis for recovery with my kids and Dick's family, and everyone is thrilled at the idea of having the old Dick back. We devote all of our energy to helping him relearn what had become disconnected in his mind as a result of the stroke. Our home soon resembles a kindergarten class as I label everything to try to trigger Dick's memory about people and events. A small sign saying "table" is taped to the kitchen table; one saying "refrigerator" on the refrigerator. I tape the names of his children and mine to the family photos that adorn the hallway.

I know he's trying but, because nothing seems to make any sense to him anymore, he withdraws into routine. I try to push him because I so desperately want my old husband back, but I know it wears him out. Anything that he can grasp and is familiar with is okay. Anything new and foreign is

185

problematic. Our daily routine of getting up, having breakfast, practicing our language therapy and other rote activities are fine. But, a visit from a friend he doesn't remember or a trip to a new doctor causes nothing but fear and panic. He gets very nervous and fidgety and pleads with me to cancel our new activity.

"Please, honey," he says, while shaking his head side to side. "I can't . . . don't want . . . please . . ."

I hold his hand, calm him down and talk him through things using words that I know he understands.

"Dick," I say, "look into my eyes . . . This is going to be okay."

We sit across from each other holding hands and slowly he calms down after hearing those words over and over again. And then we get back to our reading. Today it is the newspaper, word by word, sounding every word out and pronouncing them. He plays along like a good sport, but I can tell he doesn't understand what any of it means.

One of the most troubling developments and the most difficult to watch is how Dick has lost his self-confidence. He has become fearful, shy and unsociable, which is amazing for a man who never before demonstrated any of those qualities. In the process, he has become entirely dependent on me for everything, shadowing me like a child. It seems like our roles have shifted completely—where once he was my rock, my fearless, jolly, outgoing partner, now he's retreated into a shell of his former self. Still, he tries so hard. I admire him more and more each day as we work so hard to master tasks that only recently had been so easy for him.

Dick gets so sad and disheartened by his lack of progress and his constant state of confusion that I make little 3x5 cards with positive reinforcement messages. He keeps them in his shirt pocket; and when he gets particularly frustrated, I motion for him to pull out the cards. He points to the words and silently mouths, "Everything is okay. Happiness is inside me. I am very loved. I am on the road to recovery."

He then takes a deep breath, sighs, puts the cards back in his pocket and gets back to his work. My heart swells in admiration as I watch him seize control of himself and force himself back into the battle. I can't even imagine how it must feel for him. It just breaks my heart to see him this way. I love him so much.

All of the children—his and mine—help with reading lessons, going over flash cards with names of objects and working with a special computer program developed for stroke patients. We all want the old Dick back more than ever and we all do whatever we can to help him. Friends and family search on the Internet for information about his condition and forward it to me. I devour all of the new information and look into any leads that could ultimately help him. One is a research project at University of California, San Diego (UCSD), for people who have had strokes. I enroll Dick and we go religiously twice a week for a while.

Dr. Nelson also gives Dick homework. Last week it was remembering and repeating the phrase, "No ifs, ands or buts." The whole family helps him to memorize it. You would think it's the Gettysburg Address, but he is so proud when he successfully repeats it for Dr. Nelson a week later. For him it is a huge accomplishment. But this morning, after two weeks, and without the daily practice, he can no longer repeat the phrase. He says, "No buts . . ," or "No ands and no ifs . . ." but he can't put the whole thing together.

An unbelievable outpouring of love and support showers down on us every day via phone calls, cards and emails. If I didn't know before, I certainly understand now how loved Dick is by his friends, family and coworkers. Still, because Dick has such difficulty remembering so many things, it becomes a big trauma for him when his friends want to visit.

Just now, I got a call from Bill Nork, one of Dick's commercial real estate associates from the Bay Area.

"Kris, this is Bill," he says. "We'd like to come to San Diego to visit Dick next week. What day would work for you both? We'd like to take you guys to lunch. We want to catch up with our old buddy. How's he doing?"

"He's good, he's good," I say with some hesitance, "but one thing you have to know is that he can't remember things the way he used to, so he might not seem the same to you. We take things real slow. So, if he doesn't remember something, just pretend he does. What he still really understands is hugs, so just you guys coming to see him and giving him a big hug will mean the world to him. Oh, and don't be surprised if he cries a little. The stroke has loosened up the water works and he is a lot more sentimental."

We agree on next Tuesday. However, when I tell Dick, he immediately panics. I'm sure he's petrified of his friends seeing him in this diminished capacity over which he has so little control. Dick and I set out to make sure that doesn't happen. I know he can't remember names, so I make flash cards with photos of Bill and his wife, Susan, with their names written underneath. Then I make a very basic flow chart in great big letters, using different color ink for different criteria:

Bill Nork

CORNISH & CAREY

Emeryville

Best Friend

Wife Susan, 3 kids

By the time Bill arrives, Dick feels pretty confident that he remembers who Bill is and his relationship to him. It goes well for a while until Bill says, "Remember that incredible deal back in '89? That was classic Keane! And that party that you threw afterwards is still remembered by all of the guys in the office!"

Dick looks completely lost and I can tell he has no idea what they are talking about. Almost on cue, he reaches into his pocket and looks at his reinforcement cards. To try to calm him down, I chime in, "Gosh, it must have been great! Can you tell me about it since I wasn't there?"

That is all the prompting Bill needs to go into great detail about the events.

As I listen, I whisper key words into Dick's ear. "Oakland, big deal, you, lots of money, party . . ." He recognizes those words and smiles, nods his head and laughs, but I can tell he is getting frustrated. He abruptly excuses himself and goes upstairs.

I excuse myself, too, saying, "He gets really tired with visitors, so let me go check on him."

I follow him upstairs and find him sitting in the easy chair in our bedroom holding his head with tears running down his cheeks.

"What's wrong, sweetheart? Are you okay?" I ask, as I kneel down beside him.

Garbled words come out, "Dunno what deal . . . Bill . . . who . . ." No coherent sentences, just frustration. While he seems to remember Bill, he can't place anything Bill says in context. The look on his face makes it seem like he is so close to understanding, like it's something right there in front of him that moves farther away every time he grasps for it. It's heartbreaking to watch, and I muster all the strength and composure I have to not break down in tears with him.

When we get back downstairs, I try to think of new tactics and strategies to help him. As Bill tells more stories, I repeat key words to him to try to trigger some memory. But, just the words, "Remember, Dick, when we . . .?" triggers anxiety that tenses up his entire body. I sit next to him, hold him close to me, hold his hand and whisper in his ear, "Calm down, honey. Calm down." He tries to appear engaged and his friends are sure he is reliving those events with them. He is very happy because they never know that he really doesn't understand what they are talking about. By the time his friends leave to go back to the Bay Area, Dick is exhausted, completely drained from having to put up a façade all afternoon. The stress completely wipes him out and he naps for hours.

As I lie next to him and watch him sleep, I realize that Dick is no longer a source of support or my rock to lean on. Instead, he is a frightened child and it is my responsibility to comfort him, console him and care for him. In every sense of the word, I am his caregiver. I love Dick so much that it doesn't matter to me. I am honored to be with him in any way for this part of his journey. I love being by his side, but it is different and certainly challenging. The words "in sickness and in health" keep coming into my mind. Because of our love and commitment to each other, I will always be there for him, but I never thought this type of thing would happen to me. Does anyone?

———·•◈•·———

A small part of me, way down deep, is angry, sad and bitter that this has happened to us. Sometimes the little voice in my head gets the best of me and screams out, "Why, why is this happening to us? We just found each other!" I feel cheated, like I was given a glimpse of paradise only to have it ripped away. When I open that door, even a little, all of the bitter and angry feelings push through and the pity party starts. The tears trickle down my face and quickly turn into uncontrollable sobs.

"Why me? It's not fair. It's just not fair! I finally find my soul mate and now this happens . . . it is so unfair. What if he doesn't get better? What will we do? Neither of us is working. What's going to happen to us?"

I don't even like to think about that scenario, so I try my best not to, but sometimes I can't control the panic. It seizes my mind, tensing my body so tight that I can barely move. I allow myself a good cry, never around Dick, of course, and then, as the sobbing subsides and the tears stop falling, I bring myself back to my reality.

"Breathe, Kris, just breathe," I tell myself. And slowly I loosen up until it goes away . . . for now. Focusing on these negative feelings gets me nowhere. My life is what it is right now and I have to tackle each day with renewed energy. Again, I focus on my daily meditation for my own well-being. Without that downtime, without that silence, I know that I could not go on.

"Dick has to get better," I pray, pushing every negative thought out of my mind. My daily mantra becomes, "Today is all we have and everything is okay." I say it over and over again to make sure that we are surrounded by positive, curative energy.

An interesting human phenomenon I often ponder is that no matter how much upheaval and hardship I have been through, I always think I will be okay—that I've survived the worst, so it must be all downhill from here. After all, I deserve it! But it just doesn't always work out that way . . . life is never boring and you never know what will happen next.

"Boy," I think, "that is the story of my life!"

———— ◆ ————

Today, December 28, is our fifth wedding anniversary and Dick can't even get out of bed. It's hard to understand what is ailing him because he can't communicate with me very well; but, he keeps pointing at his stomach and grimacing, so I'm assuming his sensitive stomach is acting up. I try not to feel sorry for myself as I celebrate my anniversary over dinner with Annette, Nicholas, Jonathan and Dick's brother, Bill, instead of my husband, who gets out of bed only a few times all day to go to the bathroom. I miss the way it used to be and the fun we used to have; fun, however, doesn't seem to be a part of our lives anymore and that makes me so sad. I realize that time is passing and I can tell that Dr. Nelson's six-month prognosis for full recovery becomes more unlikely every day.

Dick spends most of his time watching television. Because of the brain damage from the stroke, he no longer is able to follow the plotlines of a television show or a movie. I imagine it's a bit like watching a foreign film without any subtitles. So thank heaven for sports. He can easily follow football and baseball. He doesn't have to hear the calls of the game to watch and follow what is happening. He doesn't even care (or maybe doesn't even know) if a game is an old replay on ESPN Classic. He only watches the game for the moment—not in terms of wins or losses, standings or playoffs—just for the joy of the game and maybe to pass the time.

It's New Year's Eve and Dick's stomach still bothers him. I'm thinking it must be the stomach flu or something like that as I've never seen his sensitive stomach problems last so long. I try to create a festive atmosphere for us to ring in the New Year but Dick is feeling so miserable that our festivities boil down to a nice dinner at home and climbing into bed to watch people on the East Coast ring in 2002 on the television. Shortly after we watch the ball drop in Times Square, Dick begins to fall asleep. I lie right next to him, hold him tight and whisper in his ear, "2002 is going to be a great year for us, you just watch." But as I lie here and watch him fade off to sleep, I can't help but wonder what 2002 really holds in store for us.

———————◦•◦•◦———————

Dick isn't getting better; in fact, he seems to be getting worse. He constantly grimaces and points to his stomach, but he still can't articulate exactly what he is feeling. Whatever it is, it sure doesn't seem like the stomach flu to me. And whatever it is, it's draining all of Dick's energy. We have had to cancel appointments with the speech therapist, and Dick just can't seem to muster the energy to do the speech and memory exercises at home. So, our progress has been very limited on getting him back to his old self.

Finally, I call Dr. Wolfe to see if he has any suggestions about Dick's stomach problems. He schedules several appointments for Dick with specialists, but they can't figure out what's wrong with him. Dick's inability to tell the doctors what he's feeling only compounds all of our frustrations. Finally, Dr. Wolfe orders a CT Scan of Dick's abdomen. A couple of days later, I get a call from Dr. Wolfe's assistant.

"Hi, Kris, it's Rebecca," she says. "Dr. Wolfe wants to see you and Dick tomorrow morning. He has cleared his schedule for the morning. What time can you come in?"

"He's cleared his schedule?" I ask, my mind spinning with possibilities. My stomach feels queasy and I get lightheaded and grab the kitchen counter to steady myself. "Why? What's going on? Can I talk to Dr. Wolfe?"

"He's with patients all afternoon, but I can ask him to give you a call later if you want."

"Yes. Definitely. I can't wait until tomorrow."

As I hang up the phone, my mind starts racing. Is this related to the stroke? Is he not going to recover? Is this something different and more serious? What the heck is happening? I try to occupy the time with busy work—helping Annette with her homework, making dinner, watching *Oprah*—but I can't escape this foreboding feeling that Dr. Wolfe has very bad news for us.

When he finally calls a little before 7:00, I run downstairs and outside to the backyard while Dick watches television in bed upstairs. I close the door behind me, try to keep my composure and get straight to the point.

"Thanks for calling me back tonight, Dr. Wolfe. I know you know that I lost my first husband ten years ago. When your assistant called earlier to schedule the appointment and said you had cleared your schedule, I got so scared and didn't feel like I could wait until tomorrow. Please tell me what is going on. What's wrong with my husband?" I ask, gasping for breath and fighting back the tears.

"I understand what you're going through, Kris," he says, and then pauses. "But, you must understand that my responsibility as Dick's doctor is to give him the results. I'm going to tell you, but you have to promise to let me tell him tomorrow. This news has to come from me, not you? Do you understand?"

"Of course, of course," I say, unable to hold back the tears any longer. "Just please tell me what's going on?"

"Okay," he says. I can almost hear him thinking this through on the other end of the line as he pauses for several seconds before continuing, "Dick has stage IV pancreatic cancer, and most likely has only about three months to live."

The words just hover around me for a few moments —did I hear him right? Dick is going to die? My husband is going to die? I hardly hear the rest of the things he's saying . . . everything starts to spin around me . . .

"I will set you up with an oncologist . . . you need to get in to see him ASAP . . , chemo may help to reduce the pain . . ."

"Pain," I mumble, still reeling from his words.

And then his final words truly bring it all home, "I'm so sorry, Kris, but there is no cure for this type of cancer. It's just a matter of time. We can only try to make him as comfortable as possible. I'm so sorry."

As I hang up the phone, I crumple onto the lounge in the backyard, tears streaming down my face. It feels like the entire world has stopped around me and the only thing I can think, feel or hear is ". . . three months to live . . ." The stroke was one thing, but I can't be losing a second husband; especially Dick, the love of my life, my soul mate, my other half—and now I only have three months left with him.

How do I face him? He's upstairs watching television, with no clue that he is so sick. Given the effects of the stroke, will he even understand it? Suddenly, relearning to read or being able to call a chair "a chair" or his glasses "glasses" instead of "lights" doesn't seem to matter much. I compose myself and go back upstairs, but just the sight of him sends me reeling; so, I slip into the bathroom, close the door, turn on the water to create some noise and start to sob again.

A box of Kleenex later, I slide next to him on the bed, lie beside him and hold his hand as we watch television together. As he drifts off to sleep, my thoughts turn to me. How am I going to make it through this again? How am I going to deal with the loneliness, the despair, the emptiness of losing a second husband? I think back to my mantra from Archbishop Oscar Romero that I relied upon so heavily after Alfonso died, "I can't; You must; I'm yours; Show me the way."

"I have to stay in the present," I tell myself. My heart aches—it physically hurts—and I think that I'm going to die, too. I vow to make his last months the best possible under the circumstances. Dick is alive now and I have to stay strong for him. As I start to cry, I realize I have no idea how.

———◆•◆•◆———

As we drive to see Dr. Wolfe, Dick asks, "Where are we going?"

"We're going to see Dr. Wolfe, honey, to get the results of all those tests they've been doing," I say, really trying to fake it and not let on how worried I am.

Dick points to his stomach and I nod.

When we arrive, Dr. Wolfe takes us both into his office and puts Dick on the exam table. He glimpses at me for a split second before turning towards Dick.

"Dick, I need to tell you some things about what's wrong with your stomach and what we found out from all those tests that we ran," he says, pointing to Dick's stomach. "Is that okay with you?"

Dick looks at me and nods.

"Unfortunately, your stomach problem is very serious. It's cancer. And it's a type of cancer that can't be cured. It's terminal. You have pancreatic cancer, which is a really bad type of cancer to get because it's usually so far advanced. Dick, I want you to listen to me very closely because this is very important. There is no cure for this, which means you don't have very long to live."

Dick looks at me with a puzzled look on his face as a tear forms and streams down his face. I reach over and hold him to me like a mother holds a scared child, but no one is there to hold me. He looks like he's going to faint or fall off the table, so I hold him up. All the while, all I can think is, "Oh my God, not again."

Dr. Wolfe presents us with two equally unappealing options, "There are really only a couple of choices here," he says. "We can do chemotherapy, which will ease your pain and prolong . . ."

Before he can finish, Dick starts shaking his head up and down rapidly in agreement.

". . . or we can just let the disease run its course and try to make you as comfortable as possible."

Upon hearing this, Dick starts shaking his head side to side to signal his opposition to the latter choice.

"Okay," Dr. Wolfe says, "then we need to get you down to the lab for some blood work right away so you can get started on the chemo."

And just like that, we are done. I look into Dick's eyes for some indication that he understands the severity of what Dr. Wolfe has told him. The tears start rolling down his cheeks as he holds me tight to him and refuses to let go. We stand there interlocked for what seems like an eternity. He understands. I know he does. Somehow I have to pull myself together and be strong.

Our lives devolve into a series of doctor appointments and chemotherapy sessions. Dick battles through it the best he can, but is so uncomfortable most of the time that it kills me when there's nothing I can do to ease his pain. I do some research online about pancreatic cancer and discover that it is one of the most painful and least curable types of cancer. In medical circles, it's sometimes called "the silent killer" because it often does not cause symptoms at the outset and the later symptoms, like Dick's, can be due to a variety of different ailments. As a result, it is very rarely cured because by the time it is detected, it's usually too late.

As news of Dick's terminal condition spreads, the outpouring of love from Dick's friends and family overwhelms us. Everyone loves and cherishes Dick, and all of his friends want to visit for a last time to let him know how important he has been to them. The bonds of love that Dick has created throughout his life with such a diverse group of people in so many different walks of life are a testament to the type of life he has lived and the type of man he is. Every day I understand more and more how special this man is and the impact he has had on so many.

The love and support manifests itself in various ways. Most surprisingly, Dick's friends in the Bay Area chip in to hire a personal chef to provide nutritional meals for Dick, me and the family. Every week, carefully planned gourmet meals, complete with instructions for heating and serving, are delivered and stored in my refrigerator. Each meal is labeled with the day it is to be eaten and even includes special treats for the children. I am floored by their thoughtfulness and generosity. What a relief it is for me, for Dick, for our families. The depth of their love for Dick has moved me deeply, and I will never forget how considerate and compassionate they have been to try to ease our burden. I have no way to thank them enough except to someday do the same for someone I love.

The chemo, the pain, the ever changing list of medications, the visitors, the meals, the confusion and the fear of the inevitable . . . all become a blur, each day running into the next and making for sleepless nights and a cloud of doom around me endlessly. I feel like I am barely holding myself together with invisible Band-Aids, safety pins and rubber bands, all ready to break at any moment.

Where is God? Where is my faith? Where is the inner strength that I have worked so hard to achieve? Where is the courage to face this horrible turn of events? Where is my God who said that everything was perfect just the way it is? Every inch of my soul screams, "No, it isn't!"

When I think of our plight, of my plight, despair creeps into my being and the only way I manage to get through the day is to stay in the present. For now, Dick is alive; for now, be strong—he needs me to face the chemo;

for now, be gracious—his friends and family want to be with him . . . and I do love him so much . . . he is here for now . . . with me . . . for now . . .

For Labor Day, we decide to drive up to Santa Barbara to spend the weekend with Dick's daughter, Sarah, for her wedding anniversary. I know this is our last trip together and probably his farewell to his beloved daughter. Just yesterday, we received word from the oncologist that Dick's results are not good and that the chemo has run its course. So, no more chemo means the pain will start to take over. Palliative care in controlling the pain is all that medical science has left to offer my poor husband. The doctors give us their blessing as well as some medication in case the pain gets worse during our three days in Santa Barbara, but there is no mistaking that the end is near.

Good-byes are always painful, but I have never felt such despair as when Dick and I stroll along a secluded beach together at sunset—alone . . . just the two of us. We stop in a private little cove and turn to each other. No words are spoken. I know. He knows. The end is near. He doesn't want to leave. I can't bear the thought of him leaving. The feeling is so overwhelming that we just look deep into each other's eyes and then hug. We can't let go. I sob and Dick comforts me.

Even through all of this, he is still so strong. I feel his arms around me and I keep sobbing until no more comes out. He keeps hugging me and I feel his spirit melt into mine. He is with me now and will always be with me. I know that. But, I selfishly want more. In silence, we look longingly into each other's eyes as our spirits refuse to let go.

The first of October has arrived; the day I have been dreading. Even though I knew it was inevitable, part of me was still holding out for a miracle. But the reality is that Dick has deteriorated to the point that I can no longer care for him adequately. So, I make the painful, yet necessary, decision to place Dick in hospice care. This morning, I tell Dick we are going to another doctor's appointment, when, in reality, I am taking him to his final resting place. As I pull out of the driveway, I realize Dick will never physically be with me in our home again. I do my best to hold back the tears, but Dick notices something is wrong. He reaches over to hold my hand as we pull out of the driveway.

"I love you so much," I whisper to him through the tears.

He just smiles and grips my hand a little tighter and puts it on his heart.

San Diego Hospice, an incredible group of caring, compassionate people, takes over Dick's day-to-day needs. I spend sixteen hours a day there, and only make it through this traumatic time because I'm confident in the knowledge that the hospice workers are doing everything in the their power to make Dick as comfortable as possible during this last part of his journey. As I come closer to the day I will lose my best friend and the love of my life, they are a great support to me as well.

Losing Dick to pancreatic cancer is a debilitating process that tests my inner resolve every day. A piece of me feels like it is being ripped off with every new crisis that he faces. His valiant fight to stay alive and combat the pain ends in conscious sedation. It breaks my heart as I give the doctor permission to sedate him. I know it is near the end and soon my dearest will be rid of all of the tortures that he has been put through. But then again, I will be alone—the grief swallows me whole, leaving me gasping for air. I can't sleep or eat. I just live to get back by his side every morning.

Dick died this afternoon, October 20, 2002. He was surrounded by loved ones all afternoon; but, as soon as everyone took a break to grab a pizza snack, he knew it was time. Without fanfare, without dramatics, he just closed his eyes and it was over. I am sure Dick's spirit has moved on to a better place. Me? I am left in a deep crevice with darkness closing in and little hope of ever seeing light again. I foolishly thought I would feel some sense of relief when it was finally over. But, as I lie in bed tonight, after saying good-bye forever to Dick this afternoon, I feel no solace even though I know his pain is over. Tears . . . unending tears that belie the depth of my grief, my helplessness, my darkness, my solitude. How can I survive this? I am not even sure I want to.

As I sit here in the first pew of Saint Thérèse of Carmel Church for Dick's funeral, I get a sense of déjà vu. Eleven years have passed since Alfonso died. This time around, I suppose I had some time to get used to the idea of losing my husband instead of finding out as I did with Alfonso. Still, the finality is setting in with no mercy.

This morning when I woke up, I rolled over and instinctively moved to cuddle next to Dick and give him a good-morning kiss. There was nothing there, just an empty place in our bed. I immediately broke down and sobbed as I saw the picture of the two of us in San Francisco on the nightstand. No more good times. No more love of my life.

Jonathan is one of several speakers at the funeral, bless his heart. With all the strength and courage he can muster, he walks up to the podium and reads a letter that he has written to Dick. There is not a dry eye in the church. Jonathan talks about what Dick meant to him, how he had become a man because of Dick's influence. He expresses his undying love and admiration for him—as a dad, as a man, as a friend, mentor and the best human being he has ever met. As he is about to end, he begins to break down, the tears pouring down his face and the words catching in his throat. Unable to continue, he just stands there. His two older brothers, Alfonso and Carl, walk up to the altar, put their arms around him and encourage him to finish.

"Save me a spot in your next foursome. I'll be there. Love always, Jonathan."

Together, the three brothers embrace and take their seats with the rest of the family. Jonathan's message touches everyone. What an incredible person Dick was—what a mark he had made—and his death will be a devastating loss for all of us.

Finally, Dick's best friend, John Landry, gets up and, with a quivering voice, talks about his relationship with Dick, the many years of companionship and the loss he already feels. He closes with a fitting tribute—a passage from Robert Frost's poem "The Road Not Taken":

> Two roads diverged in a wood, and I—
> I took the one less traveled by,
> And that has made all the difference.

Dick's friends in the Bay Area, some of whom couldn't make it down to the funeral in San Diego, want to throw him a final farewell so they can say good-bye to their beloved friend. I understand and appreciate their needs, but having been through so much, I'm dreading the trip up to the Bay Area for the event at the Orinda Country Club where Dick was a member. With all the strength and courage I can muster, I board a Southwest Airlines jet with Jonathan, Nicholas, Annette and my brother, Steve. Looking out at the clouds through the airplane window, I picture Dick, free of his earthly burdens, floating from cloud to cloud.

As a fitting farewell to a man who loved to golf so much, Jonathan and Steve, along with Dick's sons, Dayton and Kevin, and several of Dick's friends, play golf during the day at the Orinda Country Club course where Dick played so often. When they get back to the hotel, Jonathan pulls me aside as we are getting ready for the event.

"I had such a radical experience out there today, Mom," he says. "It was like Dick was right there with us at each hole. I couldn't concentrate, I didn't play well, but I didn't really care. I just didn't want it to end."

"I know, Jonny," I say. "It doesn't feel real. I can't believe he's gone."

We just stand there and hug for a while, trying to keep him with us as long as we can.

They've asked me to say a few words at the gathering tonight, but I don't think I can do it. I suggest instead that they play a song that has been summing up my feelings the last few weeks and months. As I sit here in this beautiful room, looking out at the East Bay hills sprawling in the distance, tears flow down my cheeks as I hear Josh Grobran sing "To Where You Are."

Who can say for certain
Maybe you're still here
I feel you all around me
Your memory, so clear

Deep in the stillness
I can hear you speak
You're still an inspiration
Can it be
That you are mine
Forever love
And you are watching over me from up above . . .

"Good-bye, my love," I whisper through the tears. "Good-bye."

CHAPTER 12
the aftermath

As I wake this morning, I instinctively roll over and reach to my right to put my arm around Dick. It's been nearly two years since he died and I still can't shake the habit. Two years! Has it really been two years? Can that be possible?

I wish I could say that the last two years have seen me come to terms with Dick's death, continue to evolve as a spiritual being and move forward in my life in a healthy manner. They have not. To the contrary, nothing could be further from the truth. I honestly don't remember much of it. It's as if I've sleepwalked for the last two years through a fog that refuses to lift. There is no light, only darkness and emptiness, tears and depression, confusion and despair.

I have pleaded, "God, please help me," but nothing, no answer, just more darkness, tears, then sobs and more despair. "Help me please. Help me . . ." I always whisper through the sobs, to no avail, and then more darkness. Dick's death has felt like part of me has been amputated—I can still feel his presence even though he physically isn't here. That makes it even more painful as all I'm left with are the memories, the pain and the bitterness. I just haven't been able to cope with the loss of my love, my soul mate, the one I had been waiting my whole life for. He is gone, and my life is in disarray.

This grief has encompassed my entire being, leaving me with little energy for anything else. And, after nearly two years of this, I'm exhausted. As I lay here this morning, I know in my heart that I have to break out of this somehow; I have to get better. I've been under water for two years with no idea of how to reach the surface, but now I know I need to breathe. What should I do? What can I do? What do I want to do? Certainly not anything too difficult. Anything too hard . . . well, I just couldn't even begin to face. So I grapple with these questions, wait and hope that the answer will come in some fashion.

During the past two years, San Diego Hospice has diligently kept in touch with me. Part of their mission is to make sure that the surviving spouse is doing okay. Their persistence has been impressive, particularly since I never once answered their calls or returned their messages. I can't remember how many times I would get home to find messages on the answering machine saying, "Hi, Kris, this is Susan (or Joanie, or Linda, or Sandy) from San Diego Hospice . . ." I would automatically erase the message before it even finished.

"I don't care; I don't want to hear it . . . leave me alone!"

A couple of days ago, however, I actually listened to the message. "Hi, Kris, this is Judy from San Diego Hospice just calling to see how you are doing and to see if you would like to join us for a new group that we are putting together for grief therapy. Our new group is scheduled to start in about two weeks and we have a few openings left. The group is formed of ten to fifteen men and women in your age group who have lost their spouses to illness, and want to be able to heal and accept the changes in their lives. Call me and I can tell you more about the program."

"Changes," I thought, "now that's an understatement. They have no idea."

This time, however, I did actually write the phone number down on a piece of paper, but I can't bring myself to call; so, I've just been carrying the slip of paper in my pocket for a few days. Each time I think about calling, I convince myself that I'm not ready, that I need to keep holding on to the pain. Still, here I am in the kitchen, staring at the phone thinking maybe it's time I do this. Being with people around my age who are going through similar pain almost seems comforting.

"Oh, for goodness sake," I say to myself, "just dial the phone."

With a shot of adrenaline, I dial the number ready to either hang up or leave a message when Judy answers. I am so taken back by her warm and caring voice that the dam bursts and, before I know it, I'm telling her everything. I can't believe I am doing this, but I just keep talking . . . for over an hour. She listens and listens, and I feel her compassion through the phone line. She is so understanding that I just want to reach through the phone and hug her. I need this. I need to feel that someone knows what I am going through. I need to feel understood.

The next thing I know, I've signed up for the grief therapy program. Judy faxes me a contract that requires me to commit to attend ten sessions and not to miss any sessions unless I am sick, and as she says, "Sick does not mean 'just not feeling up to it.'" This is a huge commitment . . . Yikes! Can I do this? I question myself, but with a shaky hand I sign the contract and fax it back to Judy before I can chicken out.

"Well, good for me," I think to myself as I imagine patting my own back. Maybe, just maybe this will help me. Oh God, I can only hope that it does.

<hr />

I feel like I am driving to my own execution. Every freeway exit presents a potential escape route. What had I been thinking? I signed the consent form, but what was I thinking? There is still time to chicken out as I drive down Interstate 5. I can get off here and go shopping. No wait, I'll get off at the next exit and visit my mother. Yet, I resist the temptation and find myself pulling into the driveway at San Diego Hospice. I turn off the car and put my head slowly down on the steering wheel. The tears slowly roll down my cheeks as I think of the reason I am here.

This is where my sweet, dear husband, the love of my life, died. Two years, two long years of trying to make my way through the darkness has led me back to where it all started. I haven't been back to this place since the day Dick died. I can't go on living in this bleak limbo. I know life can hold more and somehow I have to figure out how to make that happen for me. So, I get out of the car, lock the doors and slowly turn towards the front door of the Hospice. I take a few small steps forward and realize that I need to do this. I want to live again, to feel again, to see bright colors again, to see light. I open the door and walk in.

I am greeted politely by the receptionist, who guides me to the back of the building where the group is beginning to assemble. Everyone mostly keeps to themselves and I decide there's no reason for me to disturb the peace so I quietly find a seat in a circle of chairs, put my head down and pretend to check my cell phone for missed calls or messages. I want to look busy so no one will approach me. My façade of control is very fragile and I know I am barely holding it together. One mention of "death, cancer, husband, Dick, love" and the dam will break. So for now, it's better to steer away from all of those subjects for as long as possible.

Finally, after what seems like hours, Judy walks in and asks everyone to be seated. By this time, some of the people are actually speaking to each other, socializing it seems, which, in my state, I find a disturbing trend. I keep my head down, but steal glances around the room. Everyone seems normal enough, I guess. Fortunately, I don't have a lot of time to think about those things because Judy introduces herself and gives us a brief overview of what the ten-week program will cover.

"This is a sharing experience," she says. "By sharing our stories, our lives, our lost spouses with the group and actively participating in the exercises, the hope is that you all will get further down the road to accepting all these changes in your lives."

"Hmmm," I think, "sounds okay to me."

The word "changes" does give me pause though. I'm sick of change. The past twelve years have been nothing but change for me. I am sick of adapting, sick of being a strong person, sick of figuring out the "whys" and the "what fors" of life. Why can't things just be easy for once? Everyone else seems to have such an easier life than I've had. I start to fall back into my pity party when Judy interrupts my thoughts.

"I want you all to introduce yourselves to the group and tell a little bit about why you're here," she says.

I hold my breath. No way am I going first. I look down, then look away and try to avert Judy's eyes. I shrink back into my chair and try to look invisible. Thankfully, someone else volunteers.

"I'm Joe," he says, "and my wife died of cancer nine months ago. She left me alone with two teenage daughters and I'm at a total loss as to how to handle the girls, how to manage the household all without her. I just don't know how to do it. It's just so hard . . ."

He trails off as tears stream down his face. All of us cry with him and share his pain with knowing nods and soft whispers of comfort and condolence. Each person who follows tells his or her own story and is received with sorrow, understanding and tears. We know. We understand. We can relate.

Then suddenly, there is no one left but me. No place to hide now. For the first time since the session had started, I lift my head. I take in a breath, look slowly around the room making eye contact with each person, then exhale and begin my story. The tears start to flow as I tell them of my life in Mexico, our lifestyle and my husband, all leading up to March of 1991.

". . . We had finally had our little girl, after having five beautiful, handsome boys. We were so happy, so young and had so much to look forward to. March 12, 1991, changed all that."

The avalanche, his death, my sorrow . . . through sobs, I tell them of how it felt to be thirty-eight years old, a widow with six kids in a foreign country, with a greedy, evil brother-in-law who ultimately threatened my life to get what he wanted. I try to keep breathing and control the sobs, while I explain my slow process of healing and moving back to San Diego. I pause to blow my nose and look around the circle. Everyone is captivated by my story, but more than a few have somewhat confused looks on their faces as if to say, "What are you doing in this support group?"

"And then, in December 1994, at a La Jolla Country Day football game, the love of my life walked into the stadium and sat right behind me. I knew almost from that moment that he was the one, my soul mate."

The little control that I had is lost as I sob uncontrollably. Everyone sits in silence, spell bound, watching me. They wait while I try to compose myself. The woman in the chair next to me puts her arm around me and tries to calm me. Through the tears, I whisper the story . . . retelling, reliving those happy eight years, our marriage, our love, our relationship, our blended family, the weddings, graduations, the celebrations that we so happily shared. Then I break down again. Judy gets up, walks over to me and tells me to breathe. I nod at her and regain enough composure to get out a few more words, "Stroke . . . pancreatic cancer . . . died here . . ."

I can't continue so Judy mercifully announces that we will take a break. It takes me a few minutes to calm down. I feel so drained, like I've just run a marathon. During the break, nearly everyone comes by to offer condolences and support. Finally, Judy asks us to take our seats again and asks if anyone wants to share anything else. I have nothing left to say, but one of the older women in the group raises her hand. She looks like she could be a shaman by her dress and her gray hair loosely pulled back in a long braid. She lost her husband of twenty years to cancer and, as she turns to me, I can see in her eyes that she understands the pain and torment that cancer brings to a family, to a spouse and to the stricken person. She had been though the chemo, the nausea, the hair loss, the caregiver's impotence to take away the pain. With one look I know she understands.

"Please don't take this the wrong way, Kris," she says as she looks at me. "I mean this not to hurt you, but just to acknowledge you."

"Acknowledge me," I think. "What does she mean?"

"I want to say that you are our . . ." and she points slowly to everyone in the circle as she pauses. "You are our worst nightmare come true."

I'm aghast. What does she mean? I hold my breath and wait for her to finish.

She looks at me again, her eyes filled with compassion. "We all have been through hell and back in losing our spouses. But the thought that we could ever find and love someone else, start over again, love again, and then go through this pain of loss again, is everyone's worst nightmare. Going through this painful experience of loss once makes us feel like we have paid our dues, like we will never have to do it again."

She pauses for a few moments to gather herself.

"And yet you, my dear, did. God bless you. Our hearts go out to you. You've had it double."

She turns to the group, and I notice that they are all nodding in agreement.

"We admire your grit and none of us can imagine the depth of the pain you have been through."

With that, she gets up, crosses the circle and gives me a tearful, but reassuring hug. Her words and her hug cause something to shift inside of me. These people understand. They know what I'm going through and I know what they are going through. They are acknowledging my pain and tremendous loss, and I theirs. It feels good. It feels right. It feels like finally something is starting to cover and heal my gaping wound. Maybe this is the start of my healing process. For the first time, I feel validated, like a thousand-pound weight has been lifted from my shoulders. Oh thank you, God.

These sessions become the first step in my path towards healing. I fulfill my contract and attend all of the remaining sessions, all of which help me come to terms with my grief. It seems so simple; but, in reality, it has been incredibly difficult. In the end, this shared sense of loss, and the mutual acknowledgement and validation, are precisely the healing remedies I needed.

During the two years after Dick's death, my youngest children suffered with their grief as well. It was an immense challenge for me to be able to support and aid them in their recovery when I felt so incapacitated. I was basically just covering up holes. They were in pain just as I was. After all, they had lost a second father and, really, the only father they knew very well.

The boys dealt with their grief through denial and acting out their sorrow. Jonathan quit playing golf, saying he couldn't muster the interest without Dick around, and later dropped out of Cal State San Marcos. Nicholas had some behavioral issues and couldn't focus at school. I did my best but I realized there is only so much you can do to help someone. You can support them, as I tried to do with my boys, yet they have to make their own decisions, heal in their own way and according to their own time frame. I couldn't live their lives for them, but I could love them with everything I had and make sure they knew they were not alone.

Annette took Dick's death very hard as well. She had nightmares and regularly would wind up in my bed in the middle of the night. I did my best to spend as much time with her as possible, to help her through this difficult time. Late last year, we decided to join a mother-daughter philanthropic group called National Charity League (NCL) and it has proven to be a wonderful and rewarding experience for both of us. We do charity work with other mom and daughter teams, including decorating the cancer wards at Children's Hospital to try to create an upbeat environment.

Seeing these young children fighting their own cancer battles with their loving families at their side has helped put our own pain into perspective. Giving our time and energy helps Annette and I put aside our own pain by being compassionate to others who need help from people who have been through the same kind of pain. We can acknowledge and validate their pain, and in helping them heal, also heal ourselves. Annette and I strengthen our already tight bond as we cry with the family members, and offer our comfort and understanding. It's not easy, but the reward is great.

Besides the emotional and healing experiences that Annette and I are having together, I also begin making some new and wonderful friends through NCL. "Women who support women" is a mantra in NCL and I find myself surrounded by a group of strong, independent women who want to be there for me when I need a friend.

The organization is exactly what I need. I love the women, I love the purpose, I love the meetings, I love that it doesn't matter that I don't have a husband, I love the fun activities, I love the impact we make and I love the interaction with my daughter during her difficult teen years. NCL becomes an integral part of our lives. It is wonderful and I feel like it's a big part of my coming back to life. When you love what you are doing, joy has a way of seeping back into your being and you transform.

I also decide it's time to go back to work. During Dick's illness, I stopped working to care for him. Dick was very generous in providing for me and my family, but if I don't get back to work soon, I will blow through it all. I will be "out of business" as he used to say about my spending habits. So it's time.

I start back working a few hours a day and then build back up to full time over a couple months. I interpret mainly for injured Latino workers who are thrown into the Workers' Compensation system after they are injured on the job. My clients visit court-appointed doctors, get treatment, even surgeries, all without understanding English. So many of them are confused and frightened, not only by their medical prospects (many have never even been to a doctor in their entire lives), but also by the Workers' Compensation system. I become their lifeline.

Through me, they begin to understand what their injuries mean, what their proposed treatment will be and what their recovery prospects are. These people are at their most vulnerable, injured and unable to understand what their doctors are prescribing. I do my best to help them. However, my thoughts inevitably wander back to Dick and what he must have gone through after his stroke, when he fought so gallantly to understand.

Some days when I go to work feeling particularly sorry for myself, I listen to my clients' stories and suddenly my life doesn't look so bad. Incidents of poverty, ignorance, prejudice, discrimination and abuse pepper all their stories. It breaks my heart to translate for a 50-year-old man who had heat stroke resulting in brain surgery and permanent disabilities, all from picking melons in 120-degree weather day after day. Or the man who was picking avocados when he was struck by lightning, causing electricity to jolt his entire body since he couldn't escape from his steel-toed work boots.

In another case, a construction worker who had finished high school with great difficulty, so that he could better provide for his family, was hit in the head by a huge metal girder beam while working on one of the new high-rise hotels in downtown San Diego. He was so severely injured that he ended up spending his days coloring and watching cartoons with his three little children. His mental capacity was reduced to that of a four year old, but his anxiety level was out of control. The State of California paid his wife to care for him because no one else could handle the enormity of the responsibility, only someone who loved him. Helping these people becomes medicine for my soul.

All of these experiences point to a larger truth: No one is exempt from hard and trying times in their lifetimes. I remember how, after Alfonso died, I came to the conclusion that it is not the cards you are dealt, but how you play them. Everyone is dealt different cards, but cards nonetheless. Service to others is one way of playing those cards in a healing way.

When I was a child, my father used to always tell us this wise old saying: "I thought that I was down and out because I had no shoes, then I turned and the man beside me had no feet." Hard times teach us compassion. Through compassion we place ourselves into someone else's shoes, acknowledge and validate them, and align ourselves with them. It's only then that we slowly begin to realize that we are all one in this crazy life, and that we can make it through . . . together.

CHAPTER 13

the admonition

"Hey, Kris," I hear Jamie, my dear friend from NCL, say over the phone, "Gretchen's invited me and two friends to go on her boat for a harbor cruise tonight at sunset. She and her husband have hired a chef to cook dinner for us. How cool is that? I asked Amy if she wants to come with us, so you have to say yes!"

I don't have to think twice about the answer, "Oh my gosh, Jamie, that sounds fabulous. When and where?"

The thought of a relaxing cruise around the harbor with my good friends, nice wine, a great dinner and wonderful conversation sounds so enticing. What could be better? Things have been so hectic with work; and, at home, it's been an emotional roller coaster with Annette graduating from high school and soon heading off to Santa Clara University to begin college. I was so glad that she chose Santa Clara and that they had chosen her. Her years of hard work had really paid off as she was awarded a full tuition scholarship. Best of all, she will only be a short plane ride away, so I can visit whenever I want; although, since that's the last thing a college freshman wants to hear, I've decided against sharing that with her.

With Annette out of the house, I will have a (mostly) empty nest for the first time in my life. It's hard to believe that I have been parenting non-stop for thirty-four years, and often under difficult circumstances. I have to admit, the responsibility of raising six kids has worn me out. Having the day-to-day parenting duties off my platter sounds so relaxing. I know it's probably not going to be like that, but still, a girl can dream! The one thing I do know is that tonight will be nice and relaxing.

Jamie picks me up, we swing by for Amy and, before we know it, we are on the dock looking for Gretchen's boat. We don't have to look for long because before we have walked more than a few steps, we hear her scream, "Hey guys, over here!"

The three of us look up in amazement at her beautiful sixty-foot yacht. David and Gretchen are waiting for us with open arms and a glass of Veuve Clicquot, my favorite champagne. I can tell right away it's going to be a fun night. Gretchen and David use their boat as a second home. They often sail around the San Diego coast, dock near downtown and take in a concert or a Padres baseball game at Petco Park. They love being on the sea and the boat has proved to be a great escape from their busy lives. And tonight, we get to escape with them.

David prepares the boat for departure, while we are told to sit back, relax and enjoy the scenery—an order we are all too happy to follow. We sit on the upper deck and watch the flurry of activity as we pull out of the slip, head out of the dock and into the open waters of the San Diego Bay. It's a gorgeous evening and Amy, Jamie and I just smile at each other and take it all in. We sit together and clink our glasses as the sun starts to set and the lights of the city slowly start to glitter. We head south towards downtown and watch the tall buildings switch from day to night mode. Our conversation has been nice, too . . . very easy and comfortable.

We catch up on each others' lives and, by our second glass of champagne, Jamie and I are talking about the upcoming fall when our daughters will head off to college. Like Annette, Jamie's daughter Erin goes off to school in the fall, but she will be on the opposite coast in Boston.

"I'm so glad I still have a couple of years before I have to think about that," says Amy, a very successful photographer who has raised her daughter all on her own. "I don't envy you. I'm not sure what I'll do when Kelly leaves. It's hard for me to even think about Kelly being gone. I'm not sure how I'll handle that. And I'm worried about you, Kris. You'll be so lonely. Annette has been your life for so long; you won't know what to do with yourself."

"Are you kidding me," I say, "I'll be just fine, Amy. I'm looking forward to finally having a little 'me' time. I've never had that. I want to work more, build my business and maybe do some traveling. I think I will be okay with being on my own. I've always wanted more time so I can visit Dick's kids and be Grandma Kris to the grandkids. I want to visit my own kids in Mexico more, too. Alfonso and Christofer are so busy building up their business and don't have a lot of time, so it will be nice to see them in person instead of just phone calls and emails. And I also want to catch up with all my old friends in Guadalajara. Seriously, I can't envision myself being bored or lonely."

Jamie and Gretchen exchange glances and, after a long, pregnant pause, Gretchen speaks up.

"Kris, please don't take this the wrong way," she starts while hesitating and glancing back and forth at Jamie and Amy who now are looking at me, too. "We've been thinking, you know, that it might be the right time to start thinking about dating."

Jamie quickly chimes in, "It's been six years, you know. We know how much Dick meant to you, but . . ." she pauses, lowers her eyes, then slowly looks back up, right in my eyes, ". . . he's gone. It might be time to move on. He would want that . . . you know that. Remember what the last thing he said to you was?"

"I know, I know," I say, tears welling in my eyes. "He said . . . 'don't be alone.'"

I sputter for a moment, but regain my strength, shake my head and say, "But you know . . . no way, no how. There's just no way. I appreciate your thoughts and your love and your kindness."

Now I am really choking up.

"But I just can't put myself out there again. It's just too painful. I can't do it."

I look at each one of my friends and repeat, "I can't do it again. The loss is just too painful and I won't put myself through it again. I won't, I just won't. I can't."

I look down at the beautiful teak floor on the boat and then out past my friends at the sparkling skyline of the city. A few moments pass in silence while I stare at the scenery. I know that I can't possibly put myself in that situation again. I look back at each of them and smile through the tears. I get up, go over to them and hug them.

"Group hug," I whisper hoarsely. "I love you guys, but no . . . I can't do it. I just can't."

As good friends always do, we share the hug, then move on to other less emotional topics of interest.

The rest of the evening is just delightful. We dine under the stars, chat and catch up with each others' lives. During the salad, we help Jamie figure out how she is going to move Erin to Boston for college in a month. Everyone has an opinion on how to buy bedding and dorm gear, and get it all to Boston on time for move-in day. The main course—halibut prepared perfectly in a light citrus sauce with vegetables cooked just right and lightly drizzled with butter—is amazing. While we savor the meal, Amy shares with us her anxieties about having an only child who is going to be a high school sophomore when the school year begins in September.

"It's so hard being a single mom and working as much as I do," she says. "I always feel guilty, as if I don't do enough for her."

In between mouthfuls, we all nod in agreement. I admire Amy so much. She has been through so much after her divorce and has basically raised her daughter by herself. Not only that, she is one of the top wedding photographers in San Diego. Through her hard work she has bought her own home without anyone's help. To me, that is so impressive. I just love strong women like Amy, and she has always proven to be such a deep source of inspiration to me. Still, I can't help but chuckle out loud when I hear her talk about her baby growing up. Everyone notices, and looks over at me as if to say, "What's so funny?"

"Oh no . . . nothing really . . ." I say while looking at each of them and shaking my head. "No. Really, it's nothing."

I simply can't tell Amy that she hasn't seen anything yet. Her daughter is only fifteen. She doesn't drive yet. She doesn't have boy troubles. I remember all of the constant high school drama with Annette—the emotional roller coaster over grades, girlfriends and then, of course, the boys. I just smile and think to myself that Amy has no idea what she is in for.

We enjoy a delicious tiramisu with another glass of champagne as we turn around and begin the voyage back. The pier looms ahead and, as the sun has long since set, and the temperature has dropped as well, Jamie, Amy and I huddle together under a warm blanket as Gretchen and David maneuver the boat back into the slip. Once back in the slip, we gather our purses and other belongings, turn towards our hosts and, almost in unison say, "This was so great." We laugh and then one at a time give our thanks and hugs to both Gretchen and David. It has been such an exceptional evening—the perfect escape from reality that all three of us needed so badly.

We find our way through the maze of docks and are finally back safely into Jamie's car in the parking lot. All of our stuff is packed into the back of her SUV, and we pile into the front and ask her to quickly turn on the heat. Unbelievably, it's cold—at least for us thin-blooded San Diegans. Just as I am buckling my seatbelt, Jamie turns on the car's ignition and, as she gets the heat going, I notice an eerie silence. I look up to see that she's staring at me.

A bit startled, I say, "Hey, what's up?"

There is nothing but silence and the infamous "Jamie stare" straight into my eyes, which really gets my attention.

"What's up?" I insist, but again am met by nothing but her steely gaze. "Uh-oh . . . What did I do now?"

She lets the car run as she slowly sits back in her seat. She obviously has no intention of driving away just yet. Something serious is on her mind, but she can't seem to spit it out. I look back and forth between her and Amy wondering what's going on. Amy just looks at me and shrugs her shoulders. I know that somehow I have managed to annoy only Jamie as Amy doesn't look like she knows what's going on either.

"Ya know," Jamie finally begins, "you really pissed me off tonight."

She pauses for a moment while I search my mind in vain for what I could possibly have done tonight to anger her.

"You are the one who has taught me all about openness," she says as I hold my breath. "You taught me how to open myself up to all of life's possibilities, to listen to my heart, to not judge, to take each day as it comes, to live in the 'I don't know.' Remember all of those conversations we had? Remember?"

She is almost shouting now. I just nod, feeling like a child being scolded, but still not knowing why.

"Well after all of those conversations we had, I actually decided that you were on to something and that I should pay attention. I have tried . . . oh, believe me . . . I have tried to be open, open to whatever might come to me, open to new ideas, open to other people's opinions—even when I disagreed with them—open to all life has to offer. And then, here you go, my teacher—the person who taught me this concept, the person I look up to for being so open—has closed herself down completely. What the hell? Never going to date? Never going to put yourself through it again? Never going to put yourself out there? You? Really? You, my teacher?"

She finally stops, gasping for air and turning from bright red to almost purple. I am stunned by this outburst, shocked into silence as is Amy. We just sit there staring at Jamie as she tries her best to calm down. I'm paralyzed, with my mouth wide open, unable to respond in any way. The silence remains unbroken for what seems like hours. Finally, I can't take it any more.

"Oh my gosh, Jamie, you are right . . . you are so right," I say sheepishly. "So much for me being a teacher, huh? You are so right."

I take a deep breath and start to speak again, but Jamie interrupts me.

"Look, I just don't want you to close yourself down, Kris," she says. "All I'm saying is, as your friend, I want more for you. I don't want to see you lonely for the rest of your life. I just want to see you happy. I mean really happy . . . the way you used to be. And if you close off every possibility by refusing to take a chance, it's just not going to happen."

I understand what she is saying and I know that she is right. I hang my head and, without any words, slowly nod. I just keep nodding until I look up and our eyes meet. Tears are streaming down her cheeks, and I see in her eyes the deep caring and concern that only a best friend can show. I reach out to hug her and we just sit there embracing in silence.

Even though I know she's right, I also know that, right now, I just can't do it. I just can't take another chance that heartache will find me. I just can't do it. I keep those thoughts to myself, however, and whisper in her ear, "I love you, Jamie, and I so deeply appreciate your concern. And I promise to work on it."

CHAPTER 14
full circle

By far, my least favorite part of my job is the billing. For each inter-preting appointment I perform, I have to bill an insurance company; and like most insurance companies, the ones I work with do not like to part with their money. So, it often takes multiple invoices and multiple phone calls to finally get paid. It's a necessary evil but, as I sit here at my com-puter this morning, staring at this stack of unpaid invoices, I can't help but think, "There's got to be a better way." Then, a "bing," announcing the arrival of a new email, temporarily distracts me from the task at hand.

From: Ross Clark <rc@xmjc.net>
Subject: Trip to San Diego
Date: July 29, 2008, 9:30 AM PST
To: Kris Ochoa <kok@rltmx.net>

Greetings Kris. I will be in San Diego this weekend for a
conference. Haven't seen you or your family in a while.
Let me know if you are available. I would like to catch up.

Ross Clark

Whoa, now there's a voice from the past. Gosh, I haven't heard from him in years. So many memories race through my mind as I recount the lawsuit . . . the endless lawsuit. Oh well, bygones I suppose. It will be nice to see him. It's been so long, I'm not sure I will even recognize him. What the heck!

From: Kris Ochoa <kok@rltmx.net>
Subject: RE: Trip to San Diego
Date: July 29, 2008, 10:02 AM PST
To: Ross Clark <rc@xmjc.net>

Ross, that would be nice. What does your timeframe look like?
Kris

_____

From: Ross Clark <rc@xmjc.net>
Subject: RE: Trip to San Diego
Date: July 29, 2008, 10:33 AM PST
To: Kris Ochoa <kok@rltmx.net>

Kris, I have Saturday August 2nd completely free. Would like to see your kids and your family. How is your brother Steve?

Ross

_____

From: Kris Ochoa <kok@rltmx.net>
Subject: RE: Trip to San Diego
Date: July 29, 2008, 7:14 PM PST
To: Ross Clark <rc@xmjc.net>

Ross, that will work! I got in touch with Jim, Cheryl and Steve. They are available that day too, just not all at the

same time. I will pick you up and plan the day. I will figure out the who, where and when.
Kris

From: Ross Clark <rc@xmjc.net>
Subject: RE: Trip to San Diego
Date: July 29, 2008, 8:30 PM PST
To: Kris Ochoa <kok@rltmx.net>

Looking forward to it. I'm staying at The Lodge at Torrey
Pines. Thanks,

Ross

From: Kris Ochoa <kok@rltmx.net>
Subject: RE: Trip to San Diego
Date: July 29, 2008, 8:55 PM PST
To: Ross Clark <rc@xmjc.net>

OK. See you outside at 9 am! It will be nice to catch
up.
Kris

If there's one thing I am really good at, it's planning events, so putting together a day of activities for Ross will be a piece of cake. Steve can
only do breakfast, my kids are only available for lunch, and Jim and Cheryl
only have dinner open. Spread the visits over the day and maybe do some
touristy stuff in between. If nothing else, he won't leave hungry!

Ross and I had a history of spending this type of day together. Before
the trial, when Ross was taking depositions and doing interviews, he traveled quite a bit to both Guadalajara and San Diego. Many a time we would
go grab dinner or go sightseeing after business was done. I realize it's a

little different this time as it's been twelve years since we've seen each other. Those years seem like a lifetime ago.

———•·◆·•———

Saturday morning comes around and, for some reason that I can't explain, I take extra care in picking out what I wear today. I can't quite figure out why I am a little nervous about seeing Ross after all these years, but I make a special point of trying to look good. Even though I know Ross has been married for more than thirty-five years, I still feel the need to show that I look okay despite all that has happened in my life. I want to look casual, like I have just thrown something on, like I haven't spent any time at all thinking about it.

God, we women are so awful—so vain and so incredibly complicated. It cracks me up to think that men rarely notice all of the hard work women put into looking good. Still, it means a lot to me and, over the years, I have taken great care to keep myself looking halfway decent. At 56, I still weigh 108 pounds and am in decent shape thanks to regular, although not always diligent, exercise. I've always felt that my great fortune at not having to fight a weight problem was God's way of saying, "She's had enough other problems for one lifetime, fat too? I don't think so." So I do feel lucky to have remained a size two.

I decide on a white short-sleeve blouse, jeans and sandals—casual, easy and appropriate for a summer day. I am happy with my choices as I get behind the wheel of my car, but I still feel a little nervous. Will I recognize him after twelve years? Will he recognize me? My mind races a mile a minute as nervous energy flows through my body. I almost feel twitchy.

As I drive towards the hotel, I think back to the conversation with Jamie a couple weeks ago, when she criticized me for not opening myself up to life's opportunities. I'm sure this day with Ross isn't exactly what she had had in mind, but I guess it's a start. But if I'm having these kind of nerves before a platonic day out with Ross, I can't imagine what I will feel like before a date with someone on a romantic level. I really should listen to Jamie, Amy and Gretchen, but I just don't think I'm ready for that. Still, maybe now is the time to start thinking about it. I sigh and concentrate on the road in front of me.

As I pull into the driveway at The Lodge at Torrey Pines, I see all the attendants dressed in kilts and, for a moment, I feel like I have been transported to Scotland. Hundreds of majestic Torrey pine trees line the driveway and stand out against the crystal blue sky in the perfect Southern California morning. As I turn into the cul-de-sac in front of the lobby, I see Ross standing next to one of the valets, casually talking. "That's Ross all right," I think, my mind flooding with hundreds of memories of the lawsuit years.

All of the nervous jitters disappear and a sense of relief rushes over me as I pull the car towards him. It now seems so silly that I was so nervous. It's Ross. I immediately remember how calm he was and how he had been at my side through a very difficult stretch in my life. He immediately recognizes me, cracks a big smile and waves. He says good-bye to the bellman, opens my car door, gets in and says, "Well, hello again!"

He hasn't changed much. His hair has more silver in it, but, if anything, he looks more distinguished. At 6'2", he still carries himself with great dignity. He is someone you notice when he walks into a room. He reminds me of how I envision a judge would carry himself—quiet, elegant, calm, on top of the situation, someone who might sit around with his law partners sipping brandy while discussing the implications of the latest legal decision. In other words, I remind myself, nothing in common with me. The thought occurs to me that I really never knew much about his personal life even though he knew everything about mine. Oh well, chalk that up to attorney-client privilege. Maybe I will learn a little more about him today.

"So how are you, Ross?" I ask. "You haven't changed a bit!"

"Well, a little older and little grayer, but overall I can't complain too much," he says. "You look great as well."

"Thank you," I say. "The kids keep me on my toes!"

We spend the drive catching up a bit, and before we know it, we arrive at a restaurant called The Tractor Room, where we are meeting my brother, Steve, for breakfast. "Odd place he's chosen," I think, as we walk into the dark, lounge-style main dining room. We walk through the empty restaurant and choose a table on the patio with a view of the busy street below. A strategic move on my part—while Ross and Steve talk law, I can people watch, one of my favorite pastimes.

Over coffee, Steve and Ross discuss the recent cases they have been working on and, by the time we order, they are completely engrossed in each other's stories of outrageous judgments, interesting points of law and huge awards that their clients had won. I just twiddle my thumbs. "Ho hum," is all I can think, and soon my mind begins to wander from their conversation onto other, more pressing things. What the heck was that woman thinking when she got dressed this morning? Didn't she look in the mirror? Ooh, I love that gorgeous Coach purse! I've never seen that style in purple before. My mind travels further and further away from the conversation at the table and more towards the fashion oddities that pass by on the street.

As I take in the surroundings, Ross and Steve continue to talk. I hear bits and pieces but don't really pay any attention until I think I hear, "Divorce . . . three years . . . very difficult . . . I'm sorry to hear . . ." Suddenly it feels like my chair is rocking back and forth violently, the whole patio swaying, as if the Earth is shaking. The phantom movement makes me queasy and I feel like I'm going to fall off my chair.

"What's going on?" I think to myself. "What is Ross talking about?" I slowly grab the edge of the table to steady myself and I turn to face Ross. "Pay attention, Kris," I tell myself. "Pay attention."

"Yes . . . after thirty-six years of marriage, we got divorced," he says.

"Wow," Steve says. "I'm really sorry to hear that."

Holy crap, he's divorced! Never in a million years did that possibility even occur to me.

"Barbara asked me for a divorce three years ago; and after trying counseling, we came to the conclusion that it was not going to work," Ross continues, aiming his comments towards Steve, but suddenly noticing that he has my attention as well.

What! Ross is the type of man who takes "until death do us part" very seriously. He's loyal, devoted and always keeps his word. What had happened? I can't even begin to imagine.

Still reeling from the news, I try to pay attention, but I feel as if this revelation has caused the whole world to shift beneath my feet and change the entire dynamic of the day I have planned with Ross. Still, I'm not sure exactly how or why.

The rest of the breakfast is uneventful, full of small talk and legal jargon. Someone pays the bill—I'm not sure who—and the next thing I know, Ross and I are alone again in my car.

"Bye, Steve," I say through the rolled down window as Ross waves. I manage to turn on the ignition; but, before putting the car in gear, I take a deep breath, pause, slowly turn to Ross and say, "So, you have been divorced for three years?"

"Yes," he answers, not going into any detail. He looks away and out the window.

I can feel his pain. It is still raw. I can tell this had not been what he wanted. I look at him and know that this is one of those rare times when I should keep my mouth shut. He will talk about it if and when he is ready.

"I'm sorry," I say. "I am so sorry. I know what loss is and how hard it can be."

In silence, I put the car in gear and decide to change the subject.

"Well, I thought you might like to see one of our famous historical sites here in San Diego, the U.S.S. Midway museum. It is the World War II aircraft carrier and, from what I hear, makes for quite a tour. At noon we are meeting my kids for lunch, so we can check it out now for a couple hours if you feel like it."

"That sounds phenomenal," he says as the enthusiasm returns and he sounds more like himself. "I am a history buff and would love that."

"Yay," I think, "brownie points for me. I chose something that he is actually interested in!"

When we get to the Midway museum, Ross, the perfect gentleman, purchases our tickets; and, together, we walk up the ramps to the main deck of the ship where we pick up our headsets and begin our guided tour. As we put the headsets on and embark on the tour, the Midway and all of its history is the farthest thing from my mind.

"Hmm," I think, "he has really beautiful silvery hair, and he is in such good shape. He isn't even winded climbing those ramps. I never noticed those beautiful green eyes before."

All of these thoughts make my head swim. As I turn up one of the gangways, I accidentally run into him. "Geez, Kris, get yourself together here. Focus. The Midway . . . taking the tour . . . listen . . . Ross . . . lawyer . . . not married."

As much as I try, I can't help but think something is happening between us. I can't pinpoint why I feel this way. Ross hasn't said a word, but I've started to notice the way he is looking at me and it just feels different. And here I am following him around the ship feeling like a smitten teenager.

We both have our earphones on and Ross looks like he is really enjoying the tour. I, on the other hand, hope he can't see a trace of my nervousness and am so grateful he doesn't know what is going through my mind. So, I play along—when Ross nods, I nod; when his eyes look pensive, I look pensive; when he turns to take in a particular sight, so do I; and when he points at something on display that is being discussed on the tape, I turn and feign interest.

All the time, however, my thoughts return to the most startling of revelations: "He's not married. Oh my God, he's not married. What does this mean?" Ross isn't acting any differently. He continues moving along completely engrossed in the conquests of the Midway and the war in the Pacific. Maybe this is just my imagination run amok.

We conclude the tour and then meet my kids for a delightful lunch of wonderful Mexican food at a restaurant ironically called Casa Guadalajara. After lunch, I take Ross over to the Hotel Del Coronado, a San Diego landmark right on the ocean. The Hotel Del, as it's called, was the resort of choice for the rich and famous in the early 1900s and has maintained its class, style and charm over the years. To me it is almost like a trip back in time. Ross and I walk around the grounds and sit down on a bench to take in the beautiful towers of the hotel, its old wooden balconies that grace each room and the perfectly manicured gardens below.

The peace and tranquility of the afternoon opens the door to warm conversation between friends. Ross and I chat about our lives, our families and our jobs. The more we talk, the more comfortable I feel with him. He opens up about his divorce and the pain and grief that he has endured. A failed marriage had never been even a remote possibility in his mind, and I can tell it has taken its toll on him. Ross had always seemed so much like the type of man who heeds the old saying, "grin and bear it," when confronted with difficult times, so it's a revelation for me to see that he has such a vulnerable side and that he has been hurt so badly. My heart goes out to him.

Because he has been so open with me, I feel completely comfortable telling him how difficult my life has been since Dick died. Tears come into my eyes as I tell him of Dick's stroke and the debilitating and ultimately futile struggle to overcome the cancer.

"I thought I was going to die, Ross, I really did. And I really wanted to," I say. "It didn't seem like there was much to live for. The love of my life had been taken away from me . . . twice! It seemed like my life was over."

It's painful to open up and revisit these old wounds, but Ross seems to take it all in and calmly turns to me and says, "But you did it, Kris. You did it. You are a strong person. You have been dealt more than your share and yet you raised your children and you carried on. You did it. And that is what counts."

He speaks so softly and his words reveal a side of him I haven't known. I smile at him and whisper, "Thank you." With his kind, gentle expression, he acknowledges all that I have been through and admires me for it.

"Not everyone could have done what you did," he adds. "You should be very proud of yourself."

I turn and look at him for a long moment, then nod. I nod to him and to myself because, yes, I am proud of myself . . . very proud.

I drop Ross off at his hotel, and he goes up to his room to change into warmer clothes. We are joining Jim and Cheryl for the Summer Pops tonight, which is outdoors where it may be cool. As I wait for him in the lobby, I reflect on the change in the nature of our relationship since this morning. I was always a little in awe of Ross, with his commanding presence that comes from his tall sturdy frame and his quiet intelligence. But now the formidable lawyer, who I was intimidated by, is gone, replaced by an attractive, sensitive, handsome man with a vulnerable side. I'm not sure that I am supposed to even be feeling these things. It's confusing, exhilarating and frustrating all at once.

The lobby of The Lodge at Torrey Pines is beautiful with a huge stone fireplace, giving way to large bay windows that look out at the world-famous golf course and, behind that, the ocean. Even though it's August in San Diego, there is a roaring fire going. I sit in a rocking chair watching the fire crackle and contemplating the vast differences between men and women. Holy smokes, what is wrong with me? The first man who I talk to in six years and I feel like Alice in Wonderland when she falls into the rabbit's hole—round and round, down I am twirling, but where am I going?

What is wrong with me? I'll bet Ross is up in his room changing his clothes oblivious to the fact that I am in the middle of an emotional earthquake. He is so calm, cool and always seemingly in charge. I'm pulled out of my internal musings by the words, "Ready, Kris?"

I turn and nearly fall out of my chair. Ross stands to my side and his presence takes my breath away. He is so incredibly handsome. His silver gray, wavy hair is complemented perfectly by his blue and white striped tailored shirt and a navy sweater over his shoulders. His navy slacks looks so elegant and, at the same time, perfectly casual. I'm left momentarily speechless. "Holy smokes," I think, "how had I missed this before?"

As I stand up to greet him, my eyes scan the room and notice that every woman within a hundred feet has stopped dead in her tracks to stare at him. Smiling, I finally respond, "Yeah, I'm ready."

My, how things can change in a matter of hours!

We drive to my house, where it's his turn to wait while I change and get ready. As I look over the wardrobe choices, my mind races. Is it just that I am starved for male attention or do I really care about making a good impression on him? It's all so confusing. I chide myself for acting like a stupid teenager and make myself get my act together, choosing my clothes and returning downstairs in a cantaloupe colored turtleneck and some black casual corduroy pants, and cute flats. I also bring a warm coat for later when the sun goes down and the chill sets in.

As I walk down the stairs into the kitchen where Ross has been waiting for me, I feel his eyes look up over the newspaper he's reading, travel over me from head to toe, then he smiles. Yes, I see it . . . That was more than just a casual look! He mentioned earlier that I did not look my age, but now I can tell by his glance that he thinks I look attractive. With each step I descend, my smile gets bigger. "Hmm, non-verbal communication," I think as I look at him. "Okay, I can do this."

Our table is outstanding, right up close—on the side of the stage—with a perfect view. We have a wonderful dinner as the sun sets out over San Diego Bay. Boats, sailing by in the harbor, along with the Coronado Bridge in the background, make the scenery look like a postcard.

Ross entertains us all with his tales of adventure from his recent horseback safari in Kenya. "We had a fantastic time," he explains. "Every evening camp would be set up for us. There were fifteen of us guests all together and fifteen staff that consisted of guides, cooks, a chef, groomers for the horses and workers who made sure our every need was taken care of. We had fabulous dinners every night out in the savannah, great wine and the best part was getting to know the other guests. Everyone was so interesting and, by the end of the first week, we all felt like we had known each other for years."

I have not had a chance to tell Jim and Cheryl that Ross is divorced, so they innocently ask, "Did your wife enjoy being on the horse as much as you did?"

I shot them an alarming look that went right over their heads before Ross quickly answers, "Oh, she didn't go on this trip with me. You see, we divorced three years ago."

With their mouths open like they want to say something but can't formulate the words, both Jim and Cheryl in unison look at me, then back at Ross, then back to me with an odd grin frozen on their faces. Just as Jim is about to comment, Ross says, "Would you excuse me for a moment?" as he stands up, folds his napkin, puts it on the table, pushes in his chair and heads to the restroom.

The second he is out of hearing range, Cheryl immediately turns to me and starts smiling. "No wonder sparks are flying," she says as if everything now has become crystal clear.

"Excuse me?" I say, "Sparks? What sparks? I don't know what you're talking about."

"Oh get real, Kris," she says laughing. "Jim and I haven't been able to figure out what was going on here until now. I mean, if he is married, why the heck is he visiting you? But we figured, whatever, an old friend, the professional ties, all that stuff. Then when we saw you together, it didn't make sense because it really feels like you are on a date. But, oh my God . . . he's divorced. Now it all makes sense."

"What makes sense?" I say, demanding a much more detailed explanation. In my opinion, we look like two old friends catching up and filling each other in on years gone by.

"There are sparks flying between you two," Jim chimes in, while chuckling. "We can feel it. We just didn't get it until now. But now it all makes sense."

"Yeah, you two look like a perfectly matched couple from the Country Club set," Cheryl says. "Kris, he is so handsome . . ." her voice trailing off as she sees Ross coming back towards the table.

"You are out of your minds," I whisper just before he sits down. "Out of your minds," I say again while spinning my index finger around my ear.

As soon as Ross sits down, we resume our normal conversation until the announcer comes over the loud speaker to say that the show is starting in a moment. As the orchestra warms up and the lights are dimmed, all I can think about is Jim and Cheryl's words. Sparks? Really?

The music starts and everyone settles in to enjoy the concert. Ross sits on my left, where he is closer to the stage, so I turn my chair in ever so slightly to see the stage better, but also to get a better view of him. Throughout the show, I find myself stealing glances at his strong, handsome profile and just wondering what he is thinking. "This is silliness," I tell myself. "This is just two old friends catching up . . . nothing more, nothing less."

Towards the end of the show, the orchestra plays Louis Armstrong's "What a Wonderful World." Just as I begin to mouth the words, "What a wonderful world," I turn to Ross and see him mouthing the same words. Our eyes lock for an instant before he smiles and turns back towards the orchestra. What a wonderful world, indeed.

When I wake this morning, I realize Ross is probably on his way to the airport to return to Vancouver. It didn't even occur to me to offer to drive him to the airport. As I lie in bed, clutching at my pillow, I convince myself that I had imagined the whole day. It's absolutely ridiculous to think there could be anything between us. I can feel my face flush with embarrassment at even thinking he might be interested in me. He lives in Vancouver; I live here. He never once gave me any indication that he was anything but a good friend. Or did he? "I don't know," I think, as I recall the glances he gave me as I came down the staircase and later at the show.

I spend the entire morning trying to get Ross Clark out of my mind, but to no avail. I examine every detail of yesterday's events and still can't decide if there was something between us. When Jim calls later to see if I want to join him and Cheryl for a movie, the first thing he asks in almost a teasing fashion is, "So, did Ross call you today?"

"Of course not, why should he?" I ask defensively, not waiting to betray my hope that they were right.

"No reason," he says, "Just wondering . . . just wondering. No big deal."

When I hang up the phone, I realize that the fact that Ross hasn't called probably means we were all imagining the so-called sparks. Inside I am somewhat disappointed. I thought I saw something in his eyes, but I guess I was wrong. I misjudged. I should have known better. Maybe I was just being silly.

I mope through the rest of the day and try to put Ross Clark out of my mind.

Another Monday morning and I'm already running late for work when the phone rings. I pick up the phone and immediately recognize the voice of Roger, our community's front gate security guard.

"Mrs. Ochoa, there is a delivery truck here at the gate," he says. "Can I let them in?"

I try to remember what I could have ordered, but before I get too far along, Roger interrupts. "It's Adelaides. They have a delivery for you."

My heart starts pounding when I connect the dots . . . Adelaides is the best florist in San Diego. I stammer, then say, "Sure, let them in."

The two minutes it takes the truck to arrive at my doorstep seems like an eternity and the delivery man eyes me suspiciously when I greet him at the curb. He opens the back of his truck, fishes around for a few seconds, and then finally appears with the most breathtakingly beautiful summer bouquet of roses, lilies, sunflowers and alstroemeria. I thank the delivery man, while quickly ripping open the envelope to find one word:

Ross

"Yes!" I think to myself as I mimic a Tiger Woods fist pump, while the delivery man chuckles and drives away.

With much trepidation, I contemplate how to respond. Never one to mince words, I decide to seize the initiative, take the direct approach and flush him out about whether his interest in me is really on a romantic level.

From: Kris Ochoa <kok@rltmx.net>
Subject: Thanks!!
Date: August 4, 2008, 8:15 AM PST
To: Ross Clark <rc@xmjc.net>

Dear Ross,

Wow! The flowers are so beautiful. Thank you so much!

I just love getting flowers – they are my favorites. How did you know?

Flowers can mean a lot of things and I don't mean to put you on the spot, but it was so nice spending time with you on Saturday. I really enjoyed our conversations. I definitely felt a connection and I got the sense you did too. Can we talk again soon?

Kris

"Now the ball is in his court," I think, nervous as a teenager and wondering if and how he will respond.

My answer comes soon—the next evening, in fact, when a knock on the door interrupts my date with *Access Hollywood*. I scurry down the stairs in my pajamas and robe, and open the door, only to see a FedEx truck speeding off and a small package resting on my doorstep. As I pick it up, the first thing I see is my name on the front and the words Amazon.com.

"I don't remember ordering anything," I think. "Nope, I'm sure I didn't order anything from Amazon."

In the kitchen I get a sharp knife and carefully cut open the box, and see gift wrapping. My interest peaks. Should I open the card or the package first? The card wins out and I find a typewritten note inside.

> These are the 2 books that I was telling you about on Saturday. I hope you enjoy them as much as I have. Thank you for a lovely day and, of course, I'd love to talk to you again soon. Ross

"Ohhhh," I sigh. "He sent me his favorite books! Flowers, now books. I can't possibly be imagining this." As I exhale slowly, "Wow . . . wow, wow, wow . . . this is exciting!" I rush upstairs to my computer and without thinking, start typing a "thank you" email.

From: Kris Ochoa <kok@rltmx.net>
Subject: Thanks again!!
Date: August 5, 2008, 7:15 PM PST
To: Ross Clark <rc@xmjc.net>

Dear Ross,

Thank you so much!

I just got the books. I am very excited to read them especially with such a great recommendation from you. That was so nice of you.

I am so looking forward to talking with you again. I feel like we are good friends already and I really enjoyed your company last Saturday. I feel so comfortable with you and I felt like you did with me also, at least I hope you did. I would like to get to know you better.

What do you think?

Kris

––––––––––––––––––––

From: Ross Clark <rc@xmjc.net>
Subject: RE: Thanks again!!
Date: August 5, 2008, 7:45 PM PST
To: Kris Ochoa <kok@rltmx.net>

Kris, I'm glad you liked the books. I think you will enjoy reading them. Luis De Bernieres is a brilliant writer.

I look forward to getting to know you more as well. I have not had much experience in this area and am not a great phone conversationalist, but I think we will manage. We both seem to have the interest and that is an important thing. We do seem to get along quite well together and enjoy each other's company. It seems like a good place to start.

How about tomorrow night? Is 8 pm OK? If so, I will phone you then.

Ross

As I get ready to press the send button confirming our telephonic "date" for tomorrow night, I can't help but think what a strange turn of events this has been. I really do believe that when you put something out to the universe, the universe responds—not necessarily in the exact way you expect, but in such a way that, with the benefit of hindsight, makes perfect sense. That's what makes the situation with Ross so puzzling. Even though I heard Jamie's advice a few weeks ago, I truly believed I wasn't ready for another relationship with a man. So, I certainly wasn't putting out to the universe that I was looking and, yet, now here I am, giddy as a school girl, thinking about Ross. And even more than that, I just have a sense that this reunion with Ross is much more than just two old friends reconnecting. Call it female intuition or what you will, but I really feel this is the start of something big. Am I crazy?

From: Kris Ochoa <kok@rltmx.net>
Subject: RE: Thanks again!!
Date: August 5, 2008, 8:45 PM PST
To: Ross Clark <rc@xmjc.net>

So tomorrow night at 8 pm it is!

I am excited and a little nervous I have to admit. It seems like a big step even though it is just a phone call. ☺

I don't have any experience with this type of thing either so I guess we will just figure it out as we go! I think it will be great fun, this new journey! What do you think???

Kris

———————————————

From: Ross Clark <rc@xmjc.net>
Subject: RE: Thanks again!!
Date: August 5, 2008, 9:20 PM PST
To: Kris Ochoa <kok@rltmx.net>

What do I think of this new journey? Well, I think we're in trouble kid!!

Ross

EPILOGUE

As I sit here in a small aluminum fishing boat in the middle of Alta Lake in beautiful British Columbia, I can't help but think, "What the heck am I doing here?" I don't particularly like the outdoors, I certainly don't like to fish and I'm freezing my behind off. Yet, here I am with a rod and reel in hand, trying to catch rainbow trout, which aren't particularly biting on this brisk autumn day. The answer lies with my companion in the boat, who at this very moment is placing the largest and slimiest worm I've ever seen on my hook. It must be love!

Three years have passed and Ross and I are deeply in love, and happily planning our future together. Once again, I find myself in a long-distance relationship, this time shuttling back and forth between San Diego and Vancouver. The distance presents many challenges and I long for the day, which we believe is coming soon, when we can be together full time. In the meantime, Ross and I talk every night and see each other as often as we can, including this trip up to Alta Lake for our fishing expedition.

Ross' calm strength and common sense help guide me through my chaotic daily life. He is my anchor, my daily reminder that I am loved and not alone. I cherish these feelings even more after having experienced such solitude after the deaths of Alfonso and Dick. Ross makes me feel safe and loved, and I feel completely at home in his arms. We are different in so many ways, as this fishing trip illustrates, but our differences seem to bring out the best in each other and we complement each other in so many ways. I am so incredibly grateful to have Ross in my life.

I have had so many blessings in my life, too many to count. At the top of the list are the three men whom I have loved, all very different but great men who have taught me so much. I am so grateful to Alfonso, Dick and now to Ross. I know so many people who don't ever experience true love in their lifetimes and yet I have three times, and for that I know I've been blessed.

As I look back on my life, I sometimes can't help but wonder how I've made it this far. The trials, the tribulations, the challenges—they never seem to end. But as my story illustrates, when you say yes to life, yes to all of its infinite possibilities, then doors you never knew existed open up in ways you could never have imagined. I try to keep myself mindful and consciously aware of all these possibilities every day . . . because you just never know what will come next. I might even catch a fish!